Advance acclaim for *In Praise of Good Business*

"Judy Bardwick provides a practical roadmap for business executives on how to succeed in today's ever-increasing competitive environment by motivating employees to peak performance. Through numerous examples . . . she adeptly portrays the dire consequences of complacency and the competitive advantages to be gained by stimulating employees to 'move the rock' and make a difference."

> Linda A. Cardillo, Vice President, Human Resources,
> Schering-Plough Research Institute

"Compelling U.S. management issues for the 90s and a wake up call for global competitors."

> David F. Hoff, Director International Human Resources,
> Anheuser-Busch Companies

"Dr. Bardwick extends to total business management and culture change her theory that we perform best when challenged. She proposes that by defining the business we are really in, stating critical goals and objectives, and then sticking to them, we are challenged to focus on real-world needs and real-world situations. Her action-oriented approach defines clear methods for creating and implementing significant change that will help organizations 'move the rock.' "

> L. D. DeSimone, Chairman of the Board and CEO, 3M

"Judy Bardwick has brilliantly captured . . . what Marines have understood for a long time: challenge people to do more than they ever believed possible. When they succeed, as most will, they are healthier and happier. The organization of which they are a part will be equally happy and successful. Bardwick shows you the way."

> W. E. Boomer, General, U.S. Marine Corps (Ret.),
> President and CEO, Rogers Corporation

"Dr. Bardwick writes with simple compelling messages, and does not equivocate in her values. There really is no choice in business: you win through the use of skilled competitive global strategies and tactics. There is no entitlement, there is only continuous earning through continuous learning, leading to continuous success."

> Larry A. Evans, EVP, Founding Principal,
> Right Management Consultants

"Judy Bardwick fearlessly challenges much of the established wisdom about the morality of business. It's about time someone with her credentials is willing to deal with the question of what it really takes to win in a global economy."

> Stephen R. Hardis, Chairman and CEO, Eaton Corporation

"This book contains the unvarnished truth about what it takes to be competitive. It is a powerfully written analysis of resistance to change, of accountability and of leadership in action. . . . To be successful . . . put into practice the concepts spelled out so well by Judith Bardwick."

James E. Ferrell, Chairman and CEO, Ferrellgas

"*In Praise of Good Business* does a great job of explaining what the new world business is all about. It provides useful guidelines to help individuals "surf" their way through the new deal economy."

Ed Lawler, Director, Center for Effective Organizations, Marshall School of Business, USC

"Judith Bardwick's new book, *In Praise of Good Business,* contains much valuable insight. It is a wake-up call for businesses and organizations which are still operating in the no-consequence mode. That approach will not work with today's competition level, and Judith provides valuable thought on what must be changed."

Bob G. Gower, Chairman, Specified: Fuels & Chemicals, LLC

"This is not a comfortable book to read but it is important. It looks us squarely in the eye, companies and employees, and challenges us to take responsibility."

Vernon J. Ellis, Managing Director, Andersen Consulting—Europe, Middle East, Africa and India

In Praise of
Good Business

In Praise of Good Business

How Optimizing Risk Rewards Both Your Bottom Line AND Your People

Judith M. Bardwick, Ph.D.

John Wiley & Sons, Inc.

New York • Chichester • Weinheim • Brisbane • Singapore • Toronto

Published by John Wiley & Sons, Inc.

Published simultaneously in Canada.

This publication is designed to provide accurate and authoritative information in regard to the subject matter covered. It is sold with the understanding that the publisher is not engaged in rendering professional services. If professional advice or other expert assistance is required, the services of a competent professional person should be sought.

Library of Congress Cataloging-in-Publication Data:
Bardwick, Judith M., 1933–
    In praise of good business : how optimizing risk rewards both your bottom line and your people / Judith M. Bardwick.
        p.   cm.
    Includes index.
    ISBN 0-471-25407-X (cloth : alk. paper)
    1. Industrial management—United States.   2. Industrial management—Social aspects—United States.   3. Entitlement attitudes—United States.   4. Risk—Social aspects.   5. Work—Social aspects.   6. Employees—United States—Attitudes.   7. Job security—United States.   I. Title.
HD70.U58347   1998
658–DC21   97-41089
                                                     CIP

Printed in the United States of America.

10 9 8 7 6 5 4 3 2 1

This book is dedicated to my family and those friends who are as family; they are the vital *anchor to windward.*

CONTENTS

PART THREE
Implications for the Future

ACKNOWLEDGMENTS

While authors shoulder most of the work and are responsible for all of the errors, books are usually much improved by other people's input. This book owes much of its clarity to three people who served as editors. Bill Leigh, of the Leigh Bureau, is both my literary agent and the concept editor of this book. Bill's grasp of the book's message clarified it for me. Lynne Doyle, of the Leigh Bureau, was the major wordsmith editor. Lynne challenged, persisted, insisted—and achieved tremendous clarity.

The third editor is very special. For about five years I've been exchanging editing suggestions with investment banker J. Peter Bardwick, partner in Star Media Group of Dallas. After Bill Leigh, Lynne Doyle, and I had worked (and worked!) on the manuscript, Peter reedited our work. It is a testimony to his astuteness and insight that he very significantly improved what we had achieved. Peter is my son.

The following people were extraordinarily generous in giving me their time and input: James Olson, senior VP, 3Com Corporation; Christian Poindexter, chairman and CEO, and the recently retired G. Dowell Schwartz Jr., VP of general services, Baltimore Gas and Electric Company; Steve Gardiner, director, management education and development, Champion International Corporation; Regina and Peter Bidstrup, founders of Homeward Bound (Peter is the founder and former chairman and CEO of Double Tree Hotels); Craig Cantoni, consultant; Robert Newton, Ph.D., director of macrophage pathology, DuPont Merck Pharmaceutical Company; Richard Champion, director, corporate relations, Florida Power Corporation; Dennis Coleman, group personnel manager, and Ned Barnholt, executive VP and general manager, Test and Measurement Organization, Hewlett-Packard; Steven R. Peltier, president and CEO of Industrial Computer Source; Steven Mason, CEO of Mead Corporation; Michael von Poelnitz, M.D., senior director of patient marketing initiatives, Merck & Co., Inc.; Richard Wintermantel, JD, VP and director, Motorola; Walter Boomer, president and CEO of Rogers Corp., formerly CEO of Babcock-Wilcox, and General, USMC, Retired; Marisa L. Guerin, Ph.D., VP, director, human resources, Rohm & Hass; Margot Kyd, VP of human resources, marketing, and customer service, San Diego Gas and Electric Company; Mary Jane Willier, formerly of Bell Atlantic and now VP, human resources, Sierra Pacific Power; Albert L. Derden, director of quality for Texaco Refining & Marketing, Inc.; Allen W. Bell, executive VP of human resources, and David Morrison, VP, human resources development, Toronto Dominion Bank; and Norm Lorentz, VP for quality, U.S. Postal Service.

I'm delighted to acknowledge Henning Gutmann, John Wiley & Sons' new executive editor for business, who purchased a manuscript and created a book. I wish him the best of good fortune in his new position.

As ever, I am grateful for the help of Diane Nau, whose vocabulary does not include the word *impossible*.

Lastly, there are three very special people who are my biggest supporters—and sources of challenge: venture capitalist Tom Murphy; consultant Norm Schoenfeld; and Allen Armstrong, Captain, USCG, Retired, my husband and best friend.

To all of you, *many, many thanks!*

Productive Insecurity

What kind of character does a nation need
in its people?
What kind of person do you want to be?
What kind of person do you want to work with?
What kind of adult do you want your child
to become?

From pariah to prophet: Today, successful business has become the template of best practices for the rest of society's institutions.

"In Praise of Good Business" is a wake-up call. Many policies and actions that people view as "good" are in fact destructive to people and ultimately to nations. When government and business provided people with high degrees of security, they created people who were unprepared to deal with change or risk. The unintended outcome of excessive benevolence and generosity is cultures that are unprepared and unable to deal with the harsher competitive reality that began in the early 1980s and that appears to be permanent. Time has shown that what was once considered kindness is really a destructive cruelty. Giving without requiring something in return is not kind.

In the 50 years since World War II, countries as different as the United States, the former Soviet Union, Mexico, Germany, and Japan decided that security should replace fear and employment should become a basic right. Many governments and corporations set out to be honorable and fair. Both created conditions of nonaccountability for people everywhere—but especially for employees in both the private and public sectors. Over time, fairness became kindness and kindness became an attitude of being owed that produced a culture of no-consequences.

The psychology of "I am owed whatever I get," and, because I don't have to earn what I receive, "I am not responsible," creates a culture of no-consequences. In a no-consequence culture, people are not held accountable for their behavior and no differentiation is made between people who perform well and those who don't. Taken to the extreme, creating equal outcomes for everyone, irrespective of differences in behavior, is considered an expression of the highest ethical values.

While the economic costs of wasted resources in organizations, and the huge expenses of corporate, middle-class, and working-class welfare programs have become extremely painful in today's borderless economy, the psychological costs of nonaccountability are at least as great and may be greater.

Confidence may well be the single most important of human attributes, because confidence alone liberates people from inhibiting fears. Confidence is the quality that enables people to move forward into life and manage its turmoils. Without confidence, people flee from reality, continually seeking outside protection from things they must confront themselves.

The paradoxical outcome of too much security is that people are deprived of the experiences they need to become courageous. The only way people learn to handle risk is by doing it. The only way to become confident is to master challenges. When corporations and governments created risk-free environments, they denied people the experiences they need to become confident. Without confidence, life is dominated by fear and an insatiable need for safety.

The protections of no-consequence cultures and their practices must give way in the face of today's reality. Nations and organizations that back away from speaking the unspeakable about their costly practices will find themselves economically noncompetitive. Equally threatening, they have created people who are unable, and thus unwilling, to deal with the harsh competitive realities created by a borderless economy.

Worldwide, business has stepped up to the realities of borderlessness far faster and more decisively than has government. The lesson from business is that when you do step up to the harsher conditions and take action—even though it's painful and you'd rather not—you improve your chances of long-term success. When the probability of the organization succeeding is increased, and the organization creates jobs and opportunities for challenge and personal development, the conditions have also been created in which people are most likely to flourish as capable adults. That is the message of this book.

The best corporate practices of driving for significant results and celebrating their achievement, and of doing only real work that creates purpose and makes a difference, that require people to stand tall and conquer challenge, are conditions that foster a vital aspect of human nature and human existence. The work of people is work: people are injured when they are prevented from doing significant work. That is an elemental component of being human. Just observe young children, even infants. Their eyes, as big as millstones, are constantly scanning, processing the data of their universe. We start life as learning organisms and then, as we grow, we learn significance, principles, meaning, values, and ethics.

Intrinsically, people desire and prosper under conditions in which they can learn, achieve, mature, contribute, and collaborate. Any other conditions are destructive to the maturation of what most matters to people and their communities: confidence, civility, ethics, compassion, and cohesion.

In 1942, an English academic named William Beveridge released a report titled "Social Insurance and Allied Services."[1] The Beveridge report became the blueprint for the British and later the European welfare states, and it was designed to create a postwar era of full employment and freedom from poverty. In addition to poverty, the Beveridge plan was intended to eliminate disease, ignorance, squalor, and idleness. Stressing duty over dependency, the new benefits were primarily designed to see people through a crisis by giving them a basic minimum, a safety net that would end when they were on their feet.

Contrary to Beveridge's predictions, the number of British households on means-tested benefits has continued to grow instead of decline, so that in 1995 Great Britain's welfare expenditures mounted to 23 percent of the gross domestic product. In fact, wealthy British citizens have found ways to exploit the system's universality. In 1993, the government discovered that some unemployed millionaires were receiving government payments of about £1800 a week. The Beveridge system, which was designed to eliminate the worst of human vulnerabilities—being poor, sick, and ignorant—and replace those conditions with employment, education, and health, was instead corrupted to a culture and a psychology of being owed.

It is a wonderful human thing to want to be kind, to be generous, to be good. In the United States we characterized corporations as great if they were demonstrably kind, which meant they gave employees lifetime security, automatic raises, and an ever increasing roster of benefits. In a parallel judgment, government was considered good if it legalized compassion and gave people a large number of protections and advantages as a matter of right. But too much kindness destroys character. Alas, what we thought was comforting turned out to be dangerous.

Of course, sustained high levels of fear and anxiety have awful consequences. Unexpectedly, so do sustained high levels of safety and security. The "harsh" practice of having to deal with competition, of being required to be responsible, of being judged in terms of performance, serves people best. While the idea that too much security results in low confidence levels sounds strange, it's actually very simple and logical.

There is an enormously positive consequence to being required to achieve—and achieving—when the task is a challenge and the risk is real. When people are confident, they expect to succeed, which is why they are comfortable taking risks. And confident people recover quickly from the inevitable failures. The only way people achieve confidence is to succeed in many challenges when the circumstances are serious and the outcome really matters. "Serious" means that something significantly different happens when you succeed from when you don't.

Risk has two components: The first involves dealing with circumstances that haven't been mastered before. The second stipulates that nonperformance will be punished. Those who achieve will be treated differently from those who don't. If there is no punishment in the face of nonperformance, there is no real risk.

Too much security doesn't give people enough experience grappling with serious risk to learn how to manage it and learn they really can handle it. Without many experiences of succeeding when the risk is real, people can never learn that risk is more exhilarating than frightening. Without the experience of mastering risk, people remain fearful of making mistakes, of uncertainty, of responsibility, and of independence. Then people depend on external protections to keep them safe. At work, people become psychologically as well as economically dependent on their organizations to protect them.

While high levels of protection can feel good, they're not good for people. Most often, too much leniency reflects expected failure and, naturally, that deprives people of the sense that they are competent. When people are not required to perform, they can't know if they could. Being nice is not kind; it results in dependent people. When people are dependent, they play life too safely, preferring the confines of rules and procedures, cursing the status quo but never moving far from it, forever searching for protective environments. It is wrong and immoral to foster conditions that create people who, lacking confidence, are cowards.

Our organizations and our governments created unconditional security. Security is too high when it is given as a right rather than being an outcome that was earned. Safety is nearly absolute when people don't have to earn what they get, but instead receive it because of who they are. When achievement is not the precondition for getting, people get, irrespective of whether or not they achieve. The result is people don't believe they are responsible for performing. Instead, they believe they get what they get because it is owed to them.

The psychology of *I am not responsible,* and the attitude *You owe me,* raise people's expectations ever higher. Convinced they're owed whatever they get, their greed increases and they grab for everything.

It is not acceptable when national cultures and organizational actions foster a lack of confidence, fear of change, narcissism, and greed. Though many people applaud national and institutional paternalistic practices that grant safety and require nothing in return, those same people would despair if their child rearing efforts resulted in self-centered, fearful, and greedy children who thought life owed them endless goodies.

As painful as the recent loss of absolute security is, it is a good thing. The end of unconditional job security not only benefits organizations, but also people. The development of the borderless economy, which is clearly responsible for the introduction of insecurity, triggered a change that was fundamentally necessary anyway.

While human beings have a lot of control over the circumstances they create, there are certain inherent limitations that come from the essence of what we are and, therefore, what we need. Every living system, including human beings, needs a certain amount of tension to operate at its best. People achieve at the highest levels they're capable of and feel most vividly alive when they're challenged by risks that feel medium or manageable to them.

The Yerkes-Dodson Law explains the relationship between levels of risk and levels of performance.[2] People are not very motivated to perform tasks or pursue goals that are either too easy or impossibly difficult. Instead, people are most motivated to achieve when the task is challenging, but achievable. When tasks require a hard stretch, but can be accomplished, people are most gutsy. When hard goals are achieved, success is triumphant and confidence blossoms. We need a medium level of tension, of productive insecurity, to fulfill our human potential most fully.

Ending the practices of a no-consequence culture, which raises rights far above responsibility and which reinforces selfishness rather than civility, is an enormous issue because it is so widespread in American society and around the globe. But we must be careful: another issue is developing and carries the potential to be equally destructive. A new problem is generated when the values of paternalism are reversed. It has become increasingly acceptable to ignore the human factor in organizations—a stance that justifies arbitrary harsh practices and a misuse of power. The outcome is a lack of confidence, cynicism, and effective paranoia. Reversing the practice of paternalistic kindness is not an ideal; it is, instead a disaster. Organizations pay heavily when their actions destroy employee commitment and trust.

Nations have a responsibility to their citizens, organizations to their members, and parents to their children to create conditions in which all are held responsible for what they do, are expected to perform at the highest levels they can, and have the opportunity to face challenges and achieve success. That is the only way that people achieve confidence, a sense of effectiveness, autonomy, and courage. Any other set of conditions deprives people of the opportunity to grapple with life's hurdles, overcome them, and grow in confidence and courage. Like a world that is arbitrary and mean, an environment that is too protective also results in people who cannot engage in life to its fullest. That is too great a price to pay for safety.

More than any other sphere, this book concerns itself with the universe of work. Work is not a peripheral activity. Rather, work is integral to being human and is fundamental to the development of character. The best organizations are not always kind. Instead, they create conditions of productive insecurity that allow individuals to soar and organizations to succeed. Those that don't, in the long run, will fail.

When I published *Danger in the Comfort Zone* in 1991, I expected to be reviled for criticizing many corporate and government practices that others considered laudable. In short, I critiqued the psychology of being owed and practices of nonaccountability. Now, while I must admit that no union has asked me to address them, that book's popularity, and mine as a speaker and consultant, imply that the message was easy to understand and accept. Actually, I suspect that people were just waiting for someone to clarify what they already intuited. *Danger in the Comfort Zone* did just that.

Six years later, *In Praise of Good Business* significantly amplifies several themes that were introduced in the earlier book. The first is the psychology of being owed, why attitudes of nonaccountability destroy competitiveness in the borderless economy, and what practices are best for today's conditions. That constitutes Parts One and Two of this book. Part Three examines the second theme: the need to reexamine and redefine *good* in our social institutions. The second theme hammers the message home. That's why this book is important and why it will be controversial.

With a goal of achieving a healthy culture, today's imperative questions are, *What is the business of this business?* and *What is the work of those who work?* The mission of this book is to facilitate success in both economic and human terms.

The political, economic, educational, and judicial implications seem very clear to me. I am not applauding laissez-faire capitalism, as I am not proposing centrally controlled economies. I am saying that vital economies and political democracies require a continuously changing balance of power between government and business. Within that limitation, that neither government nor business can permanently dominate the other, it is clear that efforts to control the economy, and especially those practices that attempt to provide economic protection, tend to have significantly adverse outcomes if you judge high rates of long-term unemployment as something really bad. That's a judgment the great majority of Americans would make.

This book has two purposes: The first is to inform organizational leaders, especially corporate executives and management, of what they should be doing in order to make themselves competitive or keep themselves that way. The second purpose is to encourage leaders in all aspects of society to examine what they do and what they value in light of the argument this book makes. *In Praise of Good Business* argues that societies need a reinstatement of responsibility, accountability, ethics, independence, and self-reliance as the result of widespread opportunities for people to achieve meaningful success and real self-confidence.

Where Are We and How Did We Get Here?

The Borderless Economy

A FEW YEARS AGO, DURING A TALK I WAS GIVING TO A GROUP OF IBM managers, a man suddenly jumped to his feet, his body rigid with intensity, and yelled out, "Tell me what I have to know! Tell me what I have to know to be safe for the next five years!" "I'm sorry," I said, "I can't tell you that and neither can anyone else."

Nothing expresses the end of security more dramatically than downsizing when a business is profitable. *Reinventing, reengineering, downsizing, rightsizing,* and *delayering* are euphemisms used to make a tough message easier to swallow. The downsizing, layoffs, and restructuring of giant corporations like Exxon, GE, Philip Morris, DuPont, and Procter & Gamble were not the business-as-usual cuts that occur in every recession. Instead, they were structural cuts, a response to a new relentless pressure to get costs down.

There is a reason for the relentless pressure on costs. That reason is critical to our understanding of why job insecurity is replacing security and unpredictability is replacing predictability. *The core reason is the development of a borderless economy. Borderless* is more accurate than *global* because, in a deregulated economy, competition can come from the next block as well as from the other side of the world.

Here are some statistics that tell the story. Note the difference between what happened after the 1981–1982 recession and the 1990–1991 recession.

1981   Major recession.

1982   Still a recession, but white-collar employment rose by 838,000.[1]

1990   Mild recession. 316,047 jobs were cut.[2]

1991   Mild recession. Over 700,000 jobs were eliminated.[3] White collar jobs shrank by 364,000.[4] White-collar unemployment was 2,800,000.[5]

1992   The economy grew by 2.6 percent. Over 500,000 clerical and technical jobs were cut.[6] White-collar unemployment was 3,400,000[7]

1993   Corporate profit rose by 13 percent.[8] Forty-two percent of a national sample of 3,400 workers had experienced downsizing.[9] White-collar unemployment was 3,100,000.[10]

1994   Corporate profits rose 11 percent. 516,069 jobs were cut.[11]

1995   The economy and the stock market did well. By September, 212,000 people were laid off,[12] by October the total reached 343,552,[13] and by year's end the figure was 449,820.[14]

1996   From January to September, more than 300,000 people were laid off, 24 percent more than the comparable period in 1995.[15] The year's total was 459,000.[16]

1997   Job cuts in February were 20 percent higher than in February 1996.[17] Companies announced more than 50,000 job cuts in March of 1997.[18]

In 1994, a Johnson and Johnson executive visited one of his Japanese manufacturing plants. He congratulated his employees for their outstanding performance. Then he told them, "But I will have to transfer this operation to China, where the cost is ten cents against your dollar. If you want to remain in operation, you will have to find a way to use your greater technical skill to justify that extra ninety cents."

Worldwide, the 1990s have been a noninflationary period some have described as deflationary.[19] In a period of continuous cost pressure, it is not possible to raise prices significantly. Pushed to increase profits without the crutch of raising prices, management has been forced to ask: "Is it more efficient to invest in technology or hire people?" Extraordinary breakthroughs in technology, especially information technology, and the resulting organizational restructuring and reengineering have had a huge impact on the labor force. Increasingly, it is more efficient and less expensive to buy machines rather than hire people.

Downsizing may have become a permanent practice irrespective of the economic viability of an organization because organizations have taken on a permanent competitive status of being lean and mean. American unemployment is below 5 percent because companies simultaneously lay off people where the profit potential is poor while they hire and expand where opportunities are great. Pressure to keep prices and thus costs down is unremitting because in a borderless economy the customer demands and gets the best value. Organizations are achieving profits despite thin margins. Even in the midst of record profits, proactive organizations are cutting their basic cost structure, lowering their break-even point, relentlessly preparing to face softening markets and hardening competition.

What is happening? Why is business as usual no longer very usual? The most obvious factor is that there's enormous pressure to increase efficiency and get costs down. Because that's true, it's easy to see that the largest amount of change has taken place and continues to occur where profit and loss are both very important and easily visible. That's why corporations have undergone wrenching transformations while our governments and school systems have talked a lot about change but changed very little.

In a boundaryless economy, what is the border of a nation? What is the border of an organization? What is "place"? What is "speed"? Technology has made "borderlessness" a world in which you can always be reached and always be in touch, by page, by fax, by modem. A borderless economy is one in which every nation and every organization has lost the protection of distance. With boundarylessness, more and more it does not matter where you live; it does not matter where the work is done. And, as the protection of distance is gone, so too is the protection of time. Communication anywhere is instantaneous. Colleagues can be anywhere. But, without the safeguards of distance and time, competition can also come from anywhere.

In an open economy you can reach new customers, but your competitors will have equally easy access to your customers. In a borderless economy, it is both easier to find markets and harder to protect yourself from competitors. Harshly, the increase in customers created by boundarylessness is likely to be arithmetic, but the increase in competition will be geometric. That's because your competition is passionately motivated to steal your customers, but your customers are not really very passionate about who their vendor is.

Because customers have easy access to your competitors, the pressure on excellence and costs will continue relentlessly. An open economy involves unending competition to capture business and keep it. It means that if your offering is not the best, the most effective, and the most desirable, then someone, anywhere in the world, can take business from you. What's new is that there are so many *someones* and *anywheres.* Borderlessness means the competition can only continue to increase. In a boundaryless world where people can transmit and communicate instantaneously from anywhere, speed is a variable in overdrive. In a borderless economy, where distance doesn't matter and communication is instantaneous, anything, anywhere in the world, is capable of impacting you anywhere in the world. The result is that the amount of change and the rate of change will continuously increase. Everyone is in both a sprint and a marathon that has no finish line.

The Unkindness of Capitalism

Capitalism is not intrinsically kind. Instead, it is a harsh taskmaster. That's why it has a bad press, notably among political liberals. But in terms of facing and dealing with the unrelenting competition of a boundaryless economy, its harshness is an asset. It forces a disciplined pursuit of what really matters.

The American form of capitalism is much closer to the process the economist Joseph Schumpeter called "creative destruction" than are the economies of Europe, Canada, and Japan. Relative to those nations, we are less willing to support expensive social welfare programs and are more willing to give individual businesses the freedom to make their own hard choices. Thus, downsizing continues to be harsher here, and even large and profitable companies are continuing to shed large numbers of people. But at the same time, other organizations with greater potential prosper and create new jobs and wealth.

We curse the layoffs and restructuring, but they are a necessary part of capitalism's creative destruction. Creative destruction enables the economy to continuously adapt to changes in consumer demand and new technologies. In South Carolina's old economy, the fabric mills are closing, unable to compete with overseas suppliers. In the new economy, employees who used to work in the fabric mills for $10 an hour are now working in foreign-owned automobile plants for $25 an hour. Production is cheaper in South Carolina than in Germany or Japan.

Ironically, it is the harshness of the system that produces capitalism's vitality. Capitalism is a system that creates psychologically confident and resilient people because it requires that they overcome and benefit from adversity. There is more at stake than just winning the race. Facing up to hardship makes people responsible, stronger, and more complete human beings. Successful capitalism replaces the ineffective with the effective and encourages entrepreneurial initiative and growth.

In American capitalism, even the rising tide of an expanded economy will not raise all boats equally. It never has, and fundamentally it cannot. That means some organizations will succeed while others fail—and this will be true of people, too. Just as organizations need to make decisions about what they choose to do with employees who don't successfully adapt to the performance requirements of a more harshly competitive economy, so too does the nation have to come to a policy decision about the people who are not successful in this more Darwinian reality.

Will there always be some people who need powerful safety nets? Certainly. Our streets are inhabited by too many people that society abandoned. There is too little commitment to and investment in those who are genuinely and desperately needy—the mentally ill, the severely retarded, the experientially impoverished, and the addicted. There is a relatively small group of people who have long-term experiences of failing in work and in life, for whom there is only a small probability that help will turn things around. A compassionate nation should provide for those people.

But simultaneous with inadequate kindness, charity, and support for those who are the worst off, we have a national system of practices as well as a philosophy of providing enormous amounts of kindness for people who don't need it and shouldn't have it. No family, no organization, and especially no nation can afford conditions that increase the probability that people will fail because they cannot cope with reality. It is unethical to deprive people of the experiences they need to cope with the world. The "kindness" of not requiring performance backfires. And, while very human, pity is a corrosive emotion that ultimately precludes people from being able to earn the respect of others—or themselves.

I got to thinking about this when I visited a Marriott hotel. The cleaning staff was made up of severely retarded men. In addition to low IQs, most also had some physical impairment. As I walked through the corridors of the hotel and past the men, they all spoke to me in clearly rehearsed sentences. "Nice day today," they'd say, and I'd reply, "Yes, it's a very nice day today." "Yes," they'd answer, "today is better than yesterday."

There was a small card propped up on the bureau in my room in that hotel. It read: *Our Pledge—Quality is the result of my personal and individual commitment to excellence. My job is worth doing and it is worth doing right, the first time. My efforts will produce customer and personal satisfaction.* And below that the housekeeper's name was signed in painful, awkward, deliberate printed letters. The signature represented a dedicated commitment to the best that person could do. That experience was inspiring. If Marriott can get severely handicapped people enthusiastically motivated to do their best, it seems to me that we should require the same from everyone.

When, for political or humanitarian reasons, governments attempt to create job security by making it expensive to fire people, or they seek to protect industries from competition through subsidies or tariffs, or they try to equalize incomes through heavy taxation, the economic, industrial, and social outcomes are far worse than if nothing had been done. It is the freedom of creative destruction that has led to America's greater competitive success. Being in the danger zone of relentless competition is not only stressful, it's also helpful. Only by dealing with continuous risk do we develop the skills and the conviction that we can succeed with risk. Harsh competition forces us to make decisions and focus on doing what really matters while performing at ever higher levels. The markets are Darwinian; only the best will survive.

In a borderless economy nothing is permanently settled; there are no permanent solutions. These new conditions are, and should be, both exciting and scary. We are not experiencing a watershed of change. Instead, this is a time when the earth's tectonic plates are shifting and profoundly changing economies, governments, and social values. Endless competition and relentless upheaval are hard to contend with. It's hard to get used to the idea that there isn't going to be some way to solve a problem and make yourself safe. There are more people than ever in the race, and many are able to run faster and faster. Everyone, at every level, will have to learn to manage continuously increasing amounts of competition, change, and risk. While that is tough for everyone, it will be particularly difficult for those people who enjoyed the complacent, risk-averse, and safe conditions of no-consequence cultures.

The Presumption of Rights

The law of unintended consequences: With enlightenment came the presumption of rights.

Readers of the book *Danger in the Comfort Zone* will find an overlap between this chapter and my earlier book. This repetition is necessary for those who are unfamiliar with *Danger in the Comfort Zone* because a discussion of the psychology of a no-consequence culture lays the foundation for what follows.

A no-consequence culture became the dominant value, the mother culture, of the United States and most other nations of the world in the second half of the twentieth century. No-consequences is a value, a practice, and a set of beliefs that assumes security, comfort, equity of outcome, and even happiness as a matter of right.

When a no-consequence culture becomes the mother culture, a sense of being owed is "normal." That means an attitude of no-consequences is embedded in the majority of people's and organizations' assumptions, expectations, and practices. No-consequence cultures are found in every kind of organization and at every level of an organization. No-consequences is a CEO who insists on a multimillion dollar bonus and a golden parachute despite a failing business and a declining stock price. No-consequences is management that insists on many meetings, long reports, and consensual decision making in order to avoid making any decisions or taking any actions. No-consequences is the blue-collar worker who said to me, "I've worked for more than 20 years to get to a job where I don't have to work. Now where are you coming from, lady!?" No-consequences is people assuming raises, benefits, and bonuses as a matter of course.

A no-consequence culture protects people from the downside of risk. People don't experience any significant consequences if they are performing inadequately or their organization is doing badly. Even when corporations are hemorrhaging red ink, employees are protected from any hurtful outcomes of the business failure. I was, for example, at a division of one of our large corporations in the late 1980s when the business was losing billions. I asked management what its most important problems were. The answer was, "We only have 3 percent raises to give out." While the corporation was clearly losing enormous amounts of money, neither employees nor management imagined that things should be different from when the business made money. No one, for example, thought it might be appropriate for everyone to kick in some percentage of his or her salary. Though the company was in deep trouble, there was no personal imperative for anyone to notice the disaster, to change behavior, to work better and smarter in order for the organization to become profitable. As Dick Wintermantel of Motorola says, "With Entitlement you get a degeneration of mutuality."[20] Actually, you get an increase in selfishness.

No-consequence cultures reinforce the idea that the organization exists to support the employee and the employee is owed satisfaction. No-consequence cultures Manage-to-Morale and those organizations survey employee morale. Morale surveys ask people whether they are satisfied or happy with the conditions at work. By simply asking the questions *Are you satisfied? Are you happy?* the organization accepts the responsibility of making employees happy or satisfied. In morale surveys it's a one-way responsibility; the employee's responsibility to the organization is nowhere to be found. As morale surveys unwittingly reinforce a no-consequence culture, they are a destructive practice. Instead of asking, *Do you like your manager?* surveys should ask, *Does your manager push you to higher levels of performance so you are continuously achieving more significant results?*

No-consequence environments are protective. But today's reality is fluid and continuously changing, which means people can no longer be protected from risk and upheaval. Organizations are equally susceptible to no-consequence cultures. Like individuals, no-consequence organizations resist change, resist genuine accountability, and flee from risk. In the turbulent conditions that are today's reality, "protection" is self-serving and suicidal.

The technical director of one of our most esteemed corporations told me the no-consequence organization is unable to identify and make a commitment to a very few specific new products. "The process of analysis," he told me, "takes the place of decision making. The low-risk path becomes that of supplying a small amount of resources to the development of many new products. Then, every manager can always say they're working on product X because every base is covered. But, as every potential product receives only a little funding, no product has sufficient resources to really be developed."

No-consequence cultures offer two protections: First, individuals don't suffer significantly when the organization does poorly. Second, these cultures are havens for individuals who don't work. I still remember the United States Postal Service employee who was on his fifth "last chance agreement."

The culture of no-consequences is benign, protective, and parental. A no-consequence culture does not pay significant attention to the quality of performance and it does not differentiate between people on the basis of performance. It does not significantly punish nonperformance and does not significantly reward performance. In the worst case, not differentiating between people is justified by an ethic of fairness that requires equal outcomes for everyone. In other words, a no-consequence culture is not driven by performance, goals, or results.

No-consequence cultures are not driven by results; they are driven instead by relationships, processes, and rules. That means relationships, processes, and rules matter much more than results. Not long ago 14 of the top executives at a large steel mill resigned, having been recruited to run the steel mill of another company. No one could understand why anyone would have hired this group. In 1991, those 14 people managed to create a loss of $509 million. In 1992 they outdid themselves and lost $1,609,000. In 1993 they lost only $159 million.

In contrast, in the first year under new management, the mill made a profit of $176 million. That's a considerable change. Pointing to those results, someone asked the general manager: "If the 14 who were responsible for those huge losses hadn't resigned, what would have happened to them?" His answer was: "Nothing. They'd been with the company for a really long time. They're all 'good old boys.' In organizations that are driven by relationships, relationships matter more and protect you more than do results.

In no-consequence cultures, rules matter more than results. One of our most famous technology corporations was bleeding billions in the 1980s. Reversing the corporation's previous practice of merging the financial outcomes of every unit to produce a corporate outcome, the officers ordered every business unit to become a profit and loss center. This included 125 engineers and scientists who did research and product development and who published in the scientific journals. What these people had never done was sell.

Someone suggested they hire a respected consultant in their industry to do their marketing for them. Finding the right person was easy. They invited him to visit their site and look at their products. The consultant was enthusiastic. He said, "No one in the industry has products as cutting-edge as you. I would be delighted to represent you. I can think of at least a half dozen appropriate customers right now!" The R&D unit was jubilant, and the consultant returned to his office ready to follow through and start selling.

A few days later, the consultant received a phone call from a security clearance officer at the R&D lab. "It's my job," the person said, "to make sure you pass our security clearance procedures test." The consultant said, "I have an idea that might work. There's a bank in this office building. I will rent a large safety deposit box and keep the samples and drawings in the safety deposit box except when I'm showing them to customers. There will be two keys. You'll have one and I'll have the other."

The employee from the R&D group said, "That won't do. It doesn't conform to our security clearance procedures." The consultant didn't give up. He said, "Well, here's another idea. We can buy filing cabinets that are theftproof, and the samples and drawings will be kept in those locked cabinets except when I'm showing them to customers. And, of course, only you and I will know the combination."

Silence followed that suggestion. After several moments the consultant was told: "That doesn't conform to our security clearance procedures." That is the end of the story. Nothing else happened.

The security clearance officer had no idea that his actions prevented the point—selling the product—from happening because the intended outcome was lost in the process of following procedures. Interestingly, no one in the entire R&D group spoke up. Rules reigned; the security clearance officer was doing his job. People in no-consequence cultures, and the organizations themselves, become cowards.

Monopolies, like government programs or the public school system, always create no-consequence cultures. In the competitive private sector, the most common reason for the development of a no-consequence culture is sustained success. Sustained success is dangerous because it tends to blunt any sense of urgency about the market while it contributes to institutional arrogance. Institutional arrogance is the certainty that "We are successful because we know the right way to do things. Therefore, the way to be successful is to master our rules and procedures and do things exactly as we've done them before." Arrogance is the reason no-consequence cultures focus inward on their rules, processes, and relationships. When organizations focus inward, they are oblivious to the fact that they operate in ways that were once effective, but no longer are because borderlessness has created a new and very different reality. When you focus inward, you don't look outward to the customer or the competition. An inward focus contributes to missing the market. No-consequence cultures are unprepared to deal with competition, a fact they're sublimely oblivious to.

It's Expensive!

The most serious, insidious, and dangerous aspect of a no-consequence culture is that it deprives people of experiences that foster confidence, competence, and courage. Another danger is that over time there is an erosion of what actually constitutes work. The most expensive people of all are people who are truly convinced that they *are* working when, in fact, they're not. People try to keep themselves safe and increase their sense of importance by being busy and by including and elaborating everything. If you ask the people who behave in these ways, "Are you working?" to a person they will reply, "Hell, yes! Like a dog!" These are forms of not working in which people haven't a clue that they are, in fact, not working.

A friend asked if I'd be willing to review a newly created training module on empowerment. I was shocked to receive a package of 60 single-spaced pages. The package was so long and the module so confusing that I stopped reading and asked myself, "Just what is empowerment?" "Empowerment," I said, "means keeping your eyes open, seeing what's important, and doing it. For me, that's the essence of delegating authority."

For the moment, let's agree that *keeping your eyes open, seeing what's important, and doing it* is the definition of empowerment. What happens to that focused idea when it's put into 60 single-spaced pages? Obviously, the idea is destroyed. It isn't possible for people to see a central idea when it is hidden in a barrage of words and details. But if we were to ask the people who wrote the 60 single-spaced pages, "Are you working?" they'd reply, "damn right." They would have no idea that the very size of what they did made it impossible for anyone to discern what's important. Worse, those people were trying to do an excellent job. They work in an organization where there has been ongoing major downsizing for almost 10 years. Every survivor is very motivated to do excellent work. The scariest question is, If the people who wrote the 60 single-spaced pages became even more nervous about whether or not they had a job, how long would the next version of the training module be?

The core of the problem is that our criteria for determining best performance are now wrong. The old criteria, developed after World War II when the nation was very rich and time was not money, said:

- Long is better than short
- Elaborate is better than simple
- Inclusive is better than focused
- Form counts more than outcome

These criteria are no longer valid. The old criteria developed in the peacetime conditions under which we created a culture of no-consequences. Today's conditions require a transformation of our definitions of *best* and *work*.

Because no-consequence cultures are not driven by results, they are extremely expensive. No one can see what's important. Projects are too complicated, fuzzy, unfocused, and process-driven to allow people to concentrate on achieving significant results. The inexorable result is that too little is achieved that matters. The competition created by a borderless economy means that no organization and no nation can long afford no-consequence practices. More than any other factor, cost is forcing the end of environments without accountability. Today short, simple, and focused is the rule. Rather than Manage-to-Morale, organizations must Manage-to-Success, which involves Managing-to-Results. Psychologically, the healthiest conditions present continuous challenge and opportunities to achieve success in work that is significant to the business of the business.

On May 10, 1993, Steve Mason, CEO of Mead Corporation, had a 680-pound rock installed in the lobby of the corporation's headquarters building in downtown Dayton, Ohio.[21] Mead mounted a competition asking people to write a 300-word essay describing what it means to "move the rock." The winner would receive $1000. Steve Mason summed up the competition in these words: "Moving the rock means getting results. It involves doing what we need to do to satisfy customers and improve our productivity in order to become a high-performing organization. Instead of concentrating on activities, we must focus on achieving worthwhile results.

We've moved the rock whenever we deliver a valued product or service to a satisfied customer."

What does it mean to move the rock? It means to really work. What, then, is work? There is an equation in physics that says *work = force × distance*. Imagine a person standing next to a large rock, pushing on it. In this equation, force is equal to how hard did you push, how much time did you put in? In no-consequence cultures, people think they're working really hard because they put in long hours—they come early, stay late, and take stuff home at night and on the weekends. Ultimately, time becomes seniority. People expect to be rewarded because of the number of years they've been with the organization. Historically, organizations have reinforced that idea because they've rewarded employees for long service irrespective of the level of performance.

In a borderless and relentlessly competitive world, what matters in the equation is the distance the rock is moved. In

Reprinted with permission of Hewlett-Packard Corp.
Artist: Rand Kruback.

today's economic competition, the only thing that matters is results. The only important question is, "Did the rock move?"

No organization can afford any activity that doesn't move the rock. Now, and into the future, every person and every organization must challenge everything that is done and everything that is being proposed by asking, "Would this move the rock?" If the answer is no, there is a high likelihood that it shouldn't be done. Everything—values, mission, strategy, policies, and practices—must converge so everyone and everything focuses on and does only that which moves the rock.

No one can afford to have a no-consequence culture because:

- It erodes people's character and sense of needing to be responsible for themselves.

- It creates individuals and organizations who can't deal with the risk of uncertainty and competition.

- It encourages people to engage in the very expensive practice of doing things that don't matter to their organizations or themselves.

CHAPTER

2

Driven by Results: Operating in Earning

EARNING IS THE NAME I'VE GIVEN TO THE IDEAL SET OF CONDITIONS under which people and organizations succeed by pushing the edge of the envelope, by being innovative and flexible, and by driving for results that really matter. It's the necessary attitude, work style, and culture for achieving success in the boundaryless economy. Borderlessness has replaced non-competitive, predictable peacetime conditions with competitive, unpredictable conditions I call *wartime.* Succeeding in wartime requires creativity, focus, discipline, and courage. The following April 29, 1996 interview with Steven R. Peltier, CEO of Industrial Computer Source, is a portrait of an organization in earning under wartime conditions.

Industrial Computer Source's headquarters building is a modern San Diego workplace. Set in an industrial park replete with spacious grass lawns and young trees, the modern building is two stories high, faced with glass, trimmed with bright blue. Powerful pillars support the second floor and stand in front of the shiny mirrored surface that reflects shimmering green leaves. It is simultaneously lighthearted and serious.

JUDY: What is an industrial computer?

STEVE: It's a computer built to withstand rugged conditions—temperature variations, vibrations, or moisture conditions. It might sit out on an offshore oil derrick where there's going to be a lot of corrosion. Some of them will be dropped onto concrete from six feet and they have to still work. They go into tough environments. Two of our computers are going to run an unmanned lunar rover on the moon.

JUDY: It seems to me that this organization embodies an earning culture. How have you kept your employees from taking their jobs for granted after almost a decade of success?

STEVE: One thing we have going for us is that we're not that big. Worldwide, our sales are at $60 million.[1] Most companies with $60-70 million in sales would have about 500 employees. We have 175 here. We outsource *everything* so that we have the best, smallest, and most manageable workforce that we can handle. I still interview every single employee before they come to work, no matter what the job level is. Generally, the average number of people a person will interview before they are offered a job here is seven. We still spend a lot of time on bringing people in. It's very important.

JUDY: Obviously you want people who fit into your culture. What does that mean to you and how do you do it?

STEVE: We are very specific in what we expect of our employees and what they can expect from us. We have an implicit bargain in employment here. You don't have a job for life, but there is what we call a process of membership. That is, if you've been here for 10 years, you're more important than someone who has been here for a year. We have a bargain of, if you do the right work for us, we'll be there for you. We will help you grow, help you make more money, and have a better job. Since we outsource so much of our work and use temporary people when the business expands, our employees also know they won't be laid off. That's another part of the implicit bargain.

JUDY: How do the financials underscore your value system?

STEVE: The value system is the dog, the tail is the financial reiteration of it. The salesmen who are trying to increase their sales, increase their contribution, they have an absolute mathematical equation that is published in a book so that every single one of them—in every month and every quarter—can calculate the exact renumeration they're going to get for their work. We make a vast gulf between being successful or not. One dollar over your goal is a bunch of money. A dollar under your goal is very little. First prize is a new cadillac; second prize, steak knives. Third prize, you don't have a job. There is a big difference between those who are successes and also-rans. So once you hit that success of 101 percent or 100 percent plus $1, then you make nice little baby steps up from there so they can really learn to reach a little bit more, a little bit more, so that it's 101, 102, 103, 104, 105, 110, 115, so they know what greatness really is. They know how much money they get for that. We, as a staff, have an arrangement such that if they accomplish their goals, we know we're going to make proportionally more money— and we're *more* than glad to give them that dough.

JUDY: What are the other significant payoffs, Steve?

STEVE: If you ask all these employees, "Why do you like working here at Industrial Computer Source?" The first thing that's going to come out of 9 out of 10 mouths is: "Because it's fun."

JUDY: What does "fun" mean?

STEVE: Well, we have Ping-Pong tables and pool tables, we play volleyball in the parking lot, and have a beer bash every Friday. . . . But if you really pin them down and give them truth serum, it's because everyone wants to be on a winning team. That's why it's fun. People love to be on a winning team.

Last month we shipped out an extraordinary number of computers—an amount most would have said was beyond the capacity of the plant. But everyone got together and made it happen. On paper, it wasn't physically possible to ship the number of computers we shipped out our doors, but we did it. Ten days later, I chartered a 200-foot yacht and spent $40,000 on a party to celebrate what we had accomplished. People weren't just celebrating the party, but they were ceremonializing the big win. Ceremony is crucial.

We have a culture of "you can be anything you want to be, you can look anyway you want to look;" we have people here with earrings, ponytails, bones in their noses, wearing basketball shorts, because we rarely have customers here at the plant. There is a VP that I've never seen in long pants. They don't have to dress and act like everyone else. You can be yourself, anything you want to be, but you have to be a winner.

Basically, the rules are, outside of staff meetings, you have to be polite, congenial, and treat people with respect. Beyond that, you can do anything you want to do. So in our staff meetings, you can say practically anything to anyone. VPs aren't afraid to say, "You're absolutely wrong, so why don't you just shut up until I finish." I have employees coming in here telling me stuff I doubt any other CEOs hear from anybody else.

The other thing is that people perceive these perks, like dressing the way we want, or allowing departments to set their own hours as long as it doesn't interfere with the work flow of other departments. These are perks that have been earned and that can be taken away; they don't want anybody else to come in and screw up their parade. If somebody's not pulling their weight, peer pressure will generally lead to their expulsion long before my systems would pick them up and track them and try to get rid of them. Companies that have zero turnover are dying. There are people who don't belong in an organization over a period of time. One of our founders is a guy I just recently got rid of. We outgrew him, and he knew it.

JUDY: So you keep raising goals, keep raising the bar for individuals as well as the organization?

STEVE: That is the most critical thing. We've never missed an annual budget number in nine years. If you set it too high, you're going to set yourself up for a failure. You don't want to have the first failure in nine years. But if you set it too low, you're not going to get the best out of the organization.

JUDY: People always ask me, "How do you know where to set the stretch goal?" How would you answer that question?

STEVE: Well, there are two ways. One is going to be the quantitative way and the other is going to be the qualitative way. Quantitatively, in my industry, I have a very good idea of what my growth patterns have been for nine years. I also have the industry surveys that come out that you pay money for that are very in-depth for the worldwide marketplace. So, I know that I have an 18.8 percent market share in North America, I have another 4.5 percent worldwide, the market's growing at 13 percent, my compound annual growth rate is 28.8 percent. So I can come up with a pretty good range. Last year we set a goal of 27 percent growth and ended up with 31 percent. Good. Everyone felt like they knocked 'em dead.

The other is, it doesn't take very long to sit down with your sales guys and say, "OK, last year you made 102 percent of your goal. Where do you think you're going to be this next year?" Of course, he knows the bar is being set, and he tells you this number and you think, "Let me figure this out. You're going to increase gross sales 10 percent and you're going to make 30 percent more money. Why would I do that?" You get around to his own expectations.

If he thinks he can make 30 percent more money, he really thinks the organization can grow.

JUDY: Independent of his individual performance?

STEVE: Well, this entire organization has only 15 salesmen. So these are the team leaders. Each team leader is responsible for one-fourth of North American sales. It's not how I'm going to compensate him, it's another one of the factors that I'll use in assessing how much the organization is capable of growing.

JUDY: Did you just say that the salesmen anticipate their revenue on the basis of both their individual performance and the growth of the organization?

STEVE: Right. For example, every salesman here knows if his sales are the same this year as last year, he will receive zero bonus. You can't get bonus dollars with flat sales or flat profits. What I'm looking for is what their confidence level is in the growth rate of their sales. They are the ones sitting there talking to customers every day. They have the feel of the market. Is it still dynamic? Is it still going?

Each sales regional manager has between three to five guys working for him. He'll have a quarter of the United States. He's actually independent. Even if the other three-fourths do poorly, he can still make his numbers. Once all of the salesmen in his region are making their numbers, it qualifies him and his region for the quarterly incentive comp. So he has to train his guys. He can't be an individual superstar and make a bunch of money. But even if the rest of the organization falls short, he can still succeed.

JUDY: You have a system where you only reward significant success. You differentiate between good tries and major breakthroughs. Cadillacs and steak knives.

STEVE: "Cadillacs and steak knives" is a famous saying around here. It comes from a movie called *Glengarry Glen Ross*. Alec Baldwin does the famous sales speech where he goes, "Winner of the sales contest this month gets a brand new cadillac. Second place, steak knives. Third place, you're goddamn fired. Now, does everyone understand?" That is certainly not the mentality we employ here, but we use that as a model. The winners get the good stuff. The also-ran guys get another chance.

The whole thing about that movie is they're always looking for the good leads because they feel they're not given the tools they need to succeed. The key here is we make sure we give people all the tools they need to succeed.

JUDY: The way you have avoided a culture of no-consequences is . . .

STEVE: We make it very specific what the winning team looks like. We make very, very specific goals. We don't make goals we can't measure. If you can't measure it, there's something wrong with the organization.

For example, we wanted to do a new advertising program in some magazines. We already mail many, many millions of catalogs. If you advertise in magazines, you can get a nice warm feeling but you can't tell what the ads are doing. So we instituted a process called Elliot, which is the lead tracking mechanism for magazine ads. You put in a different 800 number for each magazine, you have different sales with a different code number. So if you spend $500,000 on them, you measure the exact effect of them. If anyone wants to do a new program, they know they can't propose any new program without a tracking method. If we can't measure it, we won't do it.

JUDY: And you step up to nonperformance.

STEVE: When we fail at something, we admit it. It doesn't mean the people are failures, unless there is someone who obviously fell down on the job. We take a shot at something, and if we fail, we measure it.

JUDY: The psychology in a no-consequence culture consists of at least two things. One is the sense "you owe me." Second is paying for stuff that doesn't constitute work. In no-consequence organizations there is a deterioration of the meaning of work. Busyness constitutes work. Seniority constitutes work.

STEVE: No-consequence employees believe that being with an organization for 30 years means the organization can't function without them. They see themselves as a guiding spirit, providing the vision, and that without them, people will feel lost.

JUDY: When I was here six years ago, you posted the results of all kinds of outcomes, clearly visible to everybody.

STEVE: Every single day. We show bookings by type for the day, month, YTD, order count compared to budget, number of new customers, domestic and Canadian export, international, shipments, backlog, credits, et cetera. It tells you all the main life support systems of the company every single day. I also get one from the European operation as well.

JUDY: I say, don't Manage-to-Morale, don't Manage-to-Fear, Manage-to-Success. You embody Managing-to-Success.

STEVE: I visit a lot of customers all over the world. It's a big part of my job. You can tell within 10 minutes of being in a company if they're in failure avoidance mode or success orientation. You only need to talk to three employees and you can feel it. Failure avoidance is cover your butt, manage the process, look good, smell good, walk upright, be there on time, work lots of hours. Nobody even knows what the outcome is supposed to be. Or you can tell the guys that are on top of it. They know what their goals are.

JUDY: How do you enforce ethics?

STEVE: Most companies have some inventory shrinkage. A little of this goes, a little of that goes. We deal in computer components. Some of these components are more valuable than gold. Someone easily can slip a $50,000 component into a pocket and walk out undetected. Every so often we would notice something missing. We had an employee meeting where I explained that someone who will steal one thing is someone who will steal anything. Our policy is, anyone who steals anything is a criminal and we will prosecute them to the full extent of the law. I will personally have the police come in and handcuff you and take you away from here.

Between our security cameras and a computer system that monitors the daily cycle counts and logs the employees' whereabouts, we knew there were three employees stealing from the company. We had another meeting and I said, "We know what is missing and we know who did it. If you will come to me before 5 P.M. today, we will work this out between us." Five o'clock came and went. I went over to the police station and showed them the proof. The next morning the cops came in, handcuffed the guys, and took them off. Two of the men are serving sentences in state prisons and the other is on a work furlough program. The court issues a report when someone is convicted of a crime. We posted copies of the report around the company to reinforce our intolerance of employee theft. Fortunately, we haven't had any problems since then.

JUDY: What about hierarchy? I suspect that you are not hooked on vertical power, and that you do not tolerate those who are.

STEVE: That right. We don't have the "There's the boss" sort of thing, "The department head is the boss around here." We screen those kinds of people out in the interviewing process. There are people who like having specific goals, the authority that meets a high level of responsibility, and have an attitude of "Let's go in and get it done; if I'm good, everybody knows it, and if I'm bad, everybody knows it." Some people enjoy that. Some people can't stand that. They don't want to say they can't stand that, but you can tell by the way they kind of dance around.

JUDY: These days there is so much emphasis on finding meaningful work. How do you create meaning for your employees?

STEVE: First, we have a mission and our mission is important. Our mission is that we are going to be the hands down, number one industrial computer manufacturer in the world. Which entails quality, intrinsic sales volume, profitability, quality of our staff, facility, and our products. We go over this again and again. Here's how we're going to get there. Customers, customers, customers. They're the ones who pay our paychecks. We owe them. They can stop buying if they want to. Nothing is guaranteed.

Second, every month we have a company meeting and the sales guys come in with a set of pictures and explain, "Here's a customer, and here's how they use our computers, here's why they're so incredibly important to these people, and why they're willing to pay what they pay for our stuff," because our stuff is nominally more expensive. This way, we can explain to people, "This is what we do for a living." It's not just computers going in boxes. People rely on these things.

JUDY: It's interesting, Steve, how you evolved a management style that is so effective.

STEVE: It's very effective. It's the least taxing because you're holding people accountable for results and for ethical behavior. You're not monitoring them on a continuous basis like a parent to a child. But the downside is that when things don't work right, it calls for you to make decisions that can be decidedly unpleasant. In some other organizations, you'd say, "Well, we can't do that. We can't fire them. We can't let them go. We can't enforce this." But you have to. It has to be swift, certain, and visible. People are uncomfortable doing that sometimes. But I'd rather do that on an occasional basis than forever try to manage this process where I have to drag everyone through a knothole backwards.

JUDY: How have you figured out which parts of the process add value and how to restrict the business of the business to those parts?

STEVE: Like I told you, a company this size usually would have about 500 employees and we have 175. Obviously there's some things we've chosen to do and some things we've chosen not to do. Hopefully, we've chosen well. Also, if the business were to contract or expand on a seasonal basis, between the fact that so much is farmed out and the fact that we use a lot of temporary people down here for when we get a couple of big orders or something, that way we never have to lay people off. We expand and contract based on the outside figures and the inside temps. That's another part of the implicit bargain.

JUDY: So you have a two-tier labor force. First you outsource and then you use temps when you have to. Do you have temps all the time?

STEVE: Almost always.

JUDY: Do you have any temps who work for you as individuals for any length of time?

STEVE: Yeah, and then become permanent employees? Many.

JUDY: So that's a source for hiring?

STEVE: Maybe a third of the people on the shop floor that are with me. Try them out, see if they fit and if we fit. A lot of people that start down here, for example, Lupe, who's production manager here, started as a temporary assembler and now he's running the show. Some people who have started as assemblers working integration are now working in customer service or in engineering.

JUDY: Now that you are increasingly international, are you competing with many more sources?

STEVE: Sure. When we first started this business there were probably 5 competitors and now there's 150.

JUDY: But you're growing market share?

STEVE: Oh yes, absolutely. We sell more industrial computers to more customers than anyone in North America now.

JUDY: If you look at everything you do, what matters the most?

STEVE: Everyone has the tools they need to succeed. Therefore, there are no excuses if you don't reach your goal.

> Goals are fiscal targets.
>
> We never sacrifice long-term goals for annual short-term goals.
>
> We win on this scoreboard.

There are no goals you can't measure.

Individuals have goals.

Teams have goals.

The organization has goals.

We have ever increasing success every year in both absolute and percentage terms.

When we fail, we admit it.

We step up to nonperformance.

The peer pressure is enormous.

We differentiate big time between the big winners and everyone else.

We keep raising the bar for both the organization and for every individual, but the goal is always reachable.

A results-driven culture:

- Is put up or shut up: Important accomplishments are rewarded very significantly and nonperformance is seriously punished.

- Finds fun in winning by hitting achievable, measurable, specific, stretch targets.

- Is all for one and one for all—"chained at the foot, joined at the hip, and shackled by the neck."

3

Changing an Organization's Culture Is Hard

*If you can't explain your change process on one
page, it's too complex.[1]*

STEVE MASON

This is not rocket science.[2]

NED BARNHOLT

As no-consequence organizations are guaranteed to fail in the
competitive, risky, and volatile boundaryless world, nonaccountability has to be eradicated and cultures changed. In
conversations I've had about creating major change in organizations, I've found that while every organization differs in
the details, at the core the essence of the problem and the
solution is always the same. When I ask management "What
really works?" no one brings up any of the famed processes
of the moment: team building, empowerment, reengineer-

ing, traditional training, and the like. Instead, what they say is: "Get honest. Know where you really are. Figure out where you have to go. Close the gap between where you are and where you have to be. Make sure you can measure what you're doing so you know whether you're getting there. Do only what's necessary. Make it direct, focused, clear, and simple. It's hard! Stick with it."

Ned Barnholt, general manager of Hewlett-Packard's Test and Measurement Organization, faced a crisis. TMO, Hewlett-Packard's oldest sector, had a long history of success. But in the early 1990s the sector stopped growing, profits fell, and their customer base declined because their primary customers were in aerospace and defense. As the aerospace/ defense business declined, TMO needed to change its products and create new customers. The sector needed a new answer to the question: What is the business of this business?

Ned said, "The first question is, What business do you want to be in?[3] What direction do you want to go? The second question is, What are the key success factors for that business? Do you need program management skills? Skills and processes for selling and delivering solutions? Processes for managing large R&D projects? Then, once you identify those key success factors, the third question is, What are the barriers in your organization? Do you have to make a large investment? Is it countercultural? When you look at the barriers, you can start to figure out what needs to be done. The fourth question is, What would you change? When we really looked at our barriers, we found our decision making style was too slow and we needed new leadership skills throughout the organization.

"You have to know you have to change. You have to evaluate the current organization. You have to identify the gaps between where you are and where you need to go to be successful. Then you have to start an action plan.

"We were stagnated and profits were declining. We were going through voluntary severance and had an early retirement program. People knew that if we didn't do better, that the future of the organization was at stake.

"Two things made a big difference. One was the openness with which we identified the barriers. Second was the owner-ship of what happened because the people who solved the problem were the people who identified it. We ended up giv-ing our managers more responsibility. They always had a lot of autonomy in their businesses, but they'd gotten into the mode of churning out products and managing, but not lead-ing the business.

"The key thing was saying it's okay to take risks and try new businesses. Reach out and look for growth markets that leverage our core competencies so we can grow the busi-ness. Once several divisions actually did it, everyone got the idea that it was okay to look for growth in new and different ways. Success in creating new businesses both energized people and made people aware that 'if I don't [get success-ful], I have to shrink my organization.'

"Extrapolating into the future, people started to engage and began to look differently at each business.

"Change only happens when people realize that the change involves them. An organization doesn't change. Change is the sum of individual people changing. Each per-son has to have the insight, 'I have to change. I have to behave differently.' You really have to grapple with the issue on a one-to-one basis. It takes time. That's why we really haven't gotten to all levels of the organization yet.

"I chuckle when I look at management books and the big consulting companies . . . and what they're selling. They make it sound complex. Start by looking within your own organization. The value comes from introspecting within your own organization and starting a dialogue about these issues. The learnings are personal. Change begins with your-self."

In 1995, Ned Barnholt's TMO was Hewlett-Packard's most profitable sector. Wow.

Ned makes it very clear that the basic questions are pretty simple . . .

1. What is the business of this business?
2. Do we have enough of a sense of urgency? (Do we have the drivers that create motivation for change?)
3. Where do we have to go? (What are our three highest-priority goals?)
4. What are the barriers we must overcome? (Especially those within us.)
5. What are our values? (What do we stand for?)
6. How will we measure our progress? (What are the key success indicators?)
7. How will we sustain our own and other people's motivation? (How can we achieve success?)

. . . but achieving major change in organizations and in people is usually immensely difficult.

Resistance to Change

Changing the core culture of a no-consequence organization is an imperative first step to succeeding in the open economy. While people swiftly accept that idea intellectually, in reality it's very difficult to change a no-consequence culture because people have grown emotionally dependent on its protection and because the definition of work has become so perverted that there's little identification that "I am the problem," and thus there's no self-correction. Even after years of change effort, it is normal for aspects of the no-consequence culture to persist. In terms of major change, it's usually much easier to figure out what to do than it is to make it happen.

There are at least seven major reasons why it is extremely hard to get rid of no-consequence attitudes, assumptions, and practices.

1. People don't like major change.
2. When it's the mother culture, nonaccountability is "normal."

3. The no-consequence culture co-opts efforts to change it.

4. Nonaccountability does not prepare people and organizations to deal with risk.

5. Leaders are impatient to get the change over with.

6. People don't know what you want from them.

7. Major change imposes pain on people.

1. People Don't Like Major Change

There is a natural human resistance to basic change because it is intrusive, disruptive, and just plain scary. So resistance to core change is absolutely predictable. Leaders of organizations are prone to view major change both as necessary in the face of changing reality and as an opportunity to position the organization for greater success. As such, executives and other change leaders are prone to significantly underestimate the threatening nature of change for most subordinates. Even when external realities are indeed threatening, most people prefer the status quo because they know how to manage within it. Basically, it's very simple: people don't like major change because, while change can bring gains, it will cost them the comfort of knowing how to behave and what to expect.

Moderate and appropriate fear—enough to keep people on their toes—is a necessary and healthy part of the transition to a results-driven organization. Fear is specific. It's what people feel when they can pinpoint their problem and then think of ways to solve it. When fear is moderate, people still feel they have some amount of control over the situation. In contrast to the specificity of fear, anxiety is a generalized emotion; it's what people feel when a problem is indefinable, vague, and/or outside of their control. Anxiety is significantly worse than fear, and it is always a destructive emotion.

When major change is initiated, most people at first resist changing and are preoccupied with the question, What do you want from me? Every organization I have ever known has taken people into anxiety instead of into fear when major change is required. That anxiety must be converted into fear during the transition period of change. That simply means that expectations and requirements of performance must be made as specific as possible. During the transition period, people are owed immense clarity and specificity about what is expected to happen and what is expected from them.

Employees need to know the business of the business, their contribution to it, and the goals they're expected to achieve. People need to know the targets they are expected to hit, the time frame, and the behaviors they're expected to demonstrate. Organizations must Manage-to-Success, which means highlighting successful performance. Managing-to-Success is not only a celebration of achievement, it is also a requirement of performance. Morale is highest when performance is greatest. That's especially true when the success achieved was a hard stretch. Nothing is as effective as succeeding.

A. L. Derden, director of quality for Texaco Refining and Marketing, described it this way: "Fear is not something we manage 'to,' but a natural occurrence within people when we peel back the protective layers of Entitlement.[4] The root cause of productive fear is twofold: (1) the realization that one is made visible with a specific goal, which is measurable and for which results are expected, and (2) the realization that competitive gaps exist which if not closed will undermine the financial and job security of the business unit.

"The sector of fear is something managers must not run away from, but in fact must apply their skills all the harder to lead the organization through fear into Earnings (a results-driven organization). While we don't 'Manage-to-Morale,' long-term, low morale is not good. It is a natural occurrence to be expected when an organization is first exposed to measurable accountability and moves into the sector of fear. But it's that element of measurement for which one is accountable that provides leaders the ability to give specific recognition for success, to coach and counsel and provide feedback. As one succeeds, and is recognized for improvements, one gains confidence and this confidence continues to build as one succeeds against more challenging objectives. Fear is replaced with a sense of value and pride and morale is higher as the organization sees themselves as winners and feel they own the victories."

Large change involves large risk; it can result in failure. When people are anxious, they are especially likely to hang onto old attitudes and behaviors. While some people adapt to change successfully, others are unable to do so.

2. When It's the Mother Culture, Nonaccountability Is "Normal"

When something is considered normal, it's woven into our assumptions. It doesn't provoke questions about whether or not it ought to be. Instead, the normalcy of something makes it a given. For example, for decades, unions, governments, and large corporations around the world cooperated in creating the equation that employee wages increase with seniority. That meant that while wages *might* increase because someone's skills became more valuable, wages *would* increase simply because of additional years of employment. Naturally, employees at all levels came to expect raises, and they made plans and decisions based on that. Now, value is based on a productivity scale that is worldwide and competitive. Increasingly, this is making seniority irrelevant in determining anyone's value.

When seniority is no longer valued, suddenly seniority-impacted promotions, the availability of particular jobs, wages and benefits, and people's pensions are at stake. When seniority is no longer powerful, people can no longer assume that they have jobs because of tenure, or that wages will inexorably increase every year, or that pensions are secure because of seniority. Psychologically, the end of seniority as the critical variable in determining one's worth, plus the end of the protection of nonaccountability, creates a future that is no longer predictable. And it was on the basis of a predictable future that people felt in control, knowing they could count on a job and a raise so plans could be made, homes purchased, and children educated. It is not reasonable to expect people to willingly give that up.

A particularly serious problem occurs when government programs normalize nonaccountability. While the majority of the public say they favor cutting programs in order to lower the national deficit, this same majority simultaneously opposes cuts in programs of social security, Medicare, Medicaid, and farm subsidies.[5] The congressional budget office has projected that without changes, spending for these programs will rise to 63 percent of the federal budget by the year 2004. But, while no government can afford generous Entitlement programs, no politicians feel they can afford to make serious cuts in them. As long as government reinforces the legitimacy of its programs, the difficulty of any organization changing its no-consequences culture multiplies.

3. The No-Consequence Culture Co-opts Efforts to Change It

As long as the no-consequence culture is normal, and its criteria of excellence are assumed, then change efforts typically deteriorate to no-consequence jobs and projects. For example, executives determined to increase productivity will institute a continuous quality improvement program. They hire knowledgeable people who are highly motivated to do the best job they can.

The experts typically start by assessing the processes that need improving. In the pursuit of excellence, it becomes critically important for every detail of every process to be examined and for every diagram to be printed on splendid charts that are displayed throughout the organization.

After deciding which changes are necessary, the next step is training all employees in the formal continuous quality improvement process. Now customized training modules are developed and training manuals are created. Either internal trainers are trained to teach the material or external trainers are hired. Training becomes an activity of its own. The effectiveness of the training program is measured in terms of how many people took the course and how well they liked it. What isn't measured is whether or not training and the quality process itself have increased productivity in the field.

As quality improvement activities proliferate, more people are involved and quality becomes a separate department with many jobs. In a no-consequence culture, the pursuit of improved quality becomes the pursuit of a process of excellence as well as the protection of one's job. Neither of those things has anything to do with actually improving quality and enhancing productivity in the business of the business.

4. Nonaccountability Doesn't Prepare People and Organizations to Deal with Risk

Without confidence, the core motive of people in nonaccountable cultures is a passionate desire to retain that culture. They want things to stay the same because nonaccountability gives them protection. Without the courage that confidence grants, people in no-consequence cultures often have an intellectual acceptance of the need for change—but they reject it emotionally and resist it every way they can.

Allen Bell, executive vice president of human resources for Toronto Dominion Bank, has observed two common problems when emotion is confused with understanding.[6] People can be initially motivated by an emotional call to arms, but, as they do not understand the difficulties involved, their enthusiasm quickly gives way to buyers' remorse in the face of problems. The second common trap occurs when management assumes that because people have the information about why change is necessary, they're motivated to change. *Understanding and motivation are distinctly different, and it's dangerous to ignore the distinction.*

People with a history of being nonaccountable prefer the security of peacetime and resent the current reality of competitive wartime conditions. At some psychological level they cling to the hope that after we fix this problem, things will go back to the way they were. Thus, nonaccountability does not give way easily or swiftly even under the direct assault of economic pressure and failure.[7]

5. Leaders Are Impatient to Accomplish the Change

Consultants usually expect that without a crisis, significant change in a large and complex organization will take a minimum of 5 to 10 years. I've never found a patient executive, one who could bear to contemplate a change process measured in years. Whenever I tell executives how long fundamental change takes, their response is adamantly and uniformly, "We don't have that kind of time!"

If we were discussing the development of new products based on a very innovative, experimental technology, executives would know the process could require years. But organizational change involves people and soft variables like confidence and motivation. People who lead organizations are usually not very interested in issues of people, behavior, and organizational culture. They tend to feel that the people stuff gets in the way of doing the business of the business. Therefore, executives are impatient to get the change process accomplished quickly. That's why they run from one change process to another, from one management consultant to another, in pursuit of the easiest and swiftest transformation possible—and end up looking weak and indecisive. The human element makes swift change impossible.

Changing an organization's culture and people's attitudes and behaviors takes so long that Ben Powell of GTE's Mobilnet observed, "It has been so aggravating. Finally, in the last six months or so, we have been getting to the point where we're really changing how we do business. But it's taken years. Not weeks. Not months. On a day-to-day basis, it feels like bowling in sand."[8]

The need for leaders to have self-discipline and patience came up again and again in my interviews: "After three years of change efforts I know you really need strong leadership or you end up sitting on the edge of the road. The most important thing I've learned is how hard it is to get people to change. It's very, very difficult, despite having the right reasons. Even when you spell it out, it's very hard for people to change. This is basic change, not incremental."—Dowell Schwartz[9]

"The most important thing I've learned is how tough it is to change behavior. I had some experience getting changes in behavior but never anything of this magnitude. It's extremely difficult. I'm not saying it's impossible. It is possible. It takes a lot of work and commitment. The behavior is more inbred in a regulated monopoly. It seems like you're climbing Mt. Everest. You have to come in every day with committed resolve that you can and will do it. Roll up your sleeves and work at it every single day."—Richard Champion[10]

"This is a journey and we haven't got there yet. We have the top thousand understanding but we must get the other 15,000 on board, especially on what's tough. They understand customer satisfaction, but they don't understand a high-performance organization because that's abstract. How do you describe it? I can look and know but it's hard to define. The most important thing is consistency from the top. You must decide what the message is and say it over and over, find new ways to say it and make it happen."—Steve Mason[11]

"You need persistence. The biggest failure in getting change is spending lots of time thinking about change methods and models, but people keep changing the models when change doesn't take root. Often the immediate enthusiasm dwindles and the net effect is nothing. Why? Because people like the idea but when they realize it requires a long, hard, sustained push that they didn't sign up for, they're out of there. Buyers' remorse."—Dennis Coleman[12]

"The most important thing is change takes a long time. My analogy is this: Think of a stick figure man going up the stairs with a yo-yo in his hand. The yo-yo keeps going up and down even though you keep walking up the stairs. In a change process, you have your ups and downs, just like a yo-yo. Sometimes the yo-yo may even seem to go to sleep. Perhaps we shouldn't focus on the yo-yo—but instead keep our eyes on the man who keeps going slowly but steadily up the stairs. Be careful when you get too euphoric. You get breakthroughs and highs, but then something lousy happens."—Steve Gardiner[13]

In the midst of efforts to create major change, it is normal for employees to express cynicism about management's ability to lead and make the best decisions. They blame management rather than the external environment for the need for core change. Not surprisingly, this results in hostility to and bad-mouthing of management. Executives who come from no-consequence cultures are usually made extremely uncomfortable by that kind of employee response and are in danger of backing off from the change effort.

6. People Don't Know What You Want from Them

I've always found that the organizations that talk the most about the new behaviors—empowerment, teamwork, challenging up, sharing power, and so on—are organizations that have the least experience with the behaviors they're asking for. When the new behaviors you're calling for are absent from people's experience, people cannot be certain what terms like *teamwork, empowerment, challenging up,* and *sharing power* mean. Typical training efforts to create behavioral changes are normally ineffective because they are too removed from people's actual experience in doing their work. While training can effectively create awareness that changes are needed and necessary, getting people's behavior to change requires personal experience.

I've become convinced that the only way to teach the kinds of behaviors that are now required is through one-on-one coaching, ongoing feedback, on site, in the course of people actually working. The new behaviors need to be taught and the old behaviors need to be critiqued very specifically and operationally in terms of the real work people are doing.

Learning within business is not so much a matter of practice in class as it should be a stretch in reality. Education and developmental assignments need to be interlinked. At work, the most effective teaching takes place when people are engaged in doing the hard work of the business. Organizations need a cadre of consultants-teachers-coaches who are able and confident enough to "hold up the mirror," enabling people to see what they really do. The job of the consultant-teacher-coach is to operationalize the new principles, values, and rules in the work experience in terms of very specific behaviors.

Toronto Dominion Bank is a terrific example of the kind of effective teaching that's needed. The bank has come to understand that people really learn when what they're learning is obviously relevant and important to what they do. TD has also learned that people learn most of the things they need to know when they're engaged in activities other than those that have been designated as "learning."

Toronto Dominion Bank doesn't do traditional classroom training anymore. According to David Morrison, "We've found most of what people learn, they learn when they're doing something which doesn't have learning as its purpose.[14] Our sales are way up all across the bank and coaching is a huge part of it. Branch managers now know how to coach. This process is working far beyond our expectations. It's fun and it's flexible. As part of the normal workday, people can do what they or their branch or their customers want them to do and they're engaging in the subject in a way they're comfortable with. Most important, the people themselves are making the changes happen." It's noteworthy that the changes are improvements in the bank's core business, and that makes those improvements very significant. Education at work has to result in an outstanding business outcome that reinforces a results-driven culture.

7. Major Change Imposes Pain on People

Dr. Robert Newton of DuPont Merck wrote me an extremely thoughtful letter about what happened in his organization when it began the process of moving away from a no-consequence culture.[15] He said: "For financial reasons we needed to trim all parts of the company, including research and development. The guiding principle in the research department was to maintain those employees whose skills, performance, and teamwork contributed most to the organization and then drop enough people to reach our target numbers and still be able to hire in new people with skills that the organization lacked.

"The process was run surprisingly well in that, as soon as decisions were made, they were communicated. Regardless of whether this was more unsettling to everyone or not, at least people knew what was going on, what the reasons were, and how the process was being conducted.

"The psychology of this event was rather fascinating. A voluntary retirement incentive was offered in December, with all decisions due by January 14. At that point we knew who was in the pool, what the organizational framework was, and we (management) then set about selecting people. This is when the personal nature really kicked in about what we had to do. While each person received a generous severance package, this was still hard to do on an individual basis as you thought about the impact you were about to have on people's (and their families') lives. Knowing that this was for the good of the business (and in some cases for the individual) made it possible, but not enjoyable, to do.

"Before termination announcements were made, employee reactions ranged from acceptance of the inevitable, listing and debating among cohorts of reasons why the organization had to keep them, and even concern among good performers as to whether their performance was good enough to remain. Many individuals asked questions that indicated that they had moved all the way over to Fear.

"Those who remained were relieved for the next day or so but the actual reaction set in the following week. Early in the week I began to see two feelings emerge: regret and sorrow about the loss of those who had been let go—even though their head told them it was the right thing to do (they had even debated about who was most likely to leave and had been able to predict most of the people) their hearts still felt uneasy, and anger and resentment was directed at management since we had made the decisions. Later in the week these were replaced with two new emotions which manifest in the form of minor personal conflicts: uneasiness about their role in the company and how they could work to make it successful (mostly the good performers) and uneasiness about whether, now that the company was asking them for a commitment, they could or even wanted to deliver (mostly the lower performers). Many of those who were let go the previous week due to low performance talked of doing things they had always wanted to do other than science. Their low performance seemed to be related to a bone fide lack of interest in their jobs. Those who remained and were average performers now realized that maybe they, too, needed to address whether they wanted to continue in this role.

"We have spent the last two weeks working on the final part of your process. We are showing people how they can contribute to our company being successful. Many people have risen to the challenge and have worked with us to move forward. Others are wondering if the role they play is one that they want and they are being counseled by us on a more personal level in terms of career direction."

The Sequence of Change

It's difficult to implement change because people naturally cling to old ways of doing things—an inclination so deeply instinctive that similar behavior can be observed among monkeys.[16] John Thompson described a study of how a tribe of monkeys responded to change. At night, anthropologists left a bunch of grapefruit half-buried in sand on the beaches of several islands that were inhabited only by monkeys. The next morning the monkeys found the grapefruit, ate them—and got a great deal of sand in their teeth.

For several nights more grapefruit were left on the beaches. Then one morning, one monkey remembered the sand and went down to the shore to wash the fruit in the water. The others ignored him. The following day two or three monkeys washed their fruit, the next day five or six washed theirs, and so on. When the number reached 15 to 20 monkeys, those who weren't washing tried to stop those who were; suddenly washing was perceived as dangerous. In other words, the change makers were first ignored, then suppressed.

However, Thompson tells us, following the day the hundredth monkey went to wash the grapefruit, all the monkeys—hundreds of them—washed the grapefruit. He observed: "What is ignorable, then aberrant, suddenly becomes socially acceptable."[17]

In the last few years I've observed four reasonably predictable phases that people and organizations go through as they try to cope with mega-change.

Phase 1. The first response is denial, an inability to perceive the need for change. Acknowledging that reality has changed is truly scary. It means the knowledge gained in the past is very likely to be irrelevant or ineffective because the present is fundamentally different from the past.

That's why the first phase of dealing with quantum change is normally to ignore the need for it. Explanations are put forth about why things aren't working as well as they did before based on assumptions that nothing fundamental has altered. The explanations for why things are not going well are logical and plausible—if the present is really like the past. You might hear, for example, "Mainframe computer sales are down because there's a recession in Europe and Japan."

Phase 2. The second phase occurs when the recession is over and, even though there's a recovery, sales have still not increased significantly. Now the explanation becomes: "We aren't doing it hard enough." Thus, the second phase involves buckling down. The organization continues doing what it used to do but tries to do it harder, faster, and sometimes with more people. Success is still imagined within the structure of the past. Now people might say, "Mainframe sales are still down but we're putting all of our people through an extra week of training. We're also changing their compensation. They are really going to be motivated!"

It's only after these reasonable-sounding efforts fail that people are forced to perceive that present conditions are genuinely different from what they were. The present is now seen as being significantly different from the past and this enables people to see they must do very different things.

Phase 3. During the third phase there is usually an extended period, sometimes involving several years, of flailing around. People know they can't continue as they were, but don't know what else to do. Understandably this is often a bleak time, a period of anxiety and high levels of frustration.

In this phase nothing terribly good happens; there's no major breakthrough to something positive. People have to get past the extremes of their negative emotions—their fear, anxiety, and depression—before they are able to begin to perceive opportunity. As those negative emotions moderate with time, and the mega-changes have grown more familiar and no longer seem so foreign, people begin to discern small points of light in what had seemed to be a black tunnel.

Phase 4. In the fourth phase, people begin to perceive new opportunities for success. It is the fact that success eluded them no matter how hard they tried that brings them into a future that is really different from the past. Now one might hear, "Our new chip is a real breakthrough. We can organize parallel processors and give our customers mainframe capacity at half the old price. What a marketing opportunity!"

The organizations that move into phase 4 are en route to the success of growth. That growth would not have been achieved if the organizations hadn't been forced by failure and frustration to perceive the need for major internal change. Like people, many organizations have to "hit bottom" before they can achieve success. There's a reason for the saying, "It's got to get worse before it gets better."

Major cultural changes are difficult. They involve large systems and many people, fear and resistance, denial and rationalizations. Major change is hard because habits and ideas that had become the warp and woof of the institution have to be overcome and behaviors and assumptions must be changed. Fundamental change, per se, is difficult and time consuming.

Most of the time organizational change doesn't occur because of a single, clear crisis. Instead, long-term processes of change are brought to bear and the organization adapts, sometimes almost imperceptibly, from one year to the next. That's not as thrilling or as motivating as a spectacular breakthrough. Nonetheless, it needs to be motivating enough so that people sustain their efforts to make the fundamental changes that will take them from nonaccountability to results-driven accountability.

To move from a culture of nonaccountability to one based on achieving significant results, it is necessary to:

- Get real; seek the naked truth.
- Define the issues specifically and deal with them directly, simply, forcefully, and tenaciously.
- Expect progress to be nonlinear because while the plan may be conceptually easy, realistically it's complicated by the negative emotions that change triggers.

PART TWO

Managing Now

CHAPTER

Introduction to the Interventions

Retrofitting an existing culture is tough. To get out of Entitlement you have to destabilize, and the problem for the Postal Service is it's very hard to get that after 200 years of Entitlement and patronage. Setting up an entrepreneurial culture is a relative cinch.[1]

NORM LORENTZ

After 25 years of helping to get organizations to change, I've concluded that we really got it wrong: we tried to improve an organization's performance by first changing its culture and the attitudes of its members. While that sounds plausible, it doesn't work. We use education and communication as the primary tools to achieve major change, but they are not powerful enough to make what needs to happen, happen. Education and communication are processes and are not at the core of what really matters.

Instead, the spearhead of major change has to be the achievement of significantly improved, quantitative business outcomes. People's attitudes and the general culture change naturally as an outcome of driving for quantified results in the business of the business.

The pressure to achieve important, measurable results in the core business will cause people who have better approaches and methods to succeed. They will naturally become leaders and models of how to behave. As the goals are measurable, real performance becomes the focus and differences in achievement are clear. Driving for success in the business of the business, within the values of the organization, and rewarding and punishing appropriately and powerfully is the effective way to lead people and their organizations out of a sense of being owed and into a results-driven mind-set.

The most important questions for any organization are:

1. What is the business of this business?
2. What are the critical and measurable goals of this business?

The answers to the questions, What's our business? and, What are our real goals? are the starting point for strategy, for making choices, and for changing the organization's culture as well as individuals' perspectives and behaviors.

While these are ostensibly easy questions to ask and to answer, they're not. When Walt Boomer was CEO of Babcock-Wilcox, he had to remind his engineers that "We're not an engineering company. We're a business that hires engineers. The question has to be, Will that design help or hurt profitability? Not, Is it the most elegant engineering design?"[2] Every organization must drive for results in terms of what really counts.

Reality-Driven Action

Danger in the Comfort Zone prescribed interventions using psychological force—punishment and rewards, peer pressure and support, short-term projects to achieve specific goals, and creating hope. In the ensuing years, I've observed the effectiveness of those change efforts as well as the more formal human resource techniques including variable compensation, performance evaluations, ranking, goal setting, and so on. While all of these techniques can help at the level of the individual, they're inadequate in themselves to change the cultures of organizations. For an organization to move out of the psychology of being owed, it has to move into reality-driven action.

Reality-driven action requires people to make an emotional connection to the fact that today's economic reality is (or will be) harsh, competitive, judgmental, and risky. The organization needs people to feel that reality contains threat—customers could leave, the business could fail, people could be unemployed. People should have some sense of tension about whether or not they have a job and whether or not the organization will succeed. They need to feel, as well as know, that hitting the targets of the business is the only form of security.

The sense of urgency that derives from the competitive marketplace is the most critical variable of all in terms of gaining genuine, lasting, and deep changes in the organization's culture and practices.

Too many people still don't believe their jobs depend on profitability. A machine shop's tool and die makers regarded themselves as so special that they refused to moderate their demands for raises and more vacation days and benefits during the recession of 1991. They kept threatening to walk out unless the president of the company gave them 12 percent raises at a time when the business was barely staying in the black. The president had tried reasoning with these employees for months, but had gotten nowhere. The tool and die makers just got angrier and more demanding, insisting that they be paid what they were owed. At his wits' end, the president decided to open the books and share the company's financial data with them.

He called a meeting with the tool and die makers and told them he was going to give them total access to all of the company's financial information. "But before I do that," he said, "I want to tell you a little story. Imagine," he said, "that you have money in a bank and your banker calls you up and asks you to stop by. So you go to your bank and after some small talk your banker says, 'Well, I have some news for you. I know you've been making 5 percent on your checking account. But I'm sorry to tell you that we've had some significant financial reversals and right now we can't afford to pay you that 5 percent anymore. Actually, the truth is, from now on, instead of paying you 5 percent, we're going to charge you 5 percent to keep your money here.' "

Then the boss paused, looked at the tool and die makers, and said, "What would you do?" In unison, they called out, "Move my money to another bank, of course!" Then, taking his time, the president looked each of them in the eye and said, "That's right—of course!"

Then he showed them the financial numbers. While the craftsmen knew business had slowed, they hadn't known how deeply profits had fallen. The boss then said, "Our shareholders, the people who own this company, put their money in our bank. What do you think they're going to do when we stop paying them that 5 percent?" For the first time, the tool and die makers understood why the boss found their demands outrageous, understood why the business had to be profitable, and understood the connection between the need to keep customers, profit, and the paycheck they took for granted.[3]

Sustaining a laserlike focus on succeeding and creating major change in an organization is much more likely when people are convinced that focus is critical and changes are mandatory because the real world is unendingly competitive. People need to believe that beating the competition and growing the business is the only way to be secure. They must realize that without success there'd be no organization and no jobs.

It is the sense of urgency created by competitive conditions that naturally requires members of an organization to be in touch with reality. But people much prefer to not perceive reality when that reality contains some form of threat. Instead of moving *into* reality in order to solve a problem, the tendency is to mentally move *away* from reality when reality's issues create anxiety that people try their best to avoid. Avoiding reality is further encouraged in no-consequence cultures because their inward focus naturally diverts people from external reality.

In the past few years I've learned that even when they're filled with fear and anxiety, organizations with a history of nonaccountability will retain that mind-set to some extent. Even when there have been years of churn and turmoil, red ink and downsizing, the culture and psychology of Entitlement are amazingly difficult to eradicate. In 1991, I underestimated the extent to which scared people cling, as best they can, to any of the safety the old culture provided. That's why most organizations today are having to deal with powerful legacies of nonaccountability at the same time that they're dealing with excessively high levels of fear, anxiety, and other strong negative emotions. When organizations have to manage where levels of both nonaccountability and fear are too high, they have to both sustain pressure for performance and reduce people's anxiety—while creating a sense of hope. In order for an organization to change, its people must believe that while change threatens the status quo, it also creates new, major opportunities.

Managing in the Present

Since *Danger in the Comfort Zone* was published, I've watched many organizations try to transform themselves. I now believe there are three primary things organizations must do. Specifically, an organization needs to:

1. *Get in touch with reality.* This requires (1) a sense of urgency; (2) leadership; and (3) purpose, a focus on "moving the rock."

2. *Use optimum ways to operate.* This requires organizations to (1) collaborate; (2) select the best people; and (3) use methods that increase business success.

3. *Create conditions that are critical.* This requires (1) trust; (2) commitment, or a clear understanding of the deal between employees and their organization; and (3) success, both psychological and business.

These conditions are the subject of the next nine chapters. More than anything, the nine factors are intended to get every business unit and individual in vivid touch with an ever changing reality that requires continuous and proactive responses, strategies, and innovations. While the factors are discussed primarily in terms of organizations, they are also appropriate to individuals. When, for example, the responsibilities of an organization's leadership are described, each leader can be evaluated in terms of how good the fit is between his or her performance and the qualities which have been designated as critical. That's true for all the variables.

1. *Urgency.* Does this person create a realistic sense of urgency? Does this person focus on what is happening to the business fundamentals of market share, competitive position, and costs?

2. *Leadership.* Does this person model "moving the rock," contribute to strategy, focus on "what business are we really in?," command respect, and inspire loyalty and commitment?

3. *Purpose.* Does this person do only that which is really critical to the business and has he or she identified and eliminated the garbage activities that were part of his or her position?

4. *Collaboration.* Does this person operate as part of a seamless team or is this person creating a personal fiefdom?

5. *Selection.* Does this person select others on the basis of the organization's new criteria of excellence and replace those people who don't measure up?

6. *Method.* Does this person focus on results and challenge processes that have become goals in and of themselves?

7. *Trust.* Does this person generate trust by communicating effectively and convincingly? Does this person "walk the talk"?

8. *Commitment.* Is this person clear and truthful about the implicit "contract" between employees and their organization?

9. *Success.* Does this person create conditions in which people earn psychological success as they contribute to the business success? Does this person celebrate success generously?

Although my attention moved toward an organizational focus because of the ineffectiveness of change efforts directed at individuals to change organizations, it's important to remember that managers and supervisors especially are constantly faced with having to get individuals to change their behavior. From that perspective, the techniques cited in *Danger in the Comfort Zone* remain useful.

Of the three clusters—reality-driven action, use optimum ways to operate, and create critical conditions—reality-driven action is the most important. Survival and success require reality-driven action. Individuals, organizations, and nations that refuse to perceive reality and deal with it, and that reinforce no-consequence cultures by not requiring performance, will not make it. Those that don't own up to the financial and psychological costs of nonaccountability will find themselves unable to compete for customers, deeper in incompetence, and ultimately a failure.

 Reality-driven action generates the kind of urgency you find in a start-up company; that's the urgency that motivates people to "do it!" or "move the rock!" Despite the pressures and real probability of failure, most people in start-ups will tell you that they feel their contributions matter, they are fulfilled, and they're having fun at work. Start-up companies are the model of what our institutions need to be like. Start-ups:

- Have too little money to afford much staff
- Are too precarious in terms of survival to do things that don't matter
- Remain tightly focused

That's the *only* way to go.

Reality-Driven Action: Urgency

IN THE LOBBIES, CORRIDORS, AND ROOMS OF MANY ORGANIZATIONS, one can see the charts and mantras of the management professionals. Posted for all to see are mission statements, community chest drive results, and road maps of complex processes. I'd rather see each organization's equivalent of the Conoco Wall.

In the lobby of Conoco's headquarters are two great walls of information, much of it monitored and posted continuously. No one who walks into that building can be unaware of how Conoco is doing—against itself and in comparison with its 14 major competitors. Even when Conoco is doing well, it won't be best in every category that is measured. The Conoco Wall makes certain that everyone in the organization always knows where Conoco stands in terms of what matters most. It provides goals to shoot for and competitors to beat, in a race that can never end.

Every organization needs its version of the Conoco Wall. It creates a clear and motivating message of nonstop urgency.

Urgency is the focused sense of danger that comes from a competitive reality. It is not an immobilizing panic. Instead, it's motivating. Urgency is an appropriate medium level of fear that is created by the external marketplace. Urgency is the sense that "Recast!" or "Do it better!" is absolutely necessary for survival or success. Urgency means never being able to take success for granted.

Organizations need a sense of urgency to sustain performance, to justify the end of no-consequence cultures, and to achieve results-focused organizations. The claims of urgency must reflect what is real. A sense of urgency is most easily created when reality *is* endlessly competitive, demanding, and difficult. Urgency is the natural or organic motivator for innovation and it comes from being in touch with market conditions and outcomes, with competitors as well as customers. The best organizations have the culture of an entrepreneurial start-up, one that's successful enough not to be running too scared, but scared enough to focus on what matters and do it!

Urgency can be an unfreezing process when there's a crisis. Crises naturally tend to create movement. Too often, organizations don't use the urgency that is created when things go wrong to achieve a productive outcome. And urgency isn't necessarily an unpleasant, fearful state. While urgency usually results from a clear and present danger, it can become a "zest factor," a sense of exhilaration and excitement, that unites people and breaks down old barriers and patterns as everyone is swept up in the drive to "Hit the goal! Succeed! Survive!"

When Gerald Czarnecki was IBM's senior vice president for human resources, he told advanced management classes, "Leave here with the mind-set of an entrepreneur running a five-person company who wakes at night with one great fear—the fear of not making payroll. That's not only his greatest fear, it's also his greatest strength. Every manager must be a little hungry and a little scared."[1]

Organizations and individuals need creative insecurity or constructive tension to do their best. That level of urgency should come from everyone's "getting" the idea that the battle of gaining and keeping customers is never won in an absolute or final sense. It's simple, but it's everything: in a boundaryless economy there are ever increasing competitors for anyone's customers. Urgency must be the feeling, "We have to do this extremely well because then we have a shot at attracting and keeping a customer. And if we're not excellent, we'll probably lose that customer. And if we lose that customer, I, personally, have something at risk."

Reinforcing a Sense of Urgency

Major change efforts should not be started before the urgent reasons for disruption can be articulated convincingly. If people aren't convinced there are urgent reasons for giving up old attitudes and behavior, they will resist new ways of doing things. Unless people believe that survival depends on new habits and patterns, they will not buy into the end of the status quo. People may say the right words and even chant the correct mantras, but nothing will happen.[2]

When leaders are trying to gain support for heroic efforts, it is appropriate to increase the sense of urgency by painting the danger in exaggerated pigments. Cries of alarm galvanize people to get on board. When United Airlines created United Shuttle, a carrier designed specifically to compete with Southwest Airlines, Herb Kellerman, CEO of Southwest, said, "United Shuttle is like an intercontinental ballistic missile targeted directly at Southwest."[3]

One reason it's so extraordinarily difficult to get rid of a no-consequence culture is that in the near term, a no-consequence culture protects people from negative outcomes. Fundamentally, where there's no-consequence, there's no sense of urgency. That's why no-consequence organizations try to create pressure with human resource processes like performance evaluations, ranking, pay for performance, and so on. But, unlike the natural sense of urgency that's created by a dramatic increase in competition, the human resource processes are imposed on an organization. The artificiality of that imposition blunts their effectiveness. Very simply, anything that is imposed is an add-on—and therefore, as arbitrarily as it was imposed, it can always be withdrawn. That's why human resource processes don't and can't create a sense of urgency and, therefore, can't do away with a no-consequence culture. And dangerously, employees rightly become cynical about change programs when, despite repeated effort, nothing happens because the platform for change, a sense of urgency, was never achieved.

The only effective driver for transforming a no-consequence culture is a sense of urgency that reflects reality. Without urgency, people resent management programs that increase pressure and resist, ignore, or sabotage them. Without urgency, there's no feeling that heightened pressure for performance or any other departure from the way things are is justified.

In 1991, for example, IBM imposed a performance ranking system on its employees even though the corporation's financial results were good. Announcements were made that those who were ranked in the bottom 10 percent of IBM employees were in grave danger of being fired unless their performance improved dramatically. People became incensed. Suddenly the company they had helped make successful was telling them they weren't doing enough. People's anger and resentment was so severe that the executives charged with executing the ranking system ultimately did nothing. Later, IBM had far more success ranking employees when it lost money and the need to eliminate deadwood had become unarguably obvious.

No-consequence cultures prevent any sense of urgency from developing. The height of no-consequence, of course, is the monopoly of government. An anonymous federal employee recently wrote an article that said not even serious budget cutting could change the mind-set of federal employees and create a sense of urgency, a personal imperative for them to do better.[4] The author asked some of her colleagues what would convince them that the federal government is really getting smaller and their jobs could be in jeopardy. They suggested that:

> If someone got fired, and swiftly, for running a business, like real estate, "on the side," from their desk,

> If "Solitaire" was taken out of the computers,

> If no one was in the cafeteria at two in the afternoon because people were too busy to hang out,

perhaps they might take the situation seriously.

An executive from Pacific Gas & Electric told me of the difficulties the company was having in convincing employees that they needed to increase productivity and become entrepreneurial in anticipation of the end of their monopoly status. The executive said: "Most employees are lifers. They've never worked anywhere else. Despite significant downsizing, most employees are laughing, convinced that this program, like all the other productivity efforts, will blow over." When competition only lies in a vague future, it doesn't create a real sense of alarm, of motivating urgency.[5]

Richard Champion of Florida Power observed that "At the very top of the organization, there are few that believe that sense of urgency is a problem, but the rest of the organization doesn't share that. Deregulation's been talked about for so long, it's a tired subject."[6]

In the absence of real competition, organizational leaders try to destabilize the too-comfortable status quo by cutting budgets, restructuring, downsizing, or outsourcing. The U.S. Postal Service is experiencing a very serious erosion of its market share due to electronic communications and strong competitors. When Postmaster General Marvin Runyan announced there would be no rate hikes for three years after the last one, even though the Postal Service was locked into annual increases in wages, benefits, and other costs, he forced the Postal Service into seeing that it had to do more—with less. The Postal Service has historically solved its service problems by throwing money at them, but Runyon's decision means that in order to become competitive, the USPS must put service "through the roof, while containing cost."[7] Lorentz added: "This could be our lever for change. Change is created by an extraordinary market intervention or an unreasonable CEO requirement. Cost is the part of the operation that's most visible and easy to measure along with service."

While start-up companies have the advantage of a natural urgency, established companies need to create it. Baltimore Gas and Electric Company ended the unwritten employment contract that ran: "If you showed up and were a good boy or girl, you had a job forever."[8] Dowell Schwartz elaborated, "We said we can't guarantee jobs forever. There will be downsizings. There will be acquisitions and mergers. We'll cut about 10 percent of the jobs or 1200 people. Everyone's scared to death wondering if they're going to have a job."

In anticipation of competition, some very sharp gas and electric utilities proactively created a sense of urgency despite their monopoly. Before deregulation and real competition, San Diego Gas and Electric created an arrangement with its regulators that ended the cost-plus guaranteed rate of return that utilities enjoy. Instead, SDG&E operates on a system that rewards innovation, service quality, and efficiency.

In late 1992, San Diego Gas and Electric anticipated that congress' energy act, which opened wholesale energy to competition, would later include the retail market.[9] Margot Kyd of SDG&E said: "In the early 90s, we began working with our regulatory commission to get a different set of regulations. Under traditional regulation, the more capital we spend, the more we make. We went to the commission with the idea of a performance-based regulatory framework in which our profits would be determined by our ability to pro-vide service at a competitive price. Now our incentives are based on measured customer satisfaction, the reliability of the system, the safety of the work force, and the price we charge. We have incentives for procuring gas efficiently and for bypassing our power plants if we can buy energy cheaper. These efforts have profoundly affected our vision of the com-pany and the way we do our work. It's taken us from a capital-driven culture to an environment where we spend less, improve efficiency, and improve service. We used the new performance-based regulatory structure to drive internal change. Profitability now depends on being competitive." SDG&E successfully created a sense of urgency tied to a com-petitive market before the market was competitive.

Tough Times Create Movement

In 1994, Arthur Martinez, then merchandise group chief executive, returned Sears, Roebuck & Co. to profitability by closing 113 stores that were doing badly, by giving up the catalog, which lost money, and by rebuilding Sears's image with better merchandise and catchy ads. With revenues in the black after a lengthy period of severe difficulties, Martinez observed that he was concerned because success might lead some employees to assume, falsely, that they and the company were secure again. He said, "Part of my job is to keep a vague sense of unease percolating throughout the company. The minute you say the job is done, you're dead."[10]

Sustained success precludes any sense of urgency and is, in that sense, dangerous. After I gave a talk at a unit of Merck, the response was overwhelmingly enthusiastic and the lead-ership appeared to embrace the need for a new culture. But nothing happened; there was no follow-through. An execu-tive explained it this way: "We have created a powerful sys-tem and structure, and we are very, very successful with this structure and system. So everything is functioning. There's no pressure to change the system because the mission of the business is being accomplished. The system wants to maintain its homeostasis; it resists any change. Thus, the momentary motivation generated by you threatens the homeostasis. It has to be resisted, consciously or unconsciously, and in the end it dissipates, leaving a sense of frustration. And one does not even know any longer that this frustration stems from the loss of this momentary motivation that excited and ignited the spirit in us."

Prolonged success is dangerous because it reinforces or leads to no-consequence cultures—cultures of complacency combined with arrogance. It's a short step from success to complacency. It's far better to always be a little tense, never taking success for granted.

Bob Palmer is the CEO of Digital Equipment. Like many other organizations that once enjoyed spectacular success, DEC eventually crashed in the 1980s. That motivated Palmer to research the past 15 years of American industry, because he wanted to find the explanation of why organizations that had been spectacularly successful later failed. Palmer found there is something intrinsic to success itself that leads to failure. "When you are very successful," he says, "it leads you to believe you are very bright and you understand better. You must be smart—look at how much money you're making. Then the environment changes and management goes into denial. Let's keep doing what we did to make us successful, only more aggressively."[11]

When you need to do something hard, tough times are useful. Ten years ago Robert Frey and a partner bought a small company, Cin-Made, that manufactured mailing tubes and other paper containers.[12] The company was in poor shape; its profits were marginal and its product line hadn't changed in 20 years. The labor force was unionized and the relationship between management and labor was antagonistic. Ten years later, the company was very successful, the work force was flexible and deeply motivated to achieve success, and management's relationship with the union was excellent. How was this extraordinary turnaround achieved?

Shortly after Frey bought the company, it was close to failure. Frey observed, "The people who change fastest and best are the people who have no choice."[13]

After Frey and his partner bought Cin-Made the company started losing orders, partly because it wasn't cost-competitive. Relative to its competitors, Cin-Made's labor cost was very high, as most of the competitors weren't unionized and their pay scale was much lower than Frey's. In addition, Cin-Made's employees got five to six weeks of vacation a year plus 13 holidays and a health plan that was completely paid for by the company.

Although Frey and his partner took no salary, within a short time after they bought it, the company started losing $30,000 a month. Obviously, the hemorrhage had to stop. But Frey couldn't cut management expenses because there were no managers and he and his partner, the owners, weren't paying themselves anything. The only expense that could be cut was employee wages and benefits.

Frey and his partner told the union they were going to cut wages and benefits by 25 percent. Surprise! The leaders as well as the rank and file got really angry. From the union's point of view, two rich men had bought the company so the very last thing the union would agree to was a cut in compensation. In fact, their contract had only a short time to run and the union planned to insist on pay hikes and a long list of more generous benefits in the new contract. Battle was joined and the union went on strike.

While the workers had been paid well, most didn't have much in savings and the union didn't have a large strike fund. Reluctantly, one by one, workers started coming back to work. In the meanwhile, the owners opened the books and the union leaders saw the numbers. It took time, but the union became convinced that the company really was in trouble. Word got out and workers began to worry that the company would fold. Employees were no longer worried about a raise. Instead, they were scared about their jobs. The union leaders knew the employees didn't have options because their experience and skills were too specific to Cin-Made and it would be hard for them to find other jobs. The union gave in and employees accepted a cut in wages, benefits, vacations, and holidays.

Marvelously, that was the start of what became a growth company. The fiscal crisis created a sense of urgency that the company and its employees had to change—and they did. Today, Cin-Made's autonomous and responsible employees focus on what really matters and "move the rock."

When there's a sense of crisis, that urgency can be harnessed as a significant lever for survival, for revitalization, and ultimately for success. In truth, it's usually failure, disappointment, and frustration that motivate people to reexamine that which they've taken for granted. And they rarely do this without significant bad news. It's only when the old ways of doing things are clearly not working that the path is cleared for new ways to be introduced. After all, if the old ways continue to generate success, it's immensely difficult to succeed in arguing for change. That's why proactive efforts in the midst of prosperity usually fail. In that sense, the pain of failure creates the largest opportunities for progress. Give thanks for hard times; it galvanizes urgency.

Urgency Must Be Given Shape

Allied Signal's CEO, Lawrence Bossidy, took over in July 1991. The company was hemorrhaging cash and earnings had stalled. Bossidy needed to recast the organization fast. In an interview in the *Harvard Business Review,* he said, "I believe in the 'burning platform' theory of change. When the roustabouts are standing on the offshore oil rig and the foreman yells, 'Jump into the water,' not only won't they jump but they also won't feel too kindly toward the foreman. There may be sharks in the water. They'll jump only when they themselves see the flames shooting up from the platform."[14]

One of a leader's jobs is to help everyone see that the platform is burning, whether the flames are apparent or not, because people will "jump" only after the heat has become obvious. People are rarely proactive; they have to see enough blisters on their skin before they will react. But while making the burning platform vivid is necessary, it is not sufficient. The crisis of a burning platform can lead to panic, to paralysis and no action, or to gross flailing about, none of which is useful. Leadership has to shape urgency. The "burning platform" needs a focus and priorities that lead to appropriate behavior.

Intel's CEO Andy Grove has insisted that the best thing that could have happened was the development of the Power PC in direct competition with Intel's Pentium microprocessor chip.[15] The Power PC was developed by IBM, Motorola, and Apple Computer, and it's ultrafast and inexpensive. Andy Grove said, "We needed a little threat, a good target. The juice is flowing."[16] He's pushing his factories and labs to an even higher pace than their normal ferocious one. They use a self-created identity as "competitive paranoids" to keep beating and beating and beating . . . the competition.

That reminds me of the Coke and Pepsi wars. I'll never forget standing in the lobby of the FBI training building at Quantico when a group of Coca-Cola executives arrived. As soon as they entered the lobby they dropped their luggage and fanned out into the buildings checking to see whether it was Coca-Cola or Pepsi that was being sold in the vending machines. Those Coke executives lived to defeat Pepsi in the war of beverages. And I know Pepsi feels the same way about Coke.

Urgency:

- Can unfreeze an organization
- Must be created, for without it, organizations cannot move forward
- Has to be given shape—specific direction and focus—in order to be effective

6

Reality-Driven Action: Leadership

WHEN LIFE IS ORDERLY, TASKS ARE PREDICTABLE, AND MOST THINGS are going well, people neither want nor need much leadership. When people are comfortable and secure, they want the status quo. In those circumstances, people want peacetime leadership, or more accurately, peacetime *management.* Managers manage when things are calm; in contrast, leaders lead when things are turbulent.

Calm and *Turbulence* describe the difference between conditions in which events are reasonably predictable and there's a sense of comfort and control, and conditions in which little can be anticipated accurately and there's neither comfort nor much sense of having control. Since the early 1980s, many organizations, but especially those in business, have gone from calm, peacetime conditions to those of turbulence and crisis that I call *wartime.*

In peacetime, there's neither crisis nor chaos, so there's no need for major innovations. There's no need for a major shift

72

in what people perceive as reality, nor is there a need for major change in how they behave. Instead, people are content with what already exists and change involves a gentle tweaking of an existing system in order to slowly improve it. Peacetime management involves incremental modification of what already exists, without major disruption and therefore without any major emotional consequences. When conditions are calm, when there's no sense of emergency or urgency, "leaders" don't have to be special, and they don't have to generate an emotional commitment to them and their goals. Then, "leaders" are simply people who occupy positions that have power. Anyone in those positions is seen as a "leader" irrespective of what they do because there's no need to do very much. And that's fine with their followers as long as life remains comfortable and orderly.[1]

Many who are now in positions of leadership are the wrong people. They climbed to the top of their ladders in the peacetime years of a no-consequence culture, a culture that breeds managers whose style and preference is to avoid dangerous risks and hard choices.[2] Peacetime conditions are not conducive to generating wartime leaders. In peacetime, people don't get honed on a hard stone, so they don't learn how to handle risk and they don't become confident enough to make the right—but hard—choices. Because managers and leaders, by dint of their basic personalities, are essentially very different people, peacetime managers tend not to be effective leaders.[3] As no-consequence cultures tend to attract and develop managers rather than leaders, organizations are increasingly turning to outsiders to find leaders who are mentally tough enough and psychologically free enough to make the tough calls and tackle turbulence and crises.[4]

In times of crisis and urgency people want leadership, not management. When the world is scary and the future is uncertain, people have an emotional need for a leader, a person whom they can trust and to whom they can make an emotional commitment.

This emotional neediness can be a very significant asset for a leader, but it also has a potential downside. When people are scared, they want mythic figures to believe in and lean on. Psychologically, they invest their leaders with heroic qualities because that is the grounding for their hope. Leaders must be aware that they will have to make and carry out painful decisions that may crush people's elevated expectations of how wonderful they are.

Leaders need a powerful, personal view that they are able to sell to others who become convinced of its righteousness. That view must so clearly guide their values and priorities that followers are galvanized by the constancy of their choices. Leaders gain credibility and trust by the forceful consistency of their decisions, their focus on hitting the target, and their success in making the right things happen.

Leaders convince others that they understand the issues better than anyone else.[5] People follow them because they speak about solutions with persuasive conviction, because they act decisively, and because they project confidence while others are uncertain. The prototypical leader is Winston Churchill, who, when England was expecting the Germans to invade, said, "We will fight on the beaches, . . . we shall fight in the fields and in the streets, . . . We shall never surrender."[6]

Effective leaders are focused. They severely limit their objectives to only the critical issues at any one moment in time. If leaders are too impatient, they flail about and change directions and programs too fast, long before they've had time to be effective. Leading the transformation of an organization requires a commitment to hanging in despite setbacks, following through to achieve targets. Not staying long enough with one focused process, one set of priorities and goals, leads to repetitive failure. It also creates cynicism in people who've been let down too long and too often to believe that anything is going to work.

Effective leaders stand simultaneously in today's realities and tomorrow's possibilities and they transform their ideas into forms, images, or words that generate excitement and enthusiasm in others. They make transformation positive: They evoke beliefs and create expectations that alter what other people think is possible, necessary, or desirable. While leaders must be in keen contact with reality, they must also be optimists. Leaders must really see opportunities in change and model that essential good cheer for those who follow them.

What Leaders Do in Times of Crisis

There are seven critical things leaders must do to create strong leadership and achieve success.

1. Define the business of the business
2. Create a winning strategy
3. Communicate persuasively[7]
4. Behave with integrity
5. Respect others
6. Decide and act
7. Achieve alignment

Define the Business of the Business

The most important question for any organization is, "What is the business of this business?" The answer to that question determines what that organization should and shouldn't do. Without an accurate answer to the question, "What is our core business?" you cannot know who the real customers or competitors are; you also cannot know the true measures of success.

As long as the IBM Corporation designated computers as its business, the corporate focus was on hardware. But the business of the business had to be reconceptualized from the customer's point of view. When the corporation redefined its business as "solving customer problems," it became easier to see the importance of software and services, which are two great growth opportunities, and it made it easier to perceive niche opportunities that are created by customer needs. Meeting the diverse requirements of a wide range of customers is far more likely to generate a myriad of market opportunities than can be generated by the far more restrictive "We're in the computer business."

It's hard to grasp how critically important it is to designate the business of the business both accurately and creatively. The railroads, for example, defined themselves for too long as being in the railroad business—limited, therefore, to where their tracks were—instead of perceiving themselves as being in the business of transporting people and things. As long as the railroads believed they were railroads, they were directly responsible for the huge growth of the deregulated trucking industry. Trucking declared that its business was transporting. That definition allowed truckers to be quick to perceive niche opportunities that became large growth markets. The way railroads defined their business made trucking an enormous competitor.

In defining the business, leaders must perceive forests rather than leaves. Without an overriding view, it's really easy to do the wrong things marvelously well. When Jerome York was IBM's finance chief, he visited the corporation's software production facilities in Boulder, Colorado.[8] The software executives had prepared elaborate technical presentations but the content was much too detailed to interest York. He grew more and more impatient as an executive's description of the technology needed to deliver software electronically became even more increasingly detailed. When the presentation moved to the cost of sending megabytes of software over phone lines, York exploded. He is reported to have said, "I want to get off that slide. Where do you want to take this business? Get me to the end and tell me where you want to go." York was saying, "Get off the details! You're lost in the details! Tell me clearly, what business are you in?"

In the not-so-long-ago days of peacetime, the answer to the question, *What is our core business?* never changed or changed very slowly. But in our borderless economy this question must be revisited often because the answer can change fast. But while the answer may need to change swiftly and dramatically, it's a human tendency to stay in the old grooves of thinking and doing. Without a clear crisis that obviously necessitates change, most people try, as long as they can, to stretch and pull and tug to make the past fit the present.

Only a small fraction of people have the creative imagination and ability to conceptualize the future and make it realistic enough so that they can plan for it.[9] Eckhard Pfeiffer, president of Compaq Computer, says, "Nothing is harder than casting aside the thinking, strategies, and biases that propelled a business to its current success. Companies need to learn how to unlearn, to slough off yesterday's wisdom."[10] Most of the companies that have achieved some success in transforming themselves from no-consequence cultures to cultures driven by results have had to make the most basic and difficult change—reconceptualizing what their core businesses really are.

Determining the business of the business is the first step in setting priorities. Setting priorities is a major leadership responsibility because without focused priorities, efforts are splintered and nothing gets accomplished. The best leaders get the organization to focus, to be involved only in what matters the most. The answer to that question must also be the basis for the organization's strategy—what the organization will do to achieve a market advantage. In competitive times, leaders must skillfully harness the natural sense of urgency that arises from the external threat of competition and use that to continuously reinforce a focus on doing what counts. Achieving the mission against hard odds is the glue that holds people together with a commitment to the good of all.

Create a Winning Strategy

In order to achieve market leadership and success, organizations need an innovative and dynamic idea of what they will offer customers that sets them apart and gives them a significant advantage. That idea is their strategy. Strategy is the organization's designation of the kind of value it will create for its customers. Strategy determines what the organization will focus on so it will distinguish itself from and beat the competition.

Strategy involves *what* the organization is delivering or selling to its customers that sets it apart and makes it the preferred provider. There's often a basic confusion between the strategic choice and the process of how the strategy is achieved. Process can help an organization achieve its strategy, but a process is *how* the strategy is pursued.[11] A customer doesn't care how an organization is able to offer something of greater value—only that it is. Therefore, the process of achieving the strategy must not be confused with or pursued as the strategy.[12] Strategy is best thought of very simply; it's the designation of what you're selling to your customers.

Customers simply want to know that what you're offering is a better deal than anyone else is offering. That's what strategy is all about. An organization's strategy is its decision about what it will offer in the marketplace because it believes that the customer will prefer whatever it offers to whatever its competitors are offering.

It is leadership's responsibility to create a strategy, or a line of actions that will enable the organization to succeed, grow and prosper. In a borderless economy, the questions, *How will we do this?* and *Are our competitors doing this?* must be raised and answered often because the strategy has to derive from the competitive reality of the core business. Strategy is conceptual; it is the ideas of what the organization will do better than anyone else in order to be the customer's choice. Success depends on being selected by customers.

Therefore, strategy must be constructed from the customer's point of view; the line of actions must increase the focus of all parts of the organization on the customer.

What is the business of this business?

Who are our customers?

What do our customers want?

What might our customers need?

What could delight our customers?

What can we do better than our competition?

What does the competition do better than us?

The answers to these questions are the data that enable organizations to make decisions. These decisions are the choices that become the organization's strategy. Today, these questions are posed with a new frequency and urgency because in the borderless reality, customers have ever increasing choices, so no one can count on customer loyalty. Instead, organizations have to construct a continuously evolving but consistently effective strategy because success and security have to be earned over and over again.

As strategy provides the conceptual model of choices, the strategy sets priorities. Leaders must use strategy to set priorities because organizations have to focus. They must concentrate on the few top priorities; if they don't, energy is dissipated and little is accomplished. As a negative example, in 1994 I visited a division of a technology company that claimed it was working on 20,000 new products. That was an exaggerated and ill-conceived interpretation of what it means to be customer-driven. The outcome, of course, since there were no priorities, was confusion. Different people kept pushing different products and priorities kept changing as different product champions gained or lost favor and power. Not surprisingly, the business was failing.

Many organizations that were successful and powerful in one era fail to maintain their position in the next because

they imagine the future as largely a linear projection from
the present. Their myopic internal focus and assumption of
the status quo leave them vulnerable to technological devel-
opments, shifts in customer preferences, and the sheer rate
of change in the environment. Successful organizations
work on achieving creative dissonance; they foster ideas
about the future and its possibilities that are very divergent
both from past and present scenarios.

It's easy to gain the impression from the media that ever
since 1981, the main strategy of organizations has been to
slash and burn, to defend the organization by cutting costs,
especially by downsizing the number of employees. While
cutting costs and eliminating jobs has been the most visible
response to increased competition and pricing pressures, cutting costs alone is defensive and reactive. In the long run, cutting costs cannot lead to success. A defensive strategy merely
prolongs survival and postpones failure. Management's task is
to lead the organization not only to greater efficiencies but
ultimately to greater growth and wealth creation.

Effective strategy produces growth and profit. Dennis
Coleman of Hewlett-Packard observed: "If we're not doing
that, we're not moving the rock. Cost control, process
improvement alone . . . that path is a slow death. If we're not
producing the growth rate and profitability to get the needle
off the meter, we won't succeed in the long term!"[13] Margot
Kyd adds: "Succeeding in a competitive marketplace brings a
lot of excitement, confidence, and growth. In comparison,
cutting is cautious. There's no rallying around caution."[14]

Strategy is not long-range planning. The latter is specific,
detailed, and pragmatic. A strategic plan tells people what
the goals and subgoals are, how they will be achieved, what
processes will be utilized, and how the outcomes of activities will be measured. In contrast, strategy is conceptual: it's
the big picture. Strategy uses data, but it is not confined to
whatever is quantitative and measurable.[15] Instead, strategic
thinking is imaginative, abstract, intuitive, conceptual, and,
hopefully, creative. It involves processes of synthesizing data

and ideas—of bringing together disparate pieces to create a new concept. As Richard Champion of Florida Power put it, "Strategic thinking is thinking out of the box."[16]

Far more than in peacetime, turbulent conditions put a premium on creativity, on thinking "out of the box." When conditions are turbulent, no tactical advantage will last long. In a borderless economy, there will be many more competitors, each seeking to develop an advantage before it has occurred to others. Therefore, an essential flexibility of thought has become requisite for long-term success.

Entrepreneur Edward Richardson (a pseudonym for a man who wishes to remain anonymous) balances a consistent and coherent long-term plan with short-term tactics that can turn on a dime. Richardson never loses focus that he operates in extremely competitive markets with shifting conditions that can transform advantages to liabilities in a metaphorical instant. While Richardson invests for the long haul, he's constantly scanning his universe, seeking this moment's advantage.

Strategy needs to be so clear, plausible, clever, bold, and achievable that it generates a conviction that even if the journey is hard, it's worth taking. People must see that the line of action has created a major competitive advantage. Strategy must generate the sense that "We can win!" In addition to employees, it must also convince customers and suppliers that there's more significant long-term advantage for them in your organization's plan than with any of your competitors.

Defining the business of the business shrewdly and proactively, and creating a compelling strategy for winning, are critical to getting employees, customers, and suppliers committed to your organization.

Communicate Persuasively

Leaders know that trust is a competitive advantage in a world of adversarial competition. Basically, trust is a matter of predictability. People trust others when they're told something will happen and it does. Major change, therefore, always threatens trust, and thus ultimately confidence in leadership. Ineffective or nonexistent communication, especially in times of crisis, results in an enormous increase in confusion and cynicism and a huge decline in morale, trust in the organization, and confidence in the leadership. That's why the need for accurate, forthright, and persuasive communication is especially critical in periods of major threat and change.

During periods of turbulence, most organizations send out too many communications because they think being inclusive is good. But when there are too many messages, not much gets through. Where there's too much anxiety, not much gets through either. Therefore, organizations have to limit the number of their communications and simplify the messages they send in order to communicate, persuade, and energize.

Leaders must decide which few crucial pieces of information people really need to know, and then that information must be amplified. Information must be stated far more simply and repetitiously than anyone imagines is necessary. And, when the goals are to reduce anxiety and increase commitment to the leader and the mission, the most effective communication is a face-to-face, personal dialogue.

Leaders should frame the organization's mission and values in ways that members find transcendent: The goals of the business are transmuted from the dross of ordinary work into something extraordinary. Then the organization's goals become an ambition that is worthy of heroic effort and even sacrifice. I believe that many people are more ready to make an emotional commitment if the outcome involves achieving an ennobling goal. An "ennobling goal" is one in which the achievement has an outcome that benefits more than oneself.

An often used example of transcendence involves three stonemasons: "In the days of misty towers, distressed maidens, and stalwart knights, a young man, walking down a road, came upon a laborer fiercely pounding away at a stone with hammer and chisel. The lad asked the worker, who looked frustrated and angry, 'What are you doing?' The laborer answered in a pained voice: 'I'm trying to shape this stone, and it is backbreaking work.' The youth continued his journey and soon came upon another man chipping away at a similar stone, who looked neither particularly angry nor happy. 'What are you doing?' he asked. 'I'm shaping a stone for a building.' The young man went on and before long came to a third worker chipping away at a stone, but this worker was singing happily as he worked. 'What are you doing?' The worker smiled and replied: 'I'm building a cathedral.' "[17]

Equally eloquently, Antoine de Saint-Exupéry wrote, "If you want to build a ship, then don't drum up men to gather wood, give orders, and divide the work. Rather, teach them to yearn for the far and endless sea."[18]

Behave with Integrity

Management is the message; speeches only call attention to it.[19]

Without integrity, trust is never achieved. The most important communications aren't verbal, they're behavioral. Leaders communicate their real values far more by what they do than by what they say. This is why it's imperative that leaders lead by example.

Gaining employee confidence and commitment involves clearly articulated statements of what constitutes the core business, the strategies for achieving success, and the organization's values. Leaders need to clarify the new values by embodying them in their actions even more than in their words. Leaders, especially, not only have to *do;* they must also *be* models of the new values. If they are inconsistent or duplicitous, anxious subordinates will become mistrustful and try desperately to figure out what the boss really wants, with results that are unpredictable.

Most organizations today, for example, hail the banner of being customer-focused. One company was in imminent danger of being penalized millions of dollars a day by state regulatory agencies because customer service had fallen to abysmal levels. The CEO was embarrassed and furious. He pounded on the table, face red, eyes glaring, and between clenched teeth said, "How could this happen? I told everyone: customer first!"

The CEO's mouth said, "customers," but his actions said, "shareholders." His subordinates were convinced that their primary job wasn't satisfying customers; it was getting costs down so that profits, and the price of their stock, would rise. That's why his executives downsized their units as much as they could: It naturally followed that service plummeted.

People need to know the organization's values—what it most esteems and honors—as the basis for their understanding what the real rules are. If the values are not clear under anxiety-generating conditions, people will not know what the leadership really wants from them. When they don't know what is expected of them, the majority will continue to behave according to the rules of the no-consequence culture that they know so well.

Integrity rests partly on personal courage. It requires being truthful with oneself as well as with others in terms of what is genuinely valued and what is considered important. Leaders cannot lead from ego. First, leading or making decisions on the basis of ego is likely to result in wrong decisions that lead to failure. Second, followers will not make a commitment if they perceive that defending or enhancing the leader's ego is the essential motivation underlying the leader's decisions. That renders the leader nonheroic and, therefore, not worthy of being followed.

Behaving with integrity also means being consistent in one's choices and actions. In addition to courage, this requires that leaders have some certainty about what direction to take and which path to choose, which in turn requires a clear conviction about values and a steadfastness of purpose in distinguishing between right and wrong, wise and foolish. Without a core conviction about what's right, would-be "leaders" vacillate, compromise, appease, and conciliate, with the inevitable result that they're perceived as forever bending with the wind, too weak to serve as leaders.

Respect Others

The best leaders don't waste other people's brains.

"The key lesson I've learned is the power of involving people," says HP's Dennis Coleman.[20] "If you can get them to see the need for changes and get them involved in getting them to make that happen, it's incredible what they can do." While executives normally have the broadest view, it's become very clear that organizations that operate on the basis of vertical power are deprived of the input of people who may be experts in a subject but are in subordinate positions. In the competition of a borderless economy, organizations need input from subordinates because the people doing the work usually have greater knowledge of operational reality.

Organizations with cultures that are psychologically hierarchical have a disdain for subordinates. Irrespective of what's publicly said about needing input from people lower in the hierarchy but closer to the action, those organizations tell—but don't listen to—people down the ladder. Today, many blue- and pink-collar people, in addition to white- and open-collar employees, are educated and experienced and have instant access to information. Thus, subordinates at all levels have experience, knowledge, intelligence, and skill that they could bring to the table if their bosses were psychologically able to "hear." Hearing others isn't a matter of process. It is, instead, a matter of respect.

Subordinates feel much more valuable and powerful when their input is solicited and acted on, with the result that they increase their active contribution. When people are "heard," they feel like equals—despite differences in rank. They no longer need to jockey for power in order to be heard. When people feel respected, they're naturally less defensive, and that makes it easier for them to not focus on their private agendas but, instead, on what really matters. This is positive and self-reinforcing. The more people's input is heard and utilized, the more energy and creativity they will bring to bear.

Sharing power means soliciting input from others, including subordinates, and encouraging divergent views and forthright disagreement for the purpose of hammering out better, more creative and insightful decisions. When the leadership assumes input from everyone on every rung on the ladder, and when every member has had the opportunity to earn the respect of the other members, ideas get hammered as on an anvil. The shape of the idea changes as it's beaten and the "metal" of an idea shifts in shape as it's alternately plunged between heat and cold. The only thing that's certain is that whatever opinion people had when they first got together will not be the view they hold after the discussion. Such deliberations are often exhilarating, with results that are usually surprising. In the best discussions, everyone is at least a little challenged and surprised.

When subordinates have opportunities to do significant work and earn others' respect, management can focus on the further development of those people's abilities rather than controlling their behavior. When the organization's values are clear and shared, and subordinates are deemed trustworthy, a power shift can take place, both in the kind of power that's most effective and in the focus of that power. With subordinates increasingly able to act as peers and even as authorities, information (knowledge, skill, experience, data, and intelligence) replaces formal authority (hierarchical rank, the ability to punish and reward) as the most important form of power. Then power is distributed throughout an organization, from the base up to the top, as well as horizontally. The redefinition of power as knowledge does not destroy the power of the vertical hierarchy, but blunts it.

Psychologically, with a genuine shift in power, the vertical hierarchy gets shorter; it feels like there's less distance between the top and the middle and the top and the base than there used to be. That's one reason why leaders are increasingly under the same kind of pressure as everyone else to earn the respect of the people they work with, even those who are subordinate to them. In turbulent conditions, leadership is not the automatic result of having a position high in the hierarchy. Leadership is earned by demonstrating the fact that you can deal successfully with hard and real problems, that you have judgment, and that you have the courage to do what's necessary. To win respect and trust, Mike Walsh says, "You have to make yourself vulnerable. You've got to be out there dealing with real problems, on the front line where people can watch you and personally size you up."[21]

Top management cannot succeed by itself. Line managers must be allied with the executives in order for major change to occur. Line management has hands-on responsibility for hitting the business targets. Top management must get subordinates involved because they are the people who will ultimately determine the organization's success or failure.[22] Organizational transformation that increases productivity, grows market share, satisfies customers, and increases success overall needs both direction from the leadership and a greater sense of ownership on the part of those who actually do the work of the organization. An organization cannot be transformed if the knowledge and opinions of those who do the work is largely ignored.

Successful major change in an organization involves shifts in the behaviors and responsibilities of everyone. Leaders have two divergent appearing tasks: while they do need to articulate the business of the business and the characteristics of the new culture, do need to broadcast the core strategy and values of the changed institution, simultaneously, they also need to give people a level of autonomy and responsibility to do the work that will build ownership and lead to success. Ralph S. Larsen, CEO of Johnson & Johnson, says that people criticize his management style because he insists that his subordinates figure out what they should do. "Invariably," he says, "managers come up with better solutions and set tougher standards for themselves than I would have imposed."[23] To the extent that people are knowledge-able and able, giving them appropriate control over their work is the singular evidence that they have earned authority's respect.

Decide and Act

Winston Churchill described England's prime minister Stanley Baldwin as "Decided only to be undecided, resolved to be irresolved, adamant for drift, solid for fluidity, all-powerful to be impotent."[24] In times of turbulence and crisis, that doesn't make it.

In harsh times, when conditions are ambiguous and decisions are difficult, leaders must decide, choose, and act. If they don't, they're perceived as indecisive and weak and that increases people's anxiety and insecurity. When people doubt their leaders' ability, confidence, or effectiveness, the mission is sabotaged. Thus, leaders have to be perceived as people with courage who will act.

One of the difficulties in periods of major change is that there can never be enough data for leaders to feel certain of their decisions. In reality, every innovative solution to old problems is likely to help with those old problems—while creating unexpected new ones. That's the law of unin-tended consequences. Leaders, therefore, must be both con-tinuously proactive and reactive, making decisions and taking action as they look both forward and backward. When dealing with change, the unanticipated will happen. But indecisiveness is not the answer to uncertainty.

The peacetime manager is like a supply officer: great at planning and logistics, tasks that are important and require a lot of work—but tasks in which no one gets hurt. In contrast, in crisis and turbulence, leaders must be able to consider doing the unbearable. Leadership is hard: It involves actions in which some will be injured and even die in order that the whole can live. *Injury* and *dying* refer here to painful actions like layoffs, selling or closing unprofitable units, merging with and acquiring other organizations, and so on. These are actions that threaten people's security and comfort, and, naturally, the leaders who originate and carry out these actions may well find themselves unpopular and resented. Leadership, therefore, requires a strength of character, of self-discipline, of courage, of deviance from what's popular, that peacetime managers don't need.

While soliciting input from others, including especially subordinates, and making decisions has a very important place in organizations' debate and ultimate consensus, there are times when leaders must use MBD—managing by decree.[25] MBD is especially useful when the no-consequence culture's solution is to call another meeting, or form a new task force . . . further slowing down the organization's pace to that of a giant Galapagos tortoise. Then, MBD becomes an order, with specific performance targets, usually with short time deadlines, with no excuses for failure, with no exceptions to the edict. MBD is not participatory, democratic, or subtle. But when conditions call for that style, and the CEO is personally involved and monitors progress, and the message, "Accomplish these goals or you're out," is not an empty one, MBD can be very effective.

When leaders try to create core change in an organization, says Jayme Rolls, a psychologist and management consultant, "Energy is sucked out of these people at an enormous rate—it's depleted from above and from below."[26] When you're trailblazing, by definition you have different values from those around you. Until the transformation process has achieved visible, positive results, the sense of psychological isolation can be very great. When leaders feel unsupported, it takes enormous energy, determination, and discipline to make and act on hard decisions.

While most of the time we think of resistance to change as originating from people lower in the hierarchy who lack "the big picture," the most emotionally draining source of resistance to leaders is likely to come from higher-level managers. Dowell Schwartz makes a good case that this occurs frequently: "Some people won't or don't or can't get it. The percent who get it is greatest *lower* in the organization because the stick is clearer and the tasks are more specific. The more absolute the requirements, the more specific they are, the easier it is to teach, evaluate and measure them. The stick is clear: change—or else. Initially they change because they're fearful, not because they have a vision.

"At the upper levels, there's a lot of gray. . . . There are more intangibles and it's harder to measure. It's often like playing handball with a cloud. There are no specific rules. Things are not clear. Even after four years of change, at the upper levels, among the 12 officers and the 30 direct reports to the officers, only half are with the change and the middle managers are skeptical, sure this is just another management fad that will go away."[27]

Achieve Alignment

Dowell Schwartz described nonalignment when he said only half of management, including officers, were on board with Baltimore Gas and Electric's CEO Chris Poindexter's change program. When all of management is not aligned, when a major percentage pulls in another direction or is apathetic, the difficulty of moving forward is multiplied exponentially. No organization can afford non-alignment.

The most difficult decisions don't seem to be those that involve logistics, engineering, finance, strategy, or R&D. While those decisions may actually be hard to make, they involve relatively impersonal issues, and that's easier for most people to deal with than hard decisions about people. Executives often have no tolerance for the gritty, emotional and exhausting people stuff that generates problems they really don't want to deal with. Mostly, what happens is: nothing happens. When the issues are personal and emotional, many people simply back away from doing anything. This may explain why executives often don't step up to the issue when a decision has been made but their subordinates don't abide by it.

Major change is immensely difficult to achieve. When nonalignment among executives is allowed to continue, efforts to move forward are sabotaged. The nonalignment of people close to the leadership results in passionate factionalism among subordinates. Simply stated, people choose sides.

A large company that sprawled over many states decided the way to deal with increasing competition was to build a system that would deliver seamless service to customers. Pragmatically, that involved retraining the majority of employees, reengineering their work processes, and reducing the number of existing service centers from several hundred to less than twenty. Most of the company's employees would have to move.

Not surprisingly, very intelligent and well-meaning executives disagreed on the issue of how fast they should implement the changes. Some, in essence, said: "Tear the bandage off quickly! Let's get it over with. Then we can move into the future." Others responded very differently: "We're affecting many people's lives. People have spouses who will need to change jobs, their kids are in school, and people need time to sell their houses and find somewhere else to live. Let's go slowly, one center at a time. We'll give people as much time to get ready as we can. Not only is that kind, it's also prudent. That way we won't make so many mistakes."

Between those two extreme views, there were a bunch of compromises. In truth, each view was justifiable. But until one view prevailed, no action could be taken. When there's a range of positions, word gets out and people ally with those who agree with their position. When the leadership is divided, so are the troops. As the organization splits into factions, decisions are personalized and politicized. The result is a paralysis of indecision that naturally defeats efforts to create core change. There were months of frustrating contention, and no progress was achieved until the CEO made the decision: *Full steam ahead. We'll deal with the consequences as they come up.* That's when effective change began.

Effective leaders require input from everyone involved; they prefer spirited debate before decisions are made. But once the decision is made, they require alignment, because without it progress is impossible. They require others to act enthusiastically, in line with the decision, even people who previously opposed it. As hard as it is to tell subordinates whom you know well and see often, the message has to be: *Get on the train. Now. If you're not on board, you'll be left at the station.*

Psychological Leadership

Psychologically, leaders lead because they motivate others to achieve the mission and because they convince others that they understand the issues better than anyone else. People follow them because they speak about solutions with persuasive conviction, because they project confidence when others are uncertain, and because they act decisively. Leaders must be visionaries rather than administrators. They must be immensely successful in perceiving and developing new opportunities and immensely effective in convincing people that dealing with unending change not only is necessary, but will result in far better outcomes than they've known before.

People are leaders as long as they create followers. Leadership is different from other relationships in that leaders generate hope and conviction in followers. Leaders are people whom others perceive as being able to make things better. Leaders create followers because they generate:

- Confidence in people who were frightened
- Certainty in people who were vacillating
- Action where there was hesitation
- Strength where there was weakness
- Expertise where there was floundering
- Courage where there were cowards
- Optimism where there was cynicism
- A conviction that the future will be better

Ultimately, leaders lead because they create a passionate commitment in other people to pursue the leader's strategy and succeed. In the end, leadership is not intellectual or cognitive. Leadership creates an emotional bond.

 Leadership in times of turbulence:

- Is based on conviction
- Is the result of personal courage and decisiveness
- Generates an emotional commitment in followers

Reality-Driven Action: Purpose

MAKING WORK PURPOSEFUL INVOLVES FOUR CHARACTERISTICS:

1. The work must be significant; it must be clearly relevant to the organization's goals.

2. Goals, measurements, processes, analyses, and plans need to be as simple, clear, and brief as possible.

3. Work must be focused and goals must be prioritized.

4. There must be pressure to perform and that pressure must be focused on what matters the most.

The Work Must Be Significant

Work is activity that adds value and is ultimately linked to the organization's bottom line, or the business of the business. *Garbage* is activity that is irrelevant, consumes resources, and deflects focus.

Most of the change in moving from a no-consequence culture to a results-driven one has naturally occurred in the private sector, because nothing equals competition or red ink in energizing the motive to improve. Where there's neither competitive nor financial pressure, the movement to change is glacial or nonexistent. So it's not surprising to find that although there's a lot of talk about change in the government, only government employees find the amount of change that's occurred significant and threatening. In government, the no-consequence culture can be so ingrained that the organization itself is garbage—furiously busy though thoroughly insignificant.

The federal Bureau of Mines employs about 2000 people, and its annual funding is about $175 million.[1] The Bureau was established in 1910 to promote the "safety of miners" because at that time as many as 3000 miners died each year. But the Bureau's responsibility for mine safety was transferred to the Department of Labor in the 1970s, so the Bureau of Mines had to search for a new reason to exist. It redefined its mission as making "the best possible technology available" to U.S. mineral producers, and to meeting the "information needs (of the) public and private sector alike." But the Energy Information Administration and the U.S. Geological Survey already do that. Frantically looking for a reason for being, the Bureau of Mines got into the business of extracting, stockpiling, and selling helium, stating that adequate supplies (for observation balloons?) were critically necessary for national defense. The Bureau of Mines and its activities are garbage.[2]

Faded blue and green binders filled with paper are piled up from floor to ceiling in 14 corridors as well as on the desks and chairs of the Interstate Commerce Commission Building.[3] Every day, clerks bring in an estimated 16,000 more pieces of paper from trucking companies in which truckers cite what they intend to charge for whatever they're moving. Each of those pieces of papers is a filing, and ICC examiners inspect every line of each of the pieces of paper. If they decide the filing or "tariff" is okay, it stays in the Tariff Examination Room and then, sometime in the distant future, it's hauled over to the Canceled Tariff Library. What's really wondrous is that the ICC no longer has the power to regulate shipping rates, so the tariffs don't mean anything. The ICC has had no significant function since 1980 when Congress deregulated trucking and the railroads. The ICC's mission has become the detailed processing of totally irrelevant paper. Now that is garbage raised to a higher power.[4]

Of course, purposeless work is hardly restricted to the federal government. At the same time that the Baby Bell NYNEX was downsizing relentlessly, striving as hard as it could to cut costs, it was also paying dozens of employees to paint its brand-new trucks a slightly different shade of white, at a cost of $500 a truck.[5]

Even while IBM was hemorrhaging red ink, it didn't discontinue the practice of phone mail checking until the winter of 1994. The job of the phone mail police (IBMers' own phrase) was to call IBM phone numbers in order to be sure that the message on the answering tape was in perfect IBM-speak. That's not only a blatant waste of resources—it's also not a job for a grown-up person.

Garbage can be generated by technology. In 1964 when I wrote my dissertation, a typist took my draft and retyped it. The university required five copies of the thesis. The typist would take five flimsy pages of Corrasable Bond (which was the easiest paper to erase) and put four carbons between the papers. Then she'd tap all nine of those pieces of paper so they were lined up just so and carefully roll them into the typewriter. Needless to say, everyone worked very, very hard to avoid errors because correcting one was really a big deal. But now we have computers. I recently watched one of my colleagues insist that the format of a report be changed five times. He didn't change a single word, much less an idea. Since it's so easy to make changes on the computer, the criterion of acceptability can rise to that of perfection. Since perfection is never achieved, you could continue to redo any piece of work endlessly, thus endlessly creating garbage.

Garbage is everywhere. The majority of white-collar people seem to spend most of their time in meetings, meetings that never run shorter than the time for which they were scheduled. Meetings tend to be leisurely and kind of friendly; they're more for bonding than deciding. That's why Jerre Stead, president of AT&T's Global Business Communications Systems Unit, says, "I say if you're in a meeting, any meeting, for 15 minutes, [and] they're not talking about customers or competitors, raise your hand and ask why. If it goes on for half an hour, leave! Leave the meeting!"[6]

The line members of an organization—those who actually produce the work essential to the core business—tend to become separated from staff. Staff provides support services to the core business and, as these activities are ancillary, the results of staff work are hard to evaluate quantitatively and as they pertain to the business of the business. Staff is most prone to generate garbage as they pursue things that are important to them, but are not essential to the business. This does not mean that staff members are not doing excellent work; rather, they often do a terrific job of insignificant "work." The big danger is that it's too easy for dedicated staff to become a center of activity that doesn't move the rock.

Al Derden of Texaco describes it this way: "The critical question is, What does the line organization need staff to do? Line must be very clear about what that is because if you're not careful, staff will keep throwing stuff at line and line will become overburdened with well-intended support that is actually a nonproductive activity no one has time for. Staff generates projects and programs in the spirit of support, but in the real world, many are not needed. Too often staff measures its value based on the quality, timeliness, and *quantity* of programs delivered. The first two measurements are critical, the third is harmful. Staff's value is not judged on how much they do for the line but how effective their output is aligned with line's input. Does this make the line more productive? To some staff groups this is a whole new mind-set. Here's a catch-22: We cut overhead cost by bringing staff groups in from the field and forming resource teams at one centralized point. These centralized staffs are efficient and motivated to show value. They become creative, they brainstorm ways to support the line, and they form project teams to deliver quickly. They produce good stuff. Problem is, they are not in the field, they have lost contact with the line. They fail to see the results of their last deliverable—they are too busy working on the next one. The issue is not where staff is located, but how staff's work is managed. How closely is staff's output driven by line's input? That's what's important! Well-intended, quality work which produces program and report overload on the line has negative value."[7]

In these and many other ways, garbage accrues and blurs the focus on what should be purposefully significant. Some years ago, Wal-Mart instituted a garbage program. Employees were told, "If you are required to do something that you think is garbage, you have our permission not to do it. If no one asks you, 'Why aren't you doing this?' for a week, you have permission not to do it again. If, after that time, someone challenges you with the question, 'Why aren't you doing that?' you have permission to go up two levels higher than your manager to explain why you're not doing it."

Eli Lilly awards people the "Zero Hero" ribbon when they stop doing something because it doesn't add value.[8]

Wal-Mart and Eli Lilly are marvelous examples of how garbage can be eliminated simply: Just give people permission not to do things they're required to do that they're convinced are unnecessary. People can do more significant work if they've been liberated from having to do garbage.

Every organization needs a periodic garbage removal program. People could keep a detailed journal for several weeks of exactly how they spend their time. People might, for example, find they go to a two-hour staff meeting every Monday at which on average, only 37 minutes are devoted to important business issues. Some might learn that a third of their time was spent producing magnificent-looking reports that lay, unopened, on people's bookshelves.

People don't really want to do garbage. No matter what they do and no matter where they stand on the hierarchical ladder, *people want their work to matter.* If your work doesn't matter, a big part of your life is insignificant. When you believe your work is important, and you further believe your work contributes to something that is important, then you want to do it as well as you possibly can.

Dick Wintermantel of Motorola knows people want their work to be significant, they want it to contribute to "a higher purpose, an inspiring vision."[9] He asks, "What would you dedicate your (work) life to? Not to improving the return on assets or the share price. Think of the Great Wall of China, man's longest man-made object. It's a great engineering feat and it represents the life work of tens of thousands of people. It achieved its objective of keeping the hordes out. Now imagine I'm standing on the wall and my Motorola cellular phone rings. The call is from an emergency room physician in Tempe, Arizona requesting my permission to conduct a procedure on my own daughter which literally saves her life. Not only do our phones supremely achieve the objective of letting people in, but they support what I perceive to be Motorola's higher purpose— 'Interconnecting the world for the good of humankind.' That's meaning. People want to commit to organizations which are really increasing the welfare of people's lives." In his talks to executive leadership teams around the world, Wintermantel argues that finding the higher purpose is a missed opportunity and represents the secret ingredient to organizational success.

Processes Need to Be Simple

Memos from Hell

We need to dimensionalize this management initiative.
Translation: Let's all make a plan.

We utilized a concert of cross-functional expertise.
Translation: People from different departments talked to each other.

Don't impact employee incentivization programs.
Translation: Don't screw around with people's pay.

Your job, for the time being, has been designated as "retained."
Translation: You're not fired, yet.[10]

It's hard to be simple and brief. It requires having exquisite clarity about whatever you're talking about.

Simplicity, clarity, and brevity are very rare in no-consequence cultures, first because they create no-consequence "solutions" and second because "best performance" requires length, complexity, and inclusiveness. Instead of being clear, brief, and simple, everything—programs, processes, performance measurements, plans, goals—is as long, detailed, inclusive, and complicated as possible. What was intended to be a solution to a problem usually becomes a deterrent to accomplishing anything. Whenever I see anything that's very complex, I now assume it's a product of a no-consequence culture.

Efficient, effective, innovative. You can't achieve those objectives where there's complexity, because complexity hides what matters. Anything complex lends itself to becoming a no-consequence activity in which more attention is given to process, or how things are done, then to outcome, or what is done. Therefore, plans, processes, goals, strategy, language . . . everything needs to be as simple, clear, and brief as possible.

Some years ago, I reviewed a performance appraisal form for AT&T. It took me four readings to understand what the people who had produced the form were doing. Trying to be fair and give the greatest weight to the variables they thought were more important, they weighted each question differently. As a result, the data were so complex that no one could understand, much less use, them.

It might be helpful to remember that some of the most important or impactful discourses ever given are stunning in their brevity. The Lord's Prayer contains 66 words, the Gettysburg Address 286. There are 1322 words in the Declaration of Independence. But government regulations on the sale of cabbage contain 26,911 words.

Work Must Be Focused

Focusing is the opposite of including everything. When people include everything, they stretch their attention to everything they can imagine. That means there is no focus. The inevitable outcome of trying to include everything is that no progress occurs because energies are diffused too widely.

Some years ago, I was at a Travelers Insurance meeting shortly after the company had been taken over by another organization. Understandably, everyone was scared of what the future held. The HR team had created a grid of 20 goals. Creating 20 goals intended to signify the team's thoughtfulness and thoroughness. The outcome of having 20 goals, of course, is that nothing gets accomplished. And if the people had become even more scared over the following several months, the next list of HR goals would have expanded to at least 40 and no one would have understood why nothing was getting done.

Since people in no-consequence cultures lack confidence, they cannot be courageous. Similarly, no-consequence organizations are not courageous. This is why no-consequence organizations don't focus and decision makers don't prioritize. Then, buttressed by the defense nothing was omitted, inclusiveness becomes a hallmark of comprehensiveness and instead of being perceived as a barrier to achieving, it's lauded as an asset.

Merck's former CEO Roy Vagelos says that when he first came to the lab, researchers usually worked on as many as 10 projects at the same time. They were trying to hedge their bets and not lose out by making choices early, so they did a little bit on a lot of different projects, which guaranteed that no project would have the critical mass necessary to break through to success. Vagelos says you have to focus on the 2 things out of 10 that are most likely to pay off and pay off big: "Most people work on ten projects at once and hope that one of them will succeed. Often they are unwilling to put down one of the ten because that may be the successful one. That unwillingness is the fastest way to fail."[11]

Focus and priorities are absolutely necessary in order to get anything accomplished, especially if it involves change and difficulty. Focus limits and galvanizes people's attention. Dennis Coleman of Hewlett-Packard instructs people not to try to do too many things because "They can't be assimilated. You have to have a few things you want to do, and you have to make it fast and simple. You can't have an 800-page book on simplifying your life."[12]

Experience has led me to believe that you can't focus productively on more than three priorities at any one time. Three appears to be the outside limit, and less is often better.

Lawrence Bossidy, the CEO of AlliedSignal, sets three goals every year, and those goals create the corporate focus.[13] For example, in 1994 AlliedSignal's goals were to make the numbers, to reduce cycle time, and to grow the business. Everyone knew the goals, so an assessment was simple. (1) Did the organization make its target numbers? (2) Did it make significant improvements in reducing cycle time? (3) Did the business grow? Keep it focused; keep it simple.

There Must Be Focused Pressure

Focused pressure means attention and action must be greatest where outcome matters the most. Focused pressure is an ongoing tension that forces people to work only toward the essential goals.

Often organizations get the horse before the cart when they try to generate change. The way to change people's behavior and move an organization away from a no-consequence culture is to drive for results. The other changes in culture and behavior will follow on their own. Goals must be limited to the organization's current priorities, and there must be a localized and focused pressure to achieve those targets.

The definition of what is really important must come from a clear understanding of what's most important to the business. Anything that isn't central to the business of the business is automatically less important.

Most people don't understand that. Employees tend to view all parts of their jobs as equally important and management evaluates all aspects of people's performance as though all the parts were alike in value. That's never true. People have to know what really counts.

Focused pressure must act as a lever to achieve a clear outcome. In 1995, Tom Bouchard, IBM's executive vice president of human resources, and I wrote a one-page personal business commitment and a one-page performance assessment based on CEO Lou Gerstner's three priorities—win in the marketplace, improve execution, and increase team collaboration. All employees would be asked to write down what their personal commitment would be, in their jobs, to achieve the corporation's three highest priorities. The evaluation of performance was in terms of whether or not a person achieved his or her three commitments and "got" the new corporate culture. That's focused pressure for specific performance targets.

Karin Mayhew, vice president of human resources of SNET (Southern New England Telephone), says her organization has successfully used a very tight one-page performance goal to get significant employee focus, behavioral change, and goal achievement in a very short time.[14] SNET asks for three performance measures: (1) those of the corporation; (2) the employee's two or three goals that support those of the larger organization; and (3) the few personal development goals for the year that reflect results from 360° feedback. In its one-page form, SNET has required the identification of significant goals and a focus on the very few that will be pursued for a year. Common sense supports, and SNET has found, that the outcome of focused pressure is accelerated achievement.

Especially when the goal is difficult, organizations need to create focus, set priorities, and evaluate people's contribution in terms of that focus. Everyone's efforts must be focused on very few goals, and the evaluation of any person or unit's performance must be in terms of those few priorities for a designated period of time.

A well-run company has clear priorities and goals and, after appropriate interventions, fires for nonperformance. No-consequence organizations talk a lot about measuring and rewarding differences in performance, but don't do it. If there aren't consequences to different levels of achievement, there is no pressure to perform. In order to get management to begin to differentiate between levels of performance, executives often use techniques like requiring ranking or forcing the distribution of evaluations by saying, "The top group is limited to 5 percent of employees, and you are required to have 5 percent of your subordinates in the lowest 5 percent. . . ." In these ways, managers are forced to differentiate between people and that allows management to pressure for performance.

Focused and controlled pressure involves making every person and every unit accountable for achievement. That requires specific targets, preferably with deadlines. Exerting focused pressure to perform and driving change by requiring results and paying for them is a major revolution in many industries, especially the utilities. Chris Poindexter, CEO of Baltimore Gas and Electric, said that company's change process started in 1990: "Back then we had lots of rules and people got ahead by following the rules. People were well regarded if they put in lots of effort, but I—and many others—thought we had to reward results. We were really naive and thought it would require just a little tweaking. It was a much bigger job than we anticipated because, in order to reward results, we had to first figure out what organizational structure we needed, what the goals were . . . all that stuff. Before, we had people in no-consequence cultures and others who were too scared. With clear targets, now we have more people who are into getting results."[15]

Pressure involves goals, performance evaluations, feedback, and, more and more, variable compensation. Increasingly, organizations are trying to link people's compensation and other rewards to important outcomes so people will not be rewarded when they haven't performed. Increasingly, everyone has some amount of pay actually at risk.

Dowell Schwartz of Baltimore Gas and Electric says: "We'd always talked in terms of goals, but they were just nice things you wrote in your business plans. There were no consequences if you met them or if you failed. No attention was paid to the goals until we put in consequences. You don't realize the power people bring to a job if you incent them to do something and reward them.

"The leverage to change the culture is a hefty bonus or incentive pay that's enough money to make a difference. Before, it was all based on progression through a wage range. Now we have an incentive plan based on results."[16]

San Diego Gas and Electric temporarily froze base pay in 1992 when the company started to move toward performance-based regulation. Margot Kyd says the company has established an incentive compensation plan, which includes everyone from union members to executives, that puts part of everyone's pay at risk based on corporate and team results.[17] "We're at the 75th percentile of all industries in terms of pay at risk. We reorganized into four business units for planning and budget management to better align customers and results. And over the past three and a half years since we started making changes, for the first time we're stepping up and dealing with nonperformers and moving poor performers out. We used a forced distribution on performance and we've moved the poor performers out. It's been a very difficult time."[18]

There have to be both rewards and punishments, carrots as well as sticks. Ideally, the potential of the carrot should be designed to be larger than the punishment inflicted by the stick. The stick of variable compensation is the loss of some amount of an employee's security about pay. When something is taken away, the value of what could be gained needs to be increased. And the largest part of variable pay should reflect outcomes that are under an employee's control. That is, the percentage dependent on the individual employee's performance or immediate work group should be greater than the amount that depends on the profitability of the entire organization.

In addition to achieving results, a fair system is very clear and specific about which behaviors are acceptable and which are not. When people don't abide by the code of values of the organization, it is appropriate to punish those behaviors. When, in contrast, people achieve within the guidelines of the organization's values, they should be rewarded and significantly so. The worst condition is when values are unclear and there's no response to whatever people do.

In regards to pressuring for performance, I was an expert witness in a legal case in which a man claimed the only possible reason he didn't get promoted had to be age discrimination because "throughout my career I have always been evaluated as 'excellent'." In that company, "excellent" was the third worst level of performance. In the country club atmosphere of no-consequences, performance evaluations are exaggeratedly positive.

Organizations usually have between five and nine acceptable levels of performance. I have difficulty accepting that practice. The only acceptable level of performance should be the highest level of achievement that person can do. Accepting lesser performance obviously cheats the organization of the best that its people can do—but accepting lesser performance also deprives people of the personal triumph of achieving far more than they ever imagined they could. Doing anything less cheats everyone, wherever in the hierarchy.

Purpose:

- There's a clear line of sight from what people do to a high-priority goal.

- What's emphasized is what matters most.

- *Best performance* is defined as being clear, simple, brief, and focused.

8

Operate in Optimum Ways: Collaboration

TOM WHITESIDE LEFT IBM TO JOIN SILICON GRAPHICS. HE SAID: "Nobody's dumb at IBM. But it's like herding cats; they all have their own agenda."[1]

When Lou Gerstner came to IBM in 1993, he found one of IBM's most important competitive advantages was its employees; they had a deep sense of commitment, a sense of urgency, and the right priorities.[2] But he also found that those marvelous people were stymied by the corporation's horrendous bureaucracy and its imbedded turf culture. The corporation had evolved into groups of separate and warring fiefdoms based on product, function, or location. By the time Gerstner took charge, "They were all shooting at each other, not at the enemy."[3]

When Ray Smith, CEO of Bell Atlantic, asked his top 130 people when they had felt most committed, they all identified times when they had had the opportunity to tackle whole jobs that fell entirely within their functional responsibility.[4] "That's a real problem," Smith said, "because it means meeting company-wide goals is less important to my executives than meeting their own objectives. An organization has to have people who will sacrifice their individual gain for the goals of the team."

Being individualistic and competitive can foster creativity and innovation. But it can also stifle cooperation and coordination. Effective organizations need to have room for individuality but they must also, simultaneously, reinforce the idea that the good of the whole must take precedence over the advantage of the part. Most of the time the common good must be the overriding principle that sets everyone's priorities and guides decisions.

The Iditarod Trail Dog Sled Race is a very tough race that takes place every February in Alaska under extreme conditions. Every dog is powerful and every dog is on its own long leash. Not only does every dog have to want to pull, but every dog has to want to pull together. If the dogs don't pull together, the sled leader has to waste energies—whipping, watching, forcing, disciplining, exhorting—to keep them in line. None of that helps to "move the rock." When a lot of attention must be directed to discipline, less can be accomplished. The rule must be: Pull together!

Collaboration Is a Minimum Requirement

We must indeed all hang together, or, most assuredly, we shall all hang separately.[5]

While some internal competition is useful because it fuels people's motivation to be outstanding, for the most part internal relationships must be collaborative. The wagons must form a circle. Organizations can't afford the futile activities that result when internal factions fight for power, budget, status, and turf. Organizations can't have internal boundaries because no one can afford the delays, duplication, and sheer waste that inevitably result from structural silos and territorial attitudes. Factions and turf wars use up energies toward nonproductive ends. They politicize, distract, and divide. Thus, they direct attention inward, prevent decisions or encourage erroneous ones, and waste resources in a big way.

I was recently at a meeting where the speaker asked, "What happens when you combine blue and orange?" After a pause, he chortled and said, "You get blue!" Of course, he meant *Big Blue*. All the issues of turf and factionalism are increased when organizations merge, create partnerships, outsource, and the like, because people become preoccupied with what's going to happen to them. Most people become defensive and try to dominate their counterparts to make themselves safe. While organizations join together to achieve a business outcome, the high failure rate of these mergers is largely the result of ignoring psychological factors and basic differences in the values of each culture. When Rolm was owned by IBM, the relationship failed because the Rolm people had contempt for IBM's buttoned-down culture and the IBMers had contempt for Rolm's free-swinging, shoot-'em-up-at-the-OK-Corral style. Each saw the other as the enemy, and it was inevitable that irate factions dominated.

Factionalism directs competition internally and organizations are balkanized. Organizations must recognize that the enemy is outside, not within. The absence of factionalism is a minimum requirement for organizational survival in competitive conditions. It's become very clear that having everyone working for the good of the whole is critical to every organization's success. We need cooperation and coordination between groups whose missions are aligned with that of the organization and with each other's, with relationships that are synergistic.

Walt Boomer was a four-star general in the Marine Corps.[6] He was surprised, he said, when he left the Marines and entered private industry as CEO of Babcock-Wilcox. "There was much more working together in the Marines and much more understanding of the dynamics of leadership. When I got here I found the leaders weren't aligned and they certainly weren't open with each other. Though they were all very good, they were more concerned with their own success than the success of the whole company. I just assumed there'd be more of a coordinated effort at the senior level than there was. Now they're behind me and they support the direction I'm going, but it took time for them to trust each other and me."

Jack Welch says that GE people who can't operate as team players, no matter how valuable they've been, no longer belong.[7] Welch wants people who can work up and down the hierarchy, across functions, and with customers and suppliers. At GE, he says, the culture is the opposite of the not-invented-here syndrome. "We'll go anywhere for an idea," Welch says, "because when there are no limits to whom you see, where you'll go, and what you touch, results can be remarkable because everywhere you go, someone, somewhere is doing something better. At GE, finding that better idea, wherever it is, and whoever has it and sharing it, is something we reward. At GE, collaboration across traditional turfs is becoming a requirement for employment."

The issue of collaboration is especially testy in the United States, where unions exist because of the historically adversarial relationship between labor and management. Unions developed because workers needed to unite and gain power in order to confront management's power. In today's borderless economy neither management nor labor can afford to continue the old adversarial stance.[8] The new enlightened union leadership is exemplified by Michael Bennett of Saturn, who says, "We can't afford to fight each other anymore—our job is to build the best cars we can and beat the Japanese. If we don't, there'll be no jobs for anyone!"

The new style of union and management collaboration is exemplified by U.S. Steel's Mon Valley Works. To reach its goal of becoming the leading steel supplier in the industry,[9] the company said it needed everyone's active participation to achieve significantly greater productivity. The improvement process was called *Mon Valley Tomorrow* and it was developed jointly by union employees and management.

Don Thomas was the president of the United Steel Workers of America, Local 1219, in 1993. He knew the majority of the Mon Valley workers had fathers and even grandfathers who had worked in the mill. Thomas's own son was a fourth-generation steelworker. For generations people had assumed the jobs would be there so their children and grandchildren would always be able to earn a living. But as they saw many surrounding mills close, people got worried. Fear brought the realization that keeping the mill open depended on delivering exceptional quality to customers.

In 1992, production in one Mon Valley shop stopped 24 times because of catastrophic motor failure. In 1993, the number of stoppages was reduced to 13, and in 1994 it was down to three. The shop's work teams had decided to solve the problem of catastrophic motor failure by setting up a regular schedule for testing the motors. The direct savings from the new maintenance program was $48,000 in 1995 alone. But really large financial savings were achieved by avoiding the production downtime because that results in lost sales. Workers as well as management now realize that everyone is impacted by lost revenues. The people who work at Mon Valley have come to the understanding that despite 100 years of conflict between employees and management, the truth is that the destiny of employees at all levels and the destiny of the company are totally intermingled.

Normally, creating collaboration between long-term adversaries requires an urgent sense that there's everything to lose if they continue on as before. In the steel industry, both labor and management were threatened as many major mills closed and new, specialized mills proliferated. At U.S. Steel, union and management converted from fighting to cooperating because competitiveness in the industry had increased manyfold and everyone had something in jeopardy. To beat the competition, the enemy had to be outside.

It is vested self-interest that is leading to collaboration as a normal style of interaction between factions and functions within an organization and between organizations. Replacing an adversarial relationship with a collaborative one begins with the realization by all involved that their separate goals can only be accomplished if the greater whole is successful. In order for collaboration to continue, the coordinated effort must clearly contribute to greater success than conflict would have achieved.

Joint Action

In the 1986 movie *Hoosiers,* Gene Hackman played a small-town high school basketball coach with a problem: All the players wanted to shoot. No one wanted to pass the ball to someone else so that person could score.[10]

Of late, joint action or team work has moved to center stage for several reasons, including the need to lower costs, the potential of teams to create unique answers, and the ability of collaborative people to deliver high-quality, seamless work rapidly.

With tremendous pressure on costs, there could be a significant advantage to having a workforce organized in self-directed, cooperative units. Joint action crews can be flexible, efficient, and cost-effective, because any individual's skills and knowledge are available to everyone else.

What characterizes joint action? It's flowing, interactive, and interdependent. There's lots of mutual respect and mutual help. Though all members are not created equal, where there's team spirit, there's a commitment to the triumphs of the unit, rather than those of the individual. Crew members block interference from outside as they pass to each other in order for the team to win. When there is joint action, individuals subordinate their own interests to the unity and efficiency of the group.

Small groups are not teams. The critical distinction is this: A group operates on the basis of traditional hierarchy, in which power is distributed vertically and the top of the pyramid tells the rest what to do. In contrast, a team is organized on the basis of horizontal power. A team shares a commitment to achieving significant goals by using an interactive style that takes advantage of the abilities and knowledge of each member. Within joint action crews, peer or horizontal pressure to achieve is at least as powerful as hierarchical pressure to satisfy a boss. When power is distributed horizontally, it's distributed on the basis of knowledge and skill. Horizontal power gives anyone, at any level, the opportunity to earn other people's respect. Distributing power horizontally rather than hierarchically is, therefore, a critical element of both giving people authority to make decisions and enabling people to cooperate in joint actions.

Adhering to the old silos of different functions—R&D, engineering, quality, production, marketing, and sales—is too expensive: It wastes time and resources because development proceeds in a linear instead of an integrated way. The noncooperation, noncoordination, and hoarding created by a silo mentality results in huge waste. The wheel keeps getting reinvented over and over again and progress is damned slow.

Joint action crews may have developed most dramatically in the United States in the automobile industry because they had already achieved spectacular results in the Japanese auto industry. Japanese companies had learned to assign members from all departments to work together on a project from the day development began until it was completed. That had the effect of sharply reducing turf wars and the time it took to develop new vehicles. The increase in efficiency and the opportunity for breakthroughs was clear.

In 1989, for example, Chrysler introduced platform teams when it acquired American Motors, and decided to keep AMC's 700 engineers intact as a group.[11] Rather than assigning them to different departments such as power train or steering, it put all the engineers to work developing the

1993 Grand Cherokee. The engineers and designers were put together on a single floor, along with representatives from marketing, finance, and purchasing and even outside suppliers. Hundreds of people, all of whom were working on the same project, were gathered in one place. Because the members of the development teams were in close contact, the work moved far more quickly and efficiently than had ever been the case when people threw a project over sequential walls. Clearly, crews committed to joint action could deliver a complex project far faster, and therefore far less expensively, than would have been the case with other methods.

The second reason for the emphasis on joint action is that crew members might produce more effective and innovative solutions to problems than occurs when people work individually. Team members respect each other and are, therefore, likely to "hear" each other's input. They're also likely to trust each other. Respect and trust make it far more likely that disagreements will be aired forthrightly, which encourages creative solutions. The result is a solution that's different from and better than anyone's initial ideas. Then, consensus evolves from constructive disagreement or creative confrontation.

A third reason for cooperative crews is that, in a boundaryless economy, seamless delivery has become a required part of performance. Whatever his or her function, everyone has to focus on satisfying the customer. As the organization's strategy must focus on creating an outstanding outcome for the customer, the values and structure of the organization must focus on delivering that outcome to the customer. When the focus is on solving a customer's problems, the work unit naturally evolves into a focused, cross-functional, nonhierarchical team that delivers.

Imagine you have just moved your office from Chicago to San Francisco. One of your first tasks would be to set up a telephone system, and you'd probably call Pacific Bell and ask to speak to a rep. You want someone who knows every-thing there is to know about telephone equipment and what you're most likely to need. You want to get all the information you need to make choices and you want to do that with one conversation.

After you make your selections, you want that same per-son to get them delivered. You don't want to make a second call, much less a fifth. You don't want to have to learn the phone company's organizational structure in order to get an operating phone system.

Customers are increasingly requiring large systems solu-tions. As both Dick Wintermantel of Motorola and Ned Barnholt of Hewlett-Packard observe, "That's easier to say than do because we're asking independent, free-standing competing product divisions to collaborate and share. It's really hard to get people to give up their turf. We have an extraordinary breadth of technology, but our culture is one of individual fiefdoms. We have to change from competing to collaborating if we're going to be able to design and deliver systems solutions for customers."[12]

If customers don't get what they want from one vendor, they'll "let their fingers do the walking" and go to another. It's that simple. That's why organizations must present a seamless face to the customer as they solve the customer's problems.

A Note of Caution

A very large and much admired company had people who belonged to as many as 18 teams, in addition to their job responsibilities! No team had ever disbanded, because none had a clear mandate as to what they were supposed to achieve. Teams weren't there to *do* something. Instead, belonging to teams had become an expression of loyalty and a gung-ho spirit. That's teams run amok; that's teams for teams' own sake. That's faddism. That's process over product. A virtue raised to an extreme is always a vice.[13]

Teams or groups cannot always outshine the achievement of individuals. Many people are most creative when they work alone. While joint action crews may come up with more creative ideas than individuals, it may also work in the reverse. People working together can generate fewer and less creative ideas as they move to a consensus dictated by peer pressure. Then, in addition to there being fewer ideas, the ideas that are generated may be baby steps instead of giant breakthroughs. Since small groups of people tend to become sensitive to the ideas, desires, and preferences of each other, they tend to conform rather than confront. It's emotionally very difficult for an individual to resist giving in to the group norm, especially if the group feels strongly about the issue. Thus, while making decisions or solving problems with others can increase the range of opinionated input, which can lead to greater originality and divergence from "common sense," peer pressure can also lead to group-think, the least controversial or creative "solution."

While collaborative action can make good things happen, creating teams is never the real objective. Goals have to be targets in the business of the business, and teams are only one of many processes that enable organizations to aggre-gate their collective strengths and outperform their com-petitors. It is a very serious mistake to think that creating teams is the goal.

The goal is not teamwork; it is, instead, the achievement of a significant, purposeful goal in the business of the business. Teams are often an effective way to innovate and get work done when the team is prepared to do its work, has the resources that it needs, and has a clear mandate about what it is supposed to achieve. But teams are hard to keep going because the continuous interdependence, shared power, and high-energy interaction between members require a high level of trust and openness. Thus, the rule cannot be that we always work in teams. Rather, the rule must be: Share what you know. No person or unit can hoard knowledge or resources in order to increase his or her value and power.

Cohesion

For major progress to occur, all of an organization's decision makers must be aligned, territoriality must be prohibited, and collaboration must be a mandatory requirement for being employed. But far more than collaboration, cohesion is a competitive advantage. Cooperation and collaboration are ideas; they're cognitive. In contrast, cohesion is an emotional state.

The military has long understood, created, and valued cohesion. Cohesion is an essential element of combat power and is, therefore, critical to success on the battlefield. Many well-known military leaders have talked about the effects of cohesion on their fighting men. Napoleon was certainly describing cohesion when he said: "In war, three-quarters turns on personal character and relations; the balance of manpower and materials counts only for the remaining quarter."[14] John H. John defines cohesion as "the bonding together of members of an organization/unit in such a way as to sustain their will and commitment to each other, their unit, and the mission."[15]

Cohesion is what keeps people driving forward under fire and keeps them going under the harshest of circumstances. Without it, courage departs, commitment dissolves, units don't fight, and battles are lost. In today's reality, organizations and nations would enjoy a critical advantage if they created the emotional bond of cohesion.

In order to achieve cohesion, which involves far more powerful emotions than collaboration, leaders need to articulate a vision of an extraordinary goal, a goal that has such value that the struggle to achieve it is truly worthwhile. Unless the deepest convictions of purpose are engaged, the pragmatic dominates and the best you can get is cooperation. Cohesion requires idealism.

Writing about cohesion made me wonder if I'd ever had an experience that reflected that kind of commitment. I believe I did. From 1976 to 1981, I was first a member of the executive committee and then an associate dean of the College of Literature, Science and the Arts of the University of Michigan. The dean, five associate deans, and six members of the executive committee ran the college. With 58 units—departments, centers, and institutes—the college was the largest in the university.

LS&A was a remarkable place for many reasons, one of which was the absence of politics between units. The 58 units of the college did not compete for resources. They trusted the deans and the executive committee to make the decisions that were best for the institution as a whole. The 12 people who governed the college were also professors in different departments. I never saw any of them manipulate the others to gain an advantage for their own departments. To have such an attitude govern the decisions we made was extremely rare, not only for a group of academics, but under any circumstances where groups want to protect their interests.

Economically, the late 1970s were a bad time in Michigan. The Big Three automakers were in a huge slump, so the state was in a serious recession. The college's budget was cut between 15 and 20 percent every year I was an administrator. Eighty percent of the faculty were tenured and therefore untouchable, and universities don't make money. Financially, we were in a stranglehold. We first cut fat. But, ultimately, we cut muscle. We eliminated units.

As the financial pressures got tighter and tighter and units were identified for elimination, I thought: *If ever there was a time when the college could break up into competing factions, this is it.* But it didn't happen. The college's value that decisions must benefit the institution as a whole, and the administrating professors' academic value that their responsibility was to protect and create conditions that resulted in cutting-edge knowledge, held. Those two governing values—a commitment to the greater institution and a commitment to an academic ideal—overrode any potential for factionalism. I'd call that cohesion. Key values create cohesion.

Cohesion is the ultimate in bonding. Bonding and idealism, a commitment to the greatest good, are the emotional ingredients that underlie cohesion. Like all motivation, cohesion is never cognitive. It is always emotional.

Collaboration:

• Is a minimum requirement for employment.

• Cohesion is an outcome of guiding values and ideals and it is a competitive advantage.

• Teams can be a better way to reach a goal, but they are not a goal in themselves.

Operate in Optimum Ways: Selection

No matter how long the runway, a pig can't fly.[1]

KIRK LAWRIE

Jim Ferrell, CEO of Ferrellgas, told me that when he hires people he selects them first on the basis of personality and integrity, second on the basis of intelligence, and only third on the basis of experience.[2]

A decade ago, when CEOs wanted to hire someone, they gave the greatest weight to a candidate's list of experiences and accomplishments. In the past few years, many executives have come to the realization that an employee's personality is more critical than his or her resume. While experience is obviously relevant, it's much easier to gain experience and learn a business than it is to change character or personality.

The majority of hiring decisions are made on the basis of experience, knowledge, and skills because employers prefer

employees who can swiftly go to work and solve the problems involved in a position. Another way to look at it is to
say that people prefer to make hiring and promotion decisions in terms of objective rather than subjective criteria. It's
emotionally easier to select people on the basis of their
knowledge, skills, and experiences than it is on the basis of
character and personality.

Yet, behavior is much more closely aligned with character
and personality than it is with knowledge and skill, which is
why it often proves immensely difficult to change people's
behavior. In other words, while it's relatively easy to learn
skills and information, there are very important limits to
changing people's behavior when that behavior reflects
people's character and personality. Adult character and personality are very hard to change.

Some people believe that being effective requires them
to be brutal, particularly in turnaround situations. Most
organizations cannot tolerate this kind of toughness for
long. While organizations must achieve results, personal
style counts. Corporate cultures require collaboration, col-
legiality, and geniality. Even when people must lead change,
take charge, and make hard decisions, there is still a narrow
range of behavior that will be acceptable and, therefore,
effective within the existing culture. Knowledge and skills
get people hired, but personality and character determine
success. Even if you're the boss, when you don't fit in you
tend to be spat out.

Today's Organizations Require
Different Behaviors

For decades, people learned that the way to succeed was to
master the organization's procedures, learn the rules, kiss
up, and obey their boss. Now, people are told they're supposed to think for themselves and be proactive, creative,
and gutsy enough to innovate and challenge up. People are
being asked to change from being individualistic and com-

petitive to being collegial, and organizations that always rewarded individual achievement are now requiring and rewarding people for teamwork.

San Diego Gas and Electric, for example, told its employees that the company now values people who are creative, innovative, and flexible; who embrace and thrive on change and uncertainty as an ongoing reality; who seek responsibility and accountability; who act with integrity and treat others honestly, fairly, and with respect; who enhance value through cost-effectiveness and continuous improvement; who create internal and external alliances to further company objectives; who possess and continually develop knowledge and skills; and who have a positive and constructive sense of humor. This person bears no relationship whatsoever to the obedient, conformist organization man of the 1950s, 1960s, and 1970s.

As the behavior of an ideal employee has been redefined, problem solving and decision making have become shared responsibilities between bosses and subordinates. This shift occurred because of the increased magnitude and speed of change. When there are fundamental and fast changes in the business of the business, or the ways in which an organization achieves its goals, management becomes increasingly dependent on input from others, especially people with specialized knowledge.

AT&T, for example, went from being a monopoly to needing to become competitive. It went from being a domestic business to being global; it went from transmitting only voice messages to transmitting all kinds of information, including voice; it went from being a stable organization to one that was the result of mergers, divestitures, and acquisitions. And, at the same time, there were major changes in the technologies of communication and computers. These swift mega-changes required that the officers seriously solicit and use input from subordinates with different, specialized knowledge and different management experiences than they had.

When power is distributed traditionally—hierarchically or vertically—and reserved only for those at the top, decision making is slow because information funnels up slowly, the bureaucracy grinds interminably, and decisions trickle down slowly. In the new reality, vertical power tends to be ineffective. Shared power is crucial for today's organizations to reach the levels of speed and flexibility needed to succeed.

In order to share power effectively, subordinates need to know the range of their authority and responsibility. H. J. Heinz's CEO, Anthony O'Reilly, says there's a big difference between decentralizing power and diffusing it. He believes that in order to achieve goals, power must be decentralized to those who can make the appropriate decisions quickly. The incorrect action is to dilute power so you end up with "a local planning commission, where many people can say no, but it's unclear who can say yes."[3]

Americans view power as resources—people, money, and tools. They also view power as having the authority to make things happen. When power is thought of as authority, it's not hard to think of it as coercive, dictatorial, and authoritarian. That's why power has such a bad rap for many Americans. Instead of authority, I prefer to think of power as the responsibility to make things happen, and I distinguish between the responsibility to achieve goals and the style of how that is accomplished. Today, we've rejected an authoritarian style in favor of one that's collaborative, interactive, and collegial.[4]

The importance of the new behaviors, especially in regards to a nonauthoritarian style of using power, is illustrated particularly dramatically by Jack Welch, General Electric's CEO.[5] From his reputation, Mr. Welch sounds intensely results-oriented. You would expect, then, that achieving business targets would count the most in terms of how he would regard others.

That's no longer true. Welch says that people who act in line with GE's new values, but who don't hit their business targets, should be given a second chance. But the big surprise is that Welch says that people who did achieve their goals, but who don't "get" the new values, are no longer okay in the new GE. Such people, Welch says, are usually aggressive authoritarians who force rather than inspire performance. In an intensely competitive environment, GE needs to pay attention to every good idea it can get from anyone, anywhere. That's why Welch insists GE cannot afford and will not permit management styles that suppress and intimidate subordinates. The result is that even at the highest executive levels, people who don't "get" the new values have been reassigned or asked to leave. Hitting your targets is no longer enough for you to keep your job at GE.

Some People Won't Get It

Organizations are requiring a new set of behaviors, including a new form of leadership and a new form of followership. The importance of demonstrating those behaviors or having those personal qualities has increased so much that, more and more, people who don't behave in the new ways are not being selected for positions of power and are being pressured to change or leave.

Willis Wood Jr., chairman and CEO of Pacific Enterprises, says, "You kid yourself if you think you can change another person. Especially in times of stress, we all revert to who we really are."[6] Clinton McLemore, an organizational psychologist, says the fact is: "Excepting responses to extraordinary life events that come along, people really don't change much."[7] McLemore studied the personal qualities of executives at 33 American companies, and he says the key issue is change. "It isn't that *behavior* can't change," he says. "It's just very difficult to make substantial and permanent changes in a person's basic *characteristics* or fundamental style." That's why McLemore says, we should really take a hard look at all of our organizational efforts trying to make rigid people flexible, impulsive people deliberate, and cautious people bold.

"There are three groups of people," observed Ned Barnholt; "those who get it almost immediately and they're off and running with it, those who are skeptical and not sure what to do with it, and another third who start out negative and hope it will go away. How do you know who's got it? By what they do and say. I can go out to the different divisions and I can see who's really taking the time to learn new things. It's all basically a matter of learning new skills and new ways of working. I look to see who's engaged within their organization to do that; who's making a difference and driving the change further down in their organization. In 10 minutes I can tell in which of the three buckets they fall. I used to spend most of my time with those who were the most negative, trying to convince them to change. Now I spend my time with the people in the first bucket. I'm investing in my best assets. I'm making the champions successful and I'll pick up a lot of people along the way. When the champions are successful and become the role model you'll get two-thirds because the second third usually joins in. And the last third either go along because the majority are, or you help them decide on a different career."[8]

Training is currently being asked to do more than it can accomplish. Training cannot do what many organizations expect it to, which is to change people's basic behavioral style. It's nearly impossible to change the core personality of an adult, and that the more extreme the personality, the less likely it is to change. How people use power is not likely to change through training or experience if wielding power supports a person's self-esteem and self-image. A person who proudly describes himself as a warrior is unlikely to enjoy sharing power. The man who said to me, "The golden rule is: he who has the power, rules," depends on macho to sustain his self-esteem. People who are intrinsically authoritarian as a way of propping up their egos will have great difficulty "hearing" subordinates. People who hoard information are in endless competition with everyone else and training will not make them collaborative. People who spent many years avoiding risk because they lacked self-confidence are not likely to now embrace it. People who are highly skilled in hiding are not going to be transformed from chickens to lions by a week of training. Even those who do rappel down the cliff in Outward Bound are more than likely to regress back to their previous risk-averse style when they return to the office. The artifice of training cannot create a permanent increase in confidence in the real workplace.

Organizations glibly use terms like *empowerment, teamwork,* and *sharing power,* but they vastly underestimate the gap between providing a description of the desired behavior and people really behaving in that way. Management, for example, was taught for decades to evaluate, judge, punish, and reward subordinates. Those behaviors are intrinsically different from coaching, motivating, and delegating responsibilities to subordinates. The newly desired behaviors are too foreign to many people's experience for normal training to be anything but words, words, words.

I've become convinced that getting people to behave in the new ways requires a depth of on-site coaching in real time that is rarely implemented, and, more than anything, depends on first selecting people to lead and model who already have the qualities that are desired, for whom education and work experiences will further develop and fine-tune the characteristics they already have.

The truth is, old dogs do learn new tricks as long as they're learning facts and skills. But a lot of behaviors that are now valued depend less on facts and skills and more on personality or character. The more a behavior or value is rooted in the enduring psychological characteristics of personality or character, or the more a behavior is motivated by emotional or ego considerations, or the more the behavior supports a person's sense of self-esteem, the less likely it is that training or experience will change that behavior or value. Adult personality is pretty resistant to change.

When behavior is a means for people to sustain their sense of self-esteem, then neither experience nor training is likely to change the personality, the behavior, or the values that defend it.

Select and Replace

"The people I inherited who didn't fit are gone," reports Bob Newton of DuPont Merck.[9] "I won't tolerate nonperformers. I told people they either had to grow, transfer to another part of the company, or leave. Too many people in this industry aren't hungry. They're sitting on the cash cow and enjoying it. We're trying to get rid of them and force them out. We're looking for people who are hungry, who are aggressive and not contaminated by the Entitlement culture."

Since it's very hard to change people's character, the reality is, we have to select people with the critical qualities and not cling to a misguided optimism that we will be able to train everyone to have those qualities. The other side of the coin is easy to understand, but emotionally very difficult to do. For the same reasons that we have to select the right candidates, we also have to replace or remove people who have the wrong qualities.

At a meeting of the Dial Corporation in Phoenix I heard Dial's former CEO, John Teet, challenge his human resource executives.[10] Teet was angry and pointed an irate finger at particular people. He challenged them: "Why did it take you two years to hire someone? Because you're too chicken to bring in someone really special. And why do you defend a nonperformer? Because he's been with us for a long time? He should be grateful for what he's got and now he's got to go! Why did you bring me a candidate that's done nothing successfully in the last three years? Look at what just happened with the basketball team, the Phoenix Suns. The coach traded three of their top players, people who are stars, and that really took guts. Why did he do it? Because he wanted to get the superstar, Charles Barkley. Without a superstar, the team won't be able to reach the next highest level of performance. The team feeds off the superstar's energy and he'll take them . . . up! The coach of the Suns knows that no matter how much his three stars practice, they'll never become a Charles Barkley." This is a harsh statement, but what Teet is saying is that practice alone doesn't always make it. Sometimes what is required is the enormous talent a person like Charles Barkley can bring to the table.

It's simple, but it's hard: First select people who have the qualities, talents and characteristics that are desired and deselect people whose behaviors, values, and personalities are not aligned with the new concepts of best performance. Deselecting is emotionally tough because it involves removing people from their positions, letting them go, and replacing them. Demotion is not normally an option unless the person volunteers the information that he or she is uncomfortable in a position. If people who are comfortable in their jobs and oblivious to their shortcomings are demoted, the outcome is almost always negative because they don't understand why they've failed. Demoted employees are often bitter and they create tension and increase factionalism. When that's the case, they must be removed.

Intellectually, deselecting on the basis of appropriate criteria is easy; emotionally, it's very tough because there's usually some level of friendship among the people involved. Most executives and managers are uncomfortable making hard decisions about individuals. But when they lack the courage to replace inappropriate people, their cowardice ends up sabotaging the transition from a consequence-free environment to a results-driven culture. Major organizational change requires that the people in power are models of the purpose, values, and behaviors the organization now applauds.

It's especially critical that the top people model the new values. That means issues of selection and replacement are especially important and problematic at the executive level, where old-style behaviors and values are most deeply embedded. Executives are usually people who succeeded in terms of the old patterns, before the boundaryless economy required core changes. Therefore, many experienced, long-term executives (and managers and supervisors) tend to mirror the old values, behaviors, choices, attitudes, and personal qualities. Organizations cannot afford to have people in powerful positions who are models of old and discarded values. Today's reality requires clear consistency between the values espoused, the behaviors demonstrated, and the people selected for further success.

Finding an Internal Maverick or Going Outside

Mead Corporation reengineered, outsourced, streamlined back-office processes, focused on what really mattered—and replaced quite a few managers.[11]

Organizations with no-consequence cultures characteristically "grow their own," which means executives are selected from the ranks of management, and managers are selected from the ranks of professionals and supervisors. People who have a lot of time and experience in any particular set of conditions are least able to see those conditions clearly. That's hardly surprising; no one is very good at seeing the air they breathe, nor are fish much aware of the water in which they swim.

Leading a change out of a no-consequence culture appears to require either an outsider or an internal maverick. Actually, large organizations don't usually have a lot of internal mavericks because they don't tolerate nonconformity unless the maverick is a really extraordinary performer. The issue of mavericks is well illustrated by an IBM story. Thomas Watson Jr. enjoyed telling the story of the man who liked to watch the annual migration of wild ducks.[12] In order to be sure the ducks flew where he could see them, every year he sowed a nearby lake with feed so the wild ducks would stop to eat. Eventually, some of the ducks stopped flying south and spent the winter at the lake instead. With more time they grew fat and lazy. After all, why bother to fly when everything is provided? The moral of the story is, you can make wild ducks tame, but you can never make tame ducks wild again. The phrase that I remember hearing at IBM was: "We love wild ducks as long as they fly in formation." After decades of extraordinary success, IBM became an organization of tame ducks trying to succeed in a wild duck industry.

IBM's new leadership is trying to hire wild ducks because it wants new ideas. IBM is bringing in many people who not only have the right characteristics, but cannot be bound by the IBM tradition because they weren't part of it.

Ned Barnholt says he may get more change faster if he sets up new organizations or teams with new and different cultures so he grows more people with the views and behaviors he needs, and then he'll be able to seed the older divisions with people who are role models and effective leaders of change.[13]

When major change is called for, an organization's executives or board frequently decide to bring in outsiders. Some very famous corporations have changed their leadership in the last few years by bringing in outsiders, people who had previously led corporations characterized by dynamic cultures that were very different from no-consequence cultures. Corporate boards deselected peacetime managers who were in executive roles because those people had become ineffective when external conditions changed to wartime. The examples include people who led some of our largest and most prestigious organizations. Lou Gerstner replaced John Akers as CEO of IBM; George Fisher replaced Kay Whitmore of Eastman Kodak; Jack Smith replaced Robert Stemple at General Motors. The old CEOs were incapable of leading their organizations to do battle in wartime.

Sometimes wild ducks are insiders who are simultaneously outsiders. Sol Trujillo of the Baby Bell US West is regarded as one of those people.[14] A long-term Bell system employee, he's been an agent of change in every job he has held. Instead of the gentle consensus-building style that characterizes most phone company interactions, Trujillo has a reputation as a hard-driving man determined to get where he's going. Some internal mavericks become leaders when conditions require major change. Leaders who were insiders and became superstars include Jack Welch at General Electric and the late Roberto Goizueta at Coca Cola.

To get major change you need very different kinds of thinking from what presently exists. That's why an outsider with a different background, or an internal wild duck, needs to be given the responsibility of leading and creating change. Conformists cannot lead change. People who can diverge from "common sense" are outsiders—either literally, in that they are not members of the organization, or figuratively, in that if they are members, they're not "in" because they differ significantly from the organization's norms. People who think differently must be selected for leadership roles when an organization really wants to change.

 Selection:

- The borderless economy requires new and different values and behaviors.

- Core values and personal style reflect permanent qualities and character in adults.

- Selecting the right people is more critical than training and experience.

CHAPTER

10

Operate in Optimum Ways: Method

*If you empower dummies, you get
bad decisions faster.[1]*

RICH TEERLINK

The first winner of the Malcolm Baldrige Small Business Quality Award, the Wallace Company, declared bankruptcy two years after winning the award. Critics claim the company had become so enamored of the process of pursuing the prize that it forgot to watch the business. John W. Wallace, CEO of The Wallace Company, acknowledged: "We may have gotten a little off track."[2]

In the last 15 or 20 years, process became an end in itself, a hallmark of enlightened, cutting-edge organizations. Enthralled with method, organizations made it a huge business. From the early pioneers of quality, to the mantra of empowerment, to the glories of reengineering, learning

133

organizations, 360° feedback . . . the growth in the business
of methods is stunning.

In just 10 years, from 1982 to 1992, the number of consulting firms grew from 780 to 1,533; the number of consultants increased from 30,000 people to 80,000; and revenues
jumped from $3.5 billion to $15.2 billion.[3] The number of
people who went through training increased from 33.5 million to 40.9 million and corporate spending on training rose
from $10 billion to $45 billion. Sales of business books
exploded from $225 million to $490 million.

Method Became a Growth Industry Despite Lousy Results

Organizations have many systems. They have systems, for
example, that:

- Increase quality and decrease errors
- Measure performance
- Tie compensation to achievement
- Reengineer how work is done
- Increase speed
- Create teams
- Empower people
- Increase the span of control
- Select candidates
- Train people
- Survey customers
- Assess employee morale
- Increase diversity
- Designate core competencies
- Rightsize
- Benchmark[4]

All of these systems are processes. Processes are simply the ways that organizations do things, but too often process becomes the goal. The method of how something is done gets confused with the goal. Processes are how organizations hold people accountable, compensate for performance, create teams, train and select employees, and so on. Of course, every organization needs processes and they must be effective. But the process business contributed to organizations confusing the process of how something is done with the goal of what needs to be accomplished. Too often, the process became the goal. Then, evidence of progress became a measurement of method targets instead of measurements of business goals. No organization can afford to have techniques as its goal because that deflects focus away from the critical targets of the business.

The effectiveness of the method must be measured in terms of business outcomes rather than method improvements. Process answers the question, *How should we do this?* But the imperative questions are: *What is the business of this business?* and *What is our strategy to grow and succeed?* Methods should make strategy more effective.

Faddish management methods result in more failures than successes. For example, take a look at reengineering:

- David Robinson reported that only one reengineering effort in five actually succeeds in achieving a real impact on a company's competitive position.[5]

- In a study of 100 companies, Hall, Rosenthal, and Wade found that while reengineering sometimes achieves significant success, major improvements in process don't always improve the business.[6] They found that even when companies were able to achieve major improvements in methods, usually the overall business results declined.

- By one estimate, between 50 and 70 percent of reengineering or process redesign efforts fail to achieve the goals they were created to meet.[7]

- One study of all North American and European reengineering initiatives found that only 23 percent were achieving strong results.[8]

- James Champy and Michael Hammer, authors of the best-selling *Reengineering the Corporation,* reported that three-fourths of corporate reengineering efforts fail to be carried out adequately, or even at all.[9]

- In 1995, James Champy stated that reengineering is in trouble. While reengineering has achieved some dramatic accomplishments, the majority of even substantial reengineering projects have fallen significantly short of their potential. Champy added: "I have also learned that half a revolution is not better than none. It may, in fact, be worse."[10]

Ashkenas and Shaffer summarized many studies of the effectiveness of management tools,[11] especially the quality improvement process:

Sibson and Company, a consulting firm, reported in 1993 that of 4000 focus groups they conducted, employees and customers rated the effectiveness of management fads at between 10 and 20 percent.

A 1991 survey of the membership of an American electronics association found that 73 percent reported that the ongoing TQM process had failed to achieve a significant reduction in defects. In the same year, an Electric Power Research Institute survey of more than 300 companies found that satisfaction levels for over a dozen management tools, from benchmarking to teams, ranged between 35 and 60 percent among the executives who had implemented the tools.

McKenzie and Company studied 30 quality programs and found that two-thirds had either stalled or fallen short of achieving any significant improvements.

Arthur D. Little surveyed 500 American manufacturing and service companies and found that only one-third reported that their quality programs had achieved significant results in terms of competitiveness.

An A.T. Kearney survey of over 100 British firms found that fewer than 20 percent believed their TQM programs had achieved significant results.

Clearly, there's a problem with the process. Often expectations of effectiveness are much too high, so disappointment is inevitable. Sometimes the change techniques are so complex and difficult to implement that major breakthroughs are fairly rare. In other situations, the process becomes the territory of consultants, and as a stand-apart entity, the consultants concentrate on and measure the wrong things.

Method as Absurdity

I was working for one of the Baby Bells when the human resource function became agitated because people didn't challenge each other about ideas. With justification, that was seen as a significant impediment to hammering out the best possible solutions to the company's problems. HR's solution to this problem was to create a training module to teach people how to challenge each other. Challenging was now systematized and given a name, five stages were designated that went from awareness of disagreement to resolving differences, and people were trained to challenge each other. HR taught 50 trainers to teach the challenge curriculum, so challenging became a rice bowl for 50 trainers. Over time, the technique of challenging became more detailed and elaborate, and so the training became longer and more elaborate. The trainers measured their effectiveness by counting how many people took the course in challenging. No one even thought of measuring the effectiveness of training people to challenge in terms of whether and how the business was impacted.

The usual result of such situations is an extraordinary expenditure of money and time spent doing the wrong things wondrously well or doing the right things but measuring the wrong outcomes. The danger of complex process programs is that they can become unbelievably costly helium balloons that float on high, unconnected to the business, bearing no relationship to what really matters.

HR people's use of a complicated and detailed formal quality technique made it impossible for them to maintain their focus. Their goal was to make sure that every divergent opinion would be expressed so that ideas could be challenged. When quality improvement became the focus, the process superseded finding a solution to the original problem and the real goal was lost in the process.

While each of the parts of the process may have appeared to have a logical link to the next, the ultimate outcome of such an elaborate method is the childhood game of "telephone." In that game the first person whispers a word to the next person, who whispers the word to the next . . . by the time it reaches the last person, the whispered word is either totally unidentifiable as a word or it has become an entirely different word.

Techniques have the potential to be dangerously ineffective and expensive when they are complex rather than simple, long rather than brief, murky because of details, and unfocused because every possibility is examined. Then processes endanger the goal. Moreover, the more complicated the process, the harder it is to master, so the goal becomes mastering the technique. Subsequently, prestige comes from having mastered the method rather than from having made the most progress in the business of the business.

Organizations are beginning to acknowledge disappointment with the results of expensive techniques like total quality management or reengineering. The largest reason for their disappointment is that the goals get lost in elaborate methods. People lose sight of what was important. The process becomes its own entity, serving those who need to justify their positions and salaries. A focus on processes is integral to no-consequence cultures.

No-consequence cultures typically create elaborate programs of process because in no-consequence cultures, spending money is perceived as the solution. When method is the real goal, the method is not only ineffective, it is also extravagantly expensive. The reason for that is very simple. Companies that try to create improvements with elaborate techniques usually hire specialists who are extremely motivated to do the best darn job that anyone has ever done. They're motivated to do really good work, to really turn things around. With a goal of excellence, they make certain the training program about the method is as inclusive, detailed, and thorough as possible. People are hired and trained to teach others every aspect of the technique. Classes are held and smile scores are analyzed with absurd seriousness as though the smile score was itself an assessment of improvement in the business. Measurements are made and charts are constructed. The technique is analyzed and the choice points are described. The whole is converted to a flow chart that can stretch 20 linear feet and encircle the walls of a training room. When this happens, the method is separate from the business and has become its own business, protected by those it feeds.

Keep Your Eye on the Point

After reviewing all of the literature about process improvement, especially quality improvement programs, Stratford Sherman of *Fortune* says his favorite idea about improving quality was created by Toyota's executive vice president, Taichi Ohno.[12] Ohno told workers to ask why (something went wrong) at least five times. For example, when the machine stopped because the fuse blew, the first *why* would be, "Why did the fuse blow?" The answer would be, "Because the bearing was overloaded." The second *why* is, "Why was the bearing overloaded?" The answer is, "Because the bearing wasn't lubricated." The third *why* is, "Why wasn't the bearing lubricated?" The answer is, "Because the lubrication pump wasn't working properly." The fourth *why* is, "Why was that the case?" The answer is, "Because the shaft was worn." The fifth *why* is, "Why was the shaft worn?" The answer is, "Because there was no strainer and, therefore, scraps of metal got in the pump." Ohno says that after you've asked these successive why questions you've reached the root cause of your problem and you'll know how to stop the problem from recurring. That's my kind of technique: clear, brief, focused, efficient.

Champion International Corporation started changing its culture about 10 years ago. They'd built a nontraditional mill in Michigan and the general manager had "some wild ideas about the social design of manufacturing plants," according to Steve Gardiner.[13] "They started making people who did the work more responsible for the daily activities and they had very specific ways of training and paying people for knowledge and teamwork. No one called it a change effort. They just did it. Then we found we could create change in old plants as well as new ones. We began to see improvements because of redesign and delegating responsibility to people because some numbers were being generated that told senior people something good was happening. Later we called it participative management."

Every organization needs the perspective that everything that's done must contribute to the goal of creating better products, delivering better service, lowering costs, increasing profit, growing market share, or beating the competition. That's another way of saying every method must facilitate the effectiveness of the organization's strategies. Because the process business has been so successful in selling its products, and because the media have glorified method, organizations need to continuously challenge their assumptions that technique contributes to effectiveness by asking the question: "Does this process move our rock?"

When Allen-Bradley, a manufacturer of industrial controls, first created teams in its Industrial, Computer and Communications group, it found a team delivered an innovative computer-integrated manufacturing product extremely quickly.[14] That cluster of employees began with a very clear mission and never lost focus on what the important outcome should be. Outcome always remained more important than the method of work.

Following that success, the whole company switched to teams. Teams had become a virtue and thus a goal unto themselves. The evolving rule was that all problems had to be solved through teamwork. One employee joked, "Whoever dies with the most teams wins."[15] The proliferation of teams led to an actual decline in achievement. Not surprisingly, Allen-Bradley then became much more selective about using teams to solve problems.

When organizations make delegating responsibility and authority their goal, they have made process the goal. The critical question isn't whether or not employees have power. The real question is, Does increased subordinate power improve business outcomes? Are the actions and decisions made by the people who do the work more effective than decisions made by bosses who are removed from the work? The justification for passing on more decisions to employees has to be that the employees will make better choices than their bosses about the work they're doing.

Similarly, the reengineering technique cannot be assessed, for instance, in terms of how great a consolidation of customer service units was achieved. Rather, the reengineering method must be evaluated in terms of whether or not it achieved more effective and efficient customer service that resulted in an increase in new customers and a higher retention of old ones.

Again, the technique of teams cannot be justified because people enjoy working in the high-energy, collaborative, fun interactions of teams. The effectiveness of the process of teamwork has to be judged in terms of whether or not that method cuts redundancies, increases efficiencies, results in innovation, saves time, and contributes to profits.

Typically, companies assess the effectiveness of training by counting the number of people who went to class, counting the number of trainers who are training, counting the number of dollars spent, or counting the scores on the traditional smile sheets that participants fill out at the end of a training session. While those numbers may be interesting, they're basically irrelevant. Technique cannot be justified by the peripherals of its activity. Rather, the training process must be judged in terms of whether the people who were trained improved their effectiveness. In other words, a training program needs to be evaluated by the extent to which behavioral changes helped accomplish business targets.

Processes may dramatically improve the efficiency of how the work is accomplished. When the quality process, for example, is closely tied to the business of the business, then that method can be strikingly effective in cutting costs and increasing profits. Norm Lorentz, the United States Postal Service's vice president for quality, observed: "We're delineating the relationship between core processes and enabling processes. We're focusing on the core processes which deliver to the customer and making sure the enabling methods are allied to the core techniques. The most important thing is to know where you're going and why it's imperative to get there. How you get there varies all over the map and it's best left to the doers to figure it out. This is where the quality process is very valuable. I first worked at an organization that tried to get psychological or culture change without system support. It can't work. An effective change model has a hard or statistical side. You have to have an identifiable and measurable goal or contribution, and change is demanded in that context. If you have to improve service and drive costs down, then behaviors that do that are required, and you get the culture change. A statistically based quality program is a tool set that requires the right behaviors and values. In TQM, the measure of success is customer satisfaction. In the Post Office, the quality process is the hard side of where the business has to go. When you embed the technique in the business, you won't immediately see people put an elaborate method in place because it's already there. The habit of assessing rigorously, strategic measurements as fundamentals, are already there. The process is not separate from the work."[16]

Clearly, there's powerful evidence that focused, reasonably simple, and direct processes can have a powerful effect in improving a business outcome. But I think there's a natural human tendency to take the easy road. When outcomes are measured in terms of process, especially in terms of things like money spent or people trained, it's easy to get a positive evaluation. But when the evaluation is in terms of the core business and the assessment is quantitative, there will be bad marks as well as good ones and there are likely to be clear differences in performance between different individuals and units. Since no-consequence cultures want to avoid both bad news and differentiating on the basis of performance, then measuring method instead of business outcomes enables these organizations to focus on easy goals and avoid the discomforting measurements of differences in contribution which are the hallmark of a results-driven culture.

There is, then, an unwitting reason for organizations to focus on process improvement measures rather than business outcome measures; using a technique improvement measure, which is singularly easy to achieve because it simply requires spending money, is a way to avoid evidence of failure as well as the differentiations that result in disagreeable outcomes for some people. Focusing on process reinforces the Smile City milieu of a no-consequence culture.

Process as Salvation

When gurus sell process as salvation rather than a likely solution, they increase the chances that the technique will be followed with a level of literalness that is inappropriate and dangerous. When the method is "enthroned as an institution," the guru permits no disagreements and flexibility and common sense are lost.[17] Then, followers become adherents.

All of which is reminiscent of the situation at the University of Michigan when I was a graduate student. The professors of clinical psychology were Freudians. The professors tolerated no criticism of Freudian theory, and the students happily mastered the theory by memorizing it. That gave the students some sense of security while they were feeling awfully anxious because they were therapeutic novices who were treating real patients who had big problems. When people are scared, they often request, albeit subtly, that they be told exactly how to do things. They want to be provided with a specific and comprehensive prepackaged method of how to shoulder responsibility, how to be a member of a team, how to prioritize, set goals, and evaluate performance. Psychologically, they're afraid to think for themselves and act on their own.

The difference between salvation and solution is immensely important. When a technique is viewed as providing a solution it is more likely to be considered only one method among many and judged in terms of its effectiveness. When the process is viewed as salvation it is more likely to generate a preoccupation with technique as the goal, with an absolute obedience to its rules. Blind adherence to method is a response of people who are seeking salvation rather than solutions, and those people are very motivated to not question or evaluate what they have embraced.

A couple of years ago when reengineering was just beginning to become fashionable, I chanced on a copy of *Index SMI Review* and read that no more than 20 percent of reengineering efforts succeeded.[18] At that time I was working at a communications company that had embarked on an enormous reengineering program. The company was changing all of its information technology processes at exactly the same time it was restructuring the entire organization. It is not possible to exaggerate how resentful, angry, and disturbed everyone was.

The reengineering effort was perceived as the salvation of the company as it was moving into an increasingly competitive marketplace. But the results were terrible. Basically, work stopped.

Why would organizations commence with such an expensive, painful, and disruptive process when the odds of success are apparently very small? Why do organizations embrace costly, complex, and disruptive techniques when the data say the outcome is unlikely to be a major breakthrough? One possible reason is that the leaders of the organization have become convinced that in order to succeed, they need an extraordinary change, one that involves the very fundamentals of their work methods. Another reason is that process has become an important business and people fear being left behind if they don't climb aboard the latest bandwagon. It's the lemming effect; when method is so visibly widespread, there's an assumption that those guys must know what they're doing and so we better be doing it too. A final reason is that there is something gutsy and cutting-edge when a company's history and program are abandoned for unknown and difficult territory. For many, it's a seriously thrilling and seductive image.

But something else is also going on. There is an underlying psychological reason for the proliferation and acceptance of techniques that have proved to be immensely difficult and expensive, and proportionately unsuccessful. The emergence of process as megabusiness is not only cause, it is also a symptom of what is happening. I don't think it's an accident that the processes that have developed, especially in the last 10 to 15 years, have been extraordinarily detailed in their methodology, specific in their procedures, marked by compulsive training, and obsessive in their measurements.

The 1980s, especially, were a period during which an extraordinary number of new managerial ideas were developed by people in the process business. The growth of the business of method was seriously astonishing and should have been alarming. Uncritically, organizations adopted the latest technique fads as evidence that they were on the ball. With acceptance and sales growing, naturally consultants developed more off-the-shelf, standardized programs for creating quality, customer satisfaction, time efficiencies, just-in-time methodologies, core competencies, strategic focus, alliances, global competitiveness, diversity, team building, empowerment . . . each, in turn, was uncritically accepted as *the* method to achieve success.[19]

The uncritical acceptance of the latest "wisdom" was posited as a sign of organizational health because it demonstrated the organization's willingness to change the errors of its past and move forward constructively into a future. Of course it was never an indication of organizational health. It was, instead, evidence of executive desperation for a simple solution to emerging complex problems. Management uncertainty was the real reason why the business of process prospered. Management was desperately searching for answers, preferably magical ways to handle a reality that had changed so much that old solutions were not working and their organizations were increasingly noncompetitive.

The uncertainty of organizational leaders created the fertile conditions within which purveyors of method became temporary organizational saviors. Each purveyor who became successful enough to become a guru created unreachable hope in his or her technique and inevitable disappointment as no technique is ever magical.

No process tools will allow management to be free of the responsibilities of judging, prioritizing, and deciding. Most management techniques promise far more than they can deliver because complex organizations don't get into trouble because they do one thing wrong. Rather, their problems are usually the sum of their culture, practices and assumptions, which are reflections of a reality that no longer exists.

I've watched clients go through several years of not being able to answer the question *What is the business of this business?* with any kind of confidence. That is a terrifying state of affairs, especially for those who are supposed to be the organization's leaders. If you cannot answer that question, it isn't possible to know what to do. Imagine being extremely visible within your organization, with people looking to you for the answer to *What should we do?* and not having an answer. When people are scared and they don't really know what to do, working extremely hard at something that's difficult and complex can act as a psychological defense mechanism. That is, the process activities give comfort as they appear to answer the question *What should we do?*

When the abyss of not being able to answer the question *What is the business of this business?* is reality, working very hard for long hours at a difficult task that requires detailed measurements and includes obsessive rules is very comforting. It takes all of a person's attention and psychological energy to cope with the techniques' required minutiae of measurements, rules, and charts. Thus, pursuing method becomes both a perfectly plausible behavior and a source of comfort. Dealing with the difficulties of the technique reduces feelings of uncertainty, ambiguity, confusion, anxiety, and powerlessness. But, while comforting, it's also dangerous because it facilitates the organization's remaining oblivious to the real issues.

When reality is prolonged uncertainty, no matter how difficult it is to implement an intricate technique, it's much easier than facing up to the genuinely hard and complex issues that require judgment and decisions. It's a reflection of a no-consequence culture when the goal is to create and implement elaborate process; it's a matter of fear when people cling to technique the way they cling to a life ring when a ship is going down. It's simply human to grab on to a method, especially one that's off-the-shelf, rather than face

up to the core issues for which there are no obvious or
facile answers.

 Method:

- Is a way to achieve a business goal but is never the
  goal.
- The more complex the technique, the less likely it
  is to be effective.
- Method has become a growth industry because
  frightened people seek packaged solutions.

CHAPTER

▓

11

Create Critical
Conditions: Trust

YEARS AGO IN THE 1970S, WHEN "LETTING IT ALL HANG OUT" WAS A
therapeutic prescription, I attended a National Training Lab
(NTL) workshop for women. Over the course of several days
of an emotional cauldron of very intense interactions, I was
startled by the brutal verbal attacks of normally mild, passive, introverted women on other women who had emerged
as leaders. The attacks were unexpected, inappropriate, and
out of control.

Later, when I had time to think things through, I realized I
had witnessed the difference in how people experience
power when they have it and when they don't. The women
who had become leaders had been given significant power
by their followers. They experienced that power as responsibility. If asked, they would have gravely said that their task
was to help the women who reached out to them and that
the burden of the responsibility was heavy.

In strong contrast, the women who experienced themselves as powerless did not relate to power as responsibility.
Instead, for them power was the opportunity, perhaps the
license, to manipulate and coerce others. Therefore, they
were forever scanning their environment, trying to anticipate and prevent the next time they'd be coerced and
manipulated. People who experience themselves as powerless live, essentially, in a paranoiac universe. To a dispropor-
tionate extent, their energies are directed at the imagined
and exaggerated source of threats. In the special circumstances of the workshop in which passionate emotions
evoked cheers, it's no wonder that women who felt powerless but protected in that environment lashed out at the
women with power whom they feared and resented. It was
a proactive attack intended to prevent a powerful person
from attacking them.

Trust operates in a similar way: When people are free to
use their psychological energies purposefully, they can
accomplish significant objectives. Without trust, lots of
energy is used defensively, trying to protect the self. Without
trust, people are suspicious and cynical, which makes it
nearly impossible to get collaboration or unity. Without
trust, people's energies are used to defend themselves. The
result is that even when people are present, they are not
there. Defensive, distracted, and preoccupied with themselves, they're not available for purposeful actions. A lack of
trust also makes it vastly harder to get people to buy in to
new values or actions; it prevents change from occurring; it
destroys any possibility of synergy, shared focus, and cohesion. That's why trust is a necessary condition for maximizing accomplishment. It is a competitive advantage because
when people trust an organization and its leadership, they
are psychologically free to focus on what matters. They're
not distracted by the perception that they need to fend off
the next attack or discover the next lie.

When people are scared, they become self-protective and
"hear" rumors that involve unspeakable outcomes, which

increases their dread and cynicism. Where there's too much fear, little gets communicated. First, few messages are sent out, because people are afraid to reveal the truth, they don't know what the truth is, or they don't know what to say. Second, even when the attempt is to communicate the truth, the intended listeners are usually mistrustful and cynical. The only message they might be able to "hear" is, *You're safe.* When that message cannot, in truth, be sent, nothing else gets through except the bad news, which fuels more worst-case rumors. When anxiety is expanded by the exaggeration of rumors, people are unable to believe the message or the messenger. They cannot trust.

Conditions that Generate Trust—Or the Reverse

Trust is created when people don't feel they're being manipulated for someone else's gain; when someone's word is their bond; when there's neither evasion nor lying. Trust is the result of no hidden agendas; no egoistic manipulations; no one-sided maneuverings. Trust is achieved when people are told something will happen and it in fact does happen. Trust, therefore, is the natural outcome of consistency and predictability.

Trust, today, is endangered and fragile. As trust is a natural outcome of conditions that create predictability, then major change is a potential threat to trust because major change always results in unpredictability and inconsistency. Therefore, as the borderless economy generates continuous and increasing rates of change, the boundaryless economy jeopardizes trust.

Texaco's Al Derden says: "If you're going to have trust in the midst of change, you have to have guiding principles and values, and the leaders of change must demonstrate behaviors which are in alignment with these guiding principles and values."[1] Steve Mason of Mead Corporation expresses surprise at how pivotal values are in achieving large and core changes.[2] He observes: "We had to get people to think and talk about the values we had that we needed to keep and the values we had to change in significant ways. For example, honesty and integrity are part of our heritage and we have to keep them. Values are the part of the culture that give people a relatively common frame of reference. You avoid a lot of rule books when you think this way. The values of honesty, integrity, and candor become a guideline to making a decision instead of going back to a rule book.

"What's new," Mason says, "is the need to increase the level of candor. There's a mutual obligation to communicate so we get the answers we need for the business. That takes the right environment and skills. Everyone has an obligation to be forthright and put their opinion on the table." Ned Barnholt says the most important thing in achieving major change is "involving your people, sharing ownership, and you get that by being open about whatever the problems are that you're trying to solve."[3] Achieving trust in the midst of change and unpredictability takes powerful, shared values and unusual levels of candor.

Relationships that constantly test other people jeopardize trust. When people realize they are being tested on information that has been purposely withheld from them, mistrust is the natural outcome.

Relationships in which people's loyalty, commitment, or love are continuously tested threaten trust. Several years ago a vice president of finance asked the consultant, James Wetherbe, what he thought of the company's chief information officer.[4] The vice president of finance reported that he was disgusted with the chief information officer's performance because the CIO continuously demonstrated he had no clue as to what needed to be accomplished. Wetherbe asked the vice president to write down the 10 most important things he wanted the chief information officer to achieve.

Then Wetherbe met with the chief information officer and asked him to create a list of what he believed were the 10 most important things the vice president wanted him to do.

Both men created perfectly reasonable lists, but their lists didn't match. Wetherbe showed the chief information officer the list the vice president had created. Three months later the vice president phoned Wetherbe, lauding him as a miracle worker. The chief information officer was now accomplishing everything the vice president desired. The vice president was so delighted that he asked Wetherbe to return and repeat whatever the magic process was with everyone who reported to him. Wetherbe told the vice president there was no magic. All he had done, he explained, was to show the chief information officer the vice president's list. A long silence followed. After a pause the vice president said, "Well, that explains it. Harry's been cheating."[5]

Wetherbe says that 80 percent of all of our apparent disagreements aren't disagreements; rather, they are the results of poor communication. He uses this incident as an example of the problems that result from poor communication. But I think the story is about much more than misunderstanding, noncommunication, or disagreement.

We know the vice president didn't tell Harry what he wanted him to do. The interesting questions is, *Why* didn't he? Sometimes people revel in their power, and they enjoy it when subordinates stand nervously on the uneven playing field. But equally likely, the vice president may have been constantly testing Harry because he believes that if people really want to please you, they will get into your head and know what you want. In other words, if people really care, you don't have to tell them what you want. How many times have you heard, "If (s)he really loved me, (s)he'd know what I wanted for my birthday."

In hierarchical organizations, subordinates are highly controlled through rules, sign-offs, inspections, and evaluations. Those are powerful communications that employees are not trusted. Teamwork, handing responsibility to subordinates, and challenging up are not management or workplace techniques; instead, they are styles of working that flow naturally when there's mutual respect and mutual trust.

Many organizations assume that employees are a source
of problems and not a significant source of solutions.
Whenever someone is seen as the source of problems, he or
she tends to be perceived with pity, contempt, or resentment. Those emotions ultimately contribute to an adversarial quality in a relationship and adversarial relationships
preclude any sense of trust.

Naturally, fear jeopardizes trust. When people feel like
they don't have a lot of control over what's going to happen
to them, they tend to become hypervigilant, seeking to
identify threat and find safety. When people are hypervigilant, they are prone to exaggerate the level of threat. Stated
another way, people who have greater control, people who
are closer to the sources of power, are naturally in a better
position to trust than are people who are distant from the
sources of power that can impact them enormously.

Executives and subordinates generally live in very different realities. The image of the pendulum is useful: Executives are at the top of the organization or pendulum and
since that is the fixed point of the pendulum, it doesn't
move. Blue- and pink-collar people are at the bottom of the
shaft. When the pendulum swings, the top remains fixed
while the bottom swings in the widest arc. Thus, people
who are nearer the bottom of the organization are far more
likely than those who are closer to the top to feel jerked
around by decisions other people make. Trust, therefore, is
hard to create and sustain among the people who are far
from the decision makers, because a structural source of
mistrust exists between the different levels of an organization. HP's Dennis Coleman observed that while TMO's
change effort was really successful and pretty widespread
horizontally, "The change has some gradients vertically.
Getting change down through the organization has generally proved very difficult."[6]

While failure diminishes trust, nothing is more reassuring
than success. Walt Boomer found that gaining trust in the
private sector is different and more difficult than it was in

the military. In the Marine Corps, he said, the battalion commander is God and the message is believed because it has to be true.[7] But in the corporate world that trust is not automatically there. "I'm new to the business," Boomer says, "and employees will keep on testing me until I take them to success."

Trust is the result of predictability, integrity, values, candor, respect, confidence, and success. Mistrust is the child of unpredictability, antagonism, contempt, pity, fear, and failure.

Don't Benefit from Imposing Pain

The rule is, Don't profit mightily from misery that you created. If you do, you've killed any sense of trust. While large layoffs may be necessary, they shouldn't be the occasion for executives to get large salary and bonus increases. In 1995, the CEOs of the 20 companies that had the largest layoffs had salary and bonus increases that averaged 25 percent. Looking at the financial results of Nynex and Digital, for example, it's hard to make the case that the CEOs earned that compensation.[8]

People naturally become fearful as well as resentful when executive self-interest appears to threaten them. When executives profit on the backs of everyone else, those executives are perceived as Machiavellian and self-serving and so they are perceived as untrustworthy. Then, no one believes what they say. If, in addition, they claim righteousness, people's response is derisive cynicism.

The issue is not whether downsizing and restructuring are necessary. Frequently, they are. The issue here is the extent to which trust is replaced by mistrust when powerful executives benefit greatly when they lay off powerless employees. AT&T's CEO, Robert Allen, learned that harshly when the press turned on him. *Newsweek* called him a "corporate killer" when he announced 40,000 *more* job cuts while he stood to collect almost $10 million in stock options.[9] William Rose of Carlsbad, California wrote: "I just wonder how long executive looting by pocketing the salaries of thousands of people tossed out in the streets can continue before either the government steps in or a revolution occurs. It takes the average worker half his lifetime to purchase a home, accumulate some savings, and take retirement benefits. It takes about six months to a year of unemployment to lose it all."[10]

In the mid-1980s, General Motors' CEO, Roger Smith, got $2.5 billion in wage and benefit cuts from workers because GM was losing to Japanese car makers.[11] Soon after he got the concession, Smith expanded a bonus program for himself and other executives. That short-term gain for officers created long-term mistrust and adversarial relations that remain powerful today. When there's a huge divergence in outcomes for different groups, trust and a willingness to work together are lost and adversarial relationships are a natural result.

"Chainsaw" Al Dunlap became the CEO of Scott Paper Company in April, 1994.[12] On December 12, 1995, the shareholders of the company approved his $9.4 billion merger with Kimberly-Clark Corporation. Dunlap won a great deal of applause for transforming Scott Paper, and the corporation's stock rose 225 percent. Dunlap cut 71 percent of Scott's headquarters staff, 50 percent of the managers, and 20 percent of the hourly workers. He also slashed spending on research and development and training by 50 percent.

Many of Dunlap's critics say the company is not nearly as healthy as Dunlap claims because the deep cuts in the workforce and in long-term investments in product innovation and employee skills endanger long-term viability. *Business Week* quoted an unnamed former high-level Scott executive as saying, "His sentence should be to run the company as it is for five years. He would never be able to do it. Scott is just a hollow core."[13]

Especially galling to Dunlap's critics is the fact that after being at Scott for less than two years, Dunlap gained nearly $100 million in salary, bonus, stock gains, and other perks.

His four direct reports left Scott with between $14.9 and $17.2 million after working less than two years. These staggering amounts of money must generate sardonic cynicism, contempt, and rage among the survivors of downsizing as well as all those long-term employees who were forced out of their jobs. Dunlap does do what he says he will do, but he profits mightily from the pain he inflicts. That's why Dunlap can break a company up and restructure it, but probably he could not run one. After all, who could trust him?

Do What You Say

The most important communication is never what is said, but what is done. When people perceive a gap between what's done and what's said, there cannot be any sense that those who speak have integrity and can be trusted.

Several years ago, a major gas and electric utility company created a big training and communication program emphasizing the critical importance of customer service. The utility measured the level of customer service received by internal as well as external customers. Year after year, the print and graphics unit was cited by the rest of the corporation as delivering the highest levels of customer service delivery of any part of the organization. Cutting costs, the first function the utility's executives eliminated and outsourced was the print and graphics unit.

Leaders must do what they say. Actions must be congruent with the values espoused. When the utility's executives decided to close the unit that was consistently best in delivering what had been declared to be the focus of the entire corporation, a chilling message was sent: Customer service is so much less important than we're saying that even if you're the best unit in the whole organization in terms of delivering service, that's not good enough to keep you safe.

Action is a vastly more powerful communication than is talk. For example, if the troops have variable compensation based on their performance as well as the organization's performance, then management must also have variable compensation and the percent of risk for management should be markedly higher than it is for the rank and file.

Compare "Chainsaw" Al Dunlap with Ken Iverson, who leads the successful steel producing company, Nucor.[14] Nucor's operating philosophy and practices have made it unusually successful in the very competitive steel industry. Nucor is equally noteworthy for its financial success and its trust in its employees. In 1993 the corporation employed a total of 22 people at headquarters, including everyone from the receptionist to Ken Iverson. Headquarters delegates day-to-day decisions to the operating facilities. There is no central control in terms of how general managers run their business, because headquarters trusts them and assumes they know their business.

Nucor's compensation plans and employee relations policies are simple, easy to understand, applied consistently, and perceived as fair. In the 1980s, during a period when business was slack, Iverson was proud that he was the Fortune 500 CEO who had the lowest compensation. Senior officers at Nucor do not have employment contracts, don't share in profits, have no pension or retirement plan, and don't get discretionary bonuses. In addition, their base salaries are less than those of executives with similar responsibilities at comparable companies. Instead, a large part of each executive's compensation is based directly on the corporation's return on shareholder equity. If the company does well, compensation is well above average; if the company does poorly, compensation is significantly lower than that of their peers. During a period when business was bad and Nucor cut back to a three-and-a-half-day workweek, Iverson never heard an employee complain. While the workers' pay was cut by 25 percent, department heads' compensation was cut by more than that, and the cut in officers' pay was even greater. Iverson calls it the "share the pain" program. Since management bears the largest responsibility for corporate performance, he says, when a company isn't successful, management should take the largest drop in pay.

Iverson does what he says; his practices follow his convictions. He is a person people can trust, leading a company that has a culture of trust. That has resulted in people being responsible, accountable, initiating, honest, and forthright—all of which contributes directly to Nucor's success. Iverson can run a company.

Communicate Effectively

Trust cannot exist when people are convinced that information is being withheld, that the truth is being manipulated, or that they are being fed lies. When organizations either have no-consequence cultures or are in turmoil, communication is both especially critical and significantly difficult to accomplish.

It's not a good idea for CEOs to lavish praise on their employees when they have had high profits, soaring stock prices—and major layoffs. That just contributes to widespread cynicism and mistrust. Among the 50 companies with the largest layoffs, here's what some of the chairmen said in their 1994 annual reports:

> *I have enormous confidence in the ability of the men and women of Boeing to meet the challenges ahead.* —Frank Shrontz and Philip Condit of Boeing[15]
>
> *I am confident because I am so proud of the job being done by AT&T people.* —Robert Allen of AT&T
>
> *Our people are . . . among the best in their fields, the most motivated and committed. . . . Their focus, discipline and teamwork will result in a stronger and more valuable Chase.* —Thomas Labrecque of Chase Manhattan.[16]

In contrast, when Walt Boomer was CEO of Babcock-Wilcox, he made a video that projected truth and thus generated trust. Looking directly into the lens of the camera and, therefore, into the eyes of every viewer, Boomer told

everyone forthrightly, logically, clearly, and simply where
the company stood in the industry, what the challenges and
the strategy would be, what had to be accomplished, and
why everyone should have a sense of urgency. It was an
honest and believable message. It was, therefore, a wise
message to send and a good thing to do.

Tell the truth. As Toronto Dominion's Allen Bell says,
"Open communication is critical, and that includes bad
news. When you give people the bad news and they don't
feel good, you have to tell them it's okay not to feel okay.
Figuring out what to do is the easy part. It's not your head,
it's your heart you have trouble with. When things aren't
good you have fear in your gut and disappointment in your
heart. But you have to step up to it."[17]

No-consequence cultures jeopardize trust because the
process of communicating drowns out any significant message under the sheer number of communications. When we
interview people in no-consequence cultures and ask them
what they've heard lately, a typical reply might be: "We're
downsizing by 15 percent this year and the average wage
increase will be 4 percent. We're selling off a business that
doesn't fit our strategy anymore. We're having a shower
tomorrow after work for Evelyn, who's getting married.
We're starting a big program on quality improvement. Jim is
leaving to take another job. The community chest is still 20
percent behind target. They're taking out a level of management." In no-consequence environments there are so many
communications and they're made so frequently, nothing
stands out as really important. The irony is that the staff of
the communication department is really trying to do excellent work, but the outcome is the paradoxical reverse.

E-mail is adding to the difficulty of communicating. With
e-mail, it's too easy to send a message to everyone. If you
watch people read their e-mail, it's obvious from their body
language that their goal is to clear the screen rather than
learn what's in the messages. E-mail can create an information deluge. Tom Steding, vice president of strategic market-

ing at 3COM Corporation, says he is forced to spend three hours every workday going through roughly 150 messages.[18] Steding says: "The volume of e-mail is so high, it's become devalued. Sending an e-mail is no longer sufficient to ensure communication. You've got to go see them nose-to-nose. It's like the old way, except back then you didn't have to send e-mail first. We're going backwards."[19]

The barrage of e-mail is not generating information; it's generating noise. People learn to ignore noise and then resent having to deal with it. While people can duck phone calls, they can't eliminate e-mail communications. They have to read it all. We haven't achieved the liberation of the paperless office by substituting electronic memoranda for paper ones—especially since the paper ones are easier to put in the bottom of a pile and ignore.

There seems to be a structural place in every organization's hierarchy where communication stops. It's appears to be around lower middle management or at the level of supervisors. As a consequence of this disconnect, communication stops so there's neither feedback upward nor communication downward.

In *Communicating Change,* communication experts T. J. Larkin and Sandar Larkin explain why that's true: In organizations undergoing major change, while middle and senior managers "hear" executives, subordinate employees distrust information from senior management.[20] Workers are prone to view executives with suspicion. The Larkins claim that communication research reveals that roughly 40 percent of front-line employees believe their executives aren't telling them the truth. Front-line employees do not believe what employee publications say; they dislike watching senior managers on video; and they have no interest in corporate-wide topics. The front-line workers' world is their local work area, and the only effective communication comes from the only person they trust, their supervisor. As many as 96 percent of workers believe their supervisor normally or always tells the truth. Therefore, the most credible source of information for the front-line employee is the immediate supervisor and not a distant executive.

The Larkins say front-line employees don't want to have to sift through thousands of words to find out what they want to know; they want specific answers to specific questions. When they don't receive that kind of focused information, they depend on rumors. Effective communication with front-line employees is achieved when supervisors have informal one-on-one exchanges with their subordinates, especially if these occur in response to a question the employee raised. Therefore, organizations must make certain that supervisors are prepared to answer questions.

The traditional cascade-down methods of communication beginning with the CEO are effective with senior and middle management. The CEO's direct reports should be in direct two-way communication with employees' supervisors. If the supervisor has not been communicated with effectively, the supervisor will not be able to communicate effectively. Then the messages and the intent of upper management will not impact the lower levels. Supervisors have to be the source of information for their subordinates. The Larkins, agreeing with Schoenfeld's observations and my own, don't expect communication to trickle down through middle management. Upper-level management must not assume that nonmanagement employees pay attention to their communications or believe them. Different levels of an organization generally coexist in separate worlds and don't realize it.

Especially when conditions are turbulent and trust is in jeopardy, the need for effective communication is immense. Effective communications have the following characteristics:

1. *Honesty about problems.* Trust requires that people believe the messenger and the message. Both the message and messenger have to be perceived as telling the truth; as not having a hidden agenda; and as being forthright rather than evasive. Thus, it is mandatory that a message acknowledge difficulties and even failures. If the topic of hard times

is avoided, and people either know about those times in the first place or learn about them later, they will be convinced that there is a hidden agenda and they are being manipulated. Manipulation and hidden agendas infer lying, and that absolutely precludes trust.

When discussing problems, management must also describe possible solutions, even if no final decisions have been made. Describing problems without addressing solutions increases anxiety and brings management competence into question.

2. *Simplicity, focus, clarity, and repetition.* Emotional responses tend to create resistance to a message or a distortion of the message. When an issue is important and is likely to generate an emotional response, and when a buy-in is necessary, the language must be simple so that the message is very clear, and the message must be so focused that people easily grasp what's important. Effective communication uses a maximum of three primary ideas. Since it is very difficult to effectively communicate when people perceive a message as threatening, the simple, focused, and clear message has to be repeated many more times than people think is necessary.

3. *Personal interaction.* Research shows clearly that the most effective communications are in person and, as often as possible, one-to-one. Some organizations use informal communications, like Hewlett-Packard's coffee talks where people at different levels gather. I think such gatherings are effective because that level of intimacy can lead to spontaneity, mutual "hearing," and, ultimately, higher levels of trust.

While important messages should be delivered in person when possible, they should be backed up with print, video, and other media because that reinforces the idea that the message is important.

4. *Clarity about good news.* When people are feeling angry and scared, their perceptions are selective; they gravitate

toward worst-case rumors and at some level deny the validity of any good news. When organizations are troubled, management must send out messages of success more effectively, more repetitiously, and more pointedly than they need to when the mood is happier. Since success is the only reality that can create optimism about the future, the rule is, When there's good news, shout it out! Loudly! Frequently!

5. *Evaluation regarding impact.* Never assume the message you sent was received. After the communication, it's absolutely necessary to go out into the field and find out whether or not anyone heard anything, and, if they did, what they believe they heard. That's the only way you can really find out whether or not you got through, and, if you got through, what it was people thought you said. You have to make sure you're heard.

Everyone also has the responsibility for making sure they have understood the message of the other person. The only way you can ever know whether you have communicated, or whether you have understood someone else's communication, is to simply ask, "What did you hear?" or, "Is this what you said?" Really, it's as simple and as easy as that.

 Trust:

- Is very hard to create and sustain in wartime when it's especially necessary.
- Requires telling the truth, acknowledging hard times, doing what you say, and not profiting from other people's misery.
- Is destroyed by poor communication but created by forthright, effective communication.

12

Create Critical Conditions: Commitment

METAPHORICALLY SPEAKING, JUST A SHORT WHILE AGO, ALL OUR great organizations had "People Are Our Most Important Resource" chiseled in stone above their entrances.

After World War II especially, an unwritten contract developed between employers and white-collar employees. Between jobs when they worked and pensions when they didn't, parental organizations gave loyal employees lifetime security. Blue-collar workers had the same deal, but it was embedded in a written contract, often arrived at after heated adversarial negotiations. While employers gave security, they also gained security because they retained seasoned, knowledgeable workers who were deeply molded by the stable culture of the organization.

The parental practices of our organizations created loyal employees who made profound emotional commitments to their employers. White-collar employees, in particular, identified themselves with the organizations where they worked. If you asked someone "What do you do?" the answer would be, "I'm with IBM/the federal government/the University of Michigan." For many, no other commitment was as important as, much less more important than, the commitment they made to their organization. People enthusiastically volunteered their lives, their careers, their well-being, their sense of self-regard, their very identity to their organization. The organization man had an implicit faith that the organization would be as interested in making use of his best qualities as he was himself. He entrusted his destiny to The Organization and cherished the idea that the relationship would be for keeps. It appeared to be a mutual and perfect arrangement.

Gradually, the emerging focus on employees led to management's preoccupation with employee morale, which was monitored frequently. Employers became extraordinarily generous toward employees, while employees developed extraordinary expectations about what employers owed them. In the 1980s, Anita Ross, Ph.D., then vice president for human resources of IBM, Canada, Ltd., said that a group of IBM retirees in Toronto were suing the corporation for breach of promise because the financially struggling corporation was trying to sell the IBM Country Club.[1] Over time, employees believed they were entitled to satisfaction and happiness at work. They concluded that the primary purpose of corporations was to create jobs.

Decades of mutual commitment led employees to believe that any threat to job security was an act of betrayal. Even if the company changed the direction of its business or ran into hard times, people who had long been loyal to the organization found it impossible to accept the idea that they no longer had a place in the organization, that the organization couldn't find some way to use them, that they could be discarded. For many long-term employees, being laid off wasn't simply the loss of a job; it was rejection by their family.

What's Happening?

As organizations keep cutting their costs, more and more are using contingent employees instead of full-time permanent workers for several reasons: Increasingly, organizations have learned that it can be psychologically devastating when large numbers of permanent people are let go; organizations want labor to be a variable, flexible cost; contingent employees are usually less expensive than permanent employees; and employers don't have the same responsibility to meet expensive government-mandated entitlements for contingent employees.

Stable jobs, which provided people with wages, benefits, pensions, and a sense of identity, are being replaced to a significant extent by contingent employees. The "contingent workforce" is a flexible labor force that includes people who work as temps, people who provide services to virtual organizations, and people who work as employees of a contractor that is providing outsourced services to another company.[2] People are teaming up in flexible groups for particular projects or assignments. Just as business created just-in-time delivery of supplies, it is creating a just-in-time work force. In less than 20 years, employers moved from delivering lifetime employment toward employment on an "as-needed" basis.

The number of temporary workers nearly doubled from 1990 to 1995, increasing from 1.2 million to more than 2 million, creating more jobs than just about any other industry.[3] The sector of the contingent labor force that has been growing fastest is the group of temps who work for contractors. Nearly 6.5 million contingent workers supply secretarial, janitorial, computer programming, engineering, and other business services to contractors. This population ranges from clerks hired to answer phones to very high-level professionals and even CEOs.

In addition to cutting costs, using contractors or outsourcing can be the easiest and fastest way to gain a very significant increase in the quality of the product or service for which you've contracted because that's the business of the business of that vendor.[4] Outsourcing allows an organization to focus its efforts and assets on what it does best in its core business.

In less than 20 years, millions of people are finding that the conditions of their employment have become increasingly fluid, and this trend is likely to continue. This has led some people, especially consultants and professors, to predict the end of stable organizations, permanent employees, and long-term relationships between employers and employees. I predict that this will turn out to be a testosterone view of exaggerated uninvolvement. Because most people need some security, new structures of employment like temp agencies for professionals and new forms of relationships will develop that will allow people to earn some sense of security while simultaneously creating the requisite organizational flexibility that a borderless economy requires.

Levels of Commitment

The job security that most Americans took for granted was predicated on their organizations' remaining in the same core business for the length of the employees' careers. It was also contingent on reasonably stable conditions, especially no quantum leap in competition. "Being in the same business" meant offering the same or similar products produced in the same or similar ways, sold to the same or similar customers. That's peacetime. The wartime that characterizes the borderless economy makes any such premises untenable.

It's really very simple. As the business of every business keeps changing, along with the ways it produces whatever it sells, and as markets, like competitors, keep changing, then the business, its management, and its employees are always somewhere on the scale of continuous reinvention. Some occupations and industries change much more profoundly and swiftly than others, but even those that are not in the vortex of change will experience evolutionary change.

Commitment on the part of employers requires some degree of predictability. If conditions are truly chaotic, the future becomes unpredictable and long-term commitment is impossible. If, instead, as is true in most organizations, change is accelerated but conditions are not really out of control, then some commitment to some people is possible. If it's possible, is it desirable?

There is a competition in values between people who believe success requires that organizations have the total freedom of a virtual organization—an organization that makes no or very few long-term commitments to employees because it has very few or no permanent employees—and people who are certain that success always depends on employees who are committed to the organization.

Philosophically, these really are two opposing points of view, both of which are justifiable. Both positions—committing to employees or not—can be seen as competitive advantages. Conceptually, this is a choice about whether or not an organization elects to be concerned about its people or chooses to make decisions solely on the basis of their impact on the business. Theoretically, people are interchangeable among temp employees or in virtual organizations, so issues of individual people's welfare do not have to impact decisions. If, on the other hand, the belief is that the organization needs commitment from its employees, then the decision maker's degrees of freedom are limited by the need to consider the impact of decisions on employees. Organizations that perceive employee loyalty and trust as serious advantages are restricted; they are not free to make decisions that jeopardize those emotions.

Psychology's Yerkes-Dodson Law tells us that people perform at their highest levels, and that their confidence level is highest, when they operate within conditions they experience as involving medium levels of risk. Conditions involving either absolute security or no security are destructive to both achievement and confidence. Since people do best with medium levels of risk, they need to be able to earn some security. It is therefore instructive to look at what happens in virtual organizations.

Virtual organizations do not lack commitment, but the level and intensity of the commitment has changed. A lack of commitment does not, practically speaking, involve a lack of relationship. Reality, even in virtual organizations, creates considerable employment stability for the human reason that people prefer to work with colleagues whom they already like and trust and it's obviously more efficient to work with colleagues who are already sharp about what to do. While it isn't formalized, commitment evolves even in virtual organizations because it's to everyone's advantage. The result is people are able to earn some security, which is as critical to their being able to function as flexibility may be to the organization.

Evading the truth is one of the worst things an organization can do. People can cope with hard times. What they can't cope with is not knowing what the deal really is. So a major rule, even if the news is bad, is that employers must tell employees the truth about the conditions of employment. Organizations communicate their respect for employees when they say, "This is what's real. This is what we offer. Now you have the information to make choices about whatever it is you think would be best for you. We consider you an adult and responsible for yourself." Reciprocally, employees owe employers the same truth.

Whether an organization makes a long-term employment commitment to employees or not, whether it's a costly commitment or a minimal one, without tremendous clarity about the philosophic stance that guides the organization's decisions about people, then decisions will be perceived as and are likely to be ad hoc, inconsistent, and expedient. That, in itself, has to increase people's sense of anxiety.

People always need to know the rules of the game in which they're playing. In fact, if the rules are new and are not clearly articulated, actions will not only appear illogical and inconsistent, they will be. That naturally increases people's feeling that their world is out of control and the only survival strategy is one of narcissistic expediency. Employment obligations and expectations, a prediction of what the business is likely to be, clarity about the hurdles ahead and the chances of success: all of these need to be spelled out so people have a sense of where they stand. Without that, people will experience far more anxiety than they can handle or conditions probably dictate.

Intel learned it had to change the nature of its commitment to employees. In the early 1980s, despite major efforts to resist them, Intel was forced to have a big round of layoffs.[5] The company found that was traumatic and learned that it needed to be more thoughtful and open about its relations with its employees. The company found it was particularly helpful to share as much information as possible with everyone so employees were better able to make intelligent career choices. Intel has developed quarterly business update meetings in which employees learn about Intel's financial status and strategic long-range plans. They learn where the business is growing and where it's shrinking. Managers know that a very important part of their job is to help people understand they must get whatever training and experience is necessary to be in a growth sector because employees are responsible for maintaining their own employability. Intel's commitment to employees does not involve a promise of permanent employment. Instead, the commitment is one of absolute openness. Intel deals in the truth.

Phony Commitment

The traditional security of lifetime employment is being replaced by a new definition that says that while organizations can no longer promise employ*ment,* they promise employ*ability.* The most common commitment organizations are making to employees is that they will give employees enough classroom education and job experience to make their skills marketable, if not to their current organization, then to another. The basic idea is that as businesses are changing the core of their business, then people will vary in terms of how important their skills are to the evolving core business. The assumption is that if people's skills and knowledge are really cutting edge, even if they're no longer valuable to an employer whose business has changed, they will surely appeal to another for whom that knowledge is very relevant.

This new form of commitment was well described by Robert Waterman and his colleagues, who wrote about the development of self-reliant workers, or a *career-resilient work force.*[6] From the perspective that a career-long commitment from the organization to its employees is essentially over, Waterman asked, "What should the employment contract involve?" His answer is a set of mutual responsibilities between the employer and the employee: employers have the responsibility to give employees the opportunity to become more employable, which involves developing skills and knowledge while employees are responsible for increasing productivity and making some commitment to the organization as a community.

Alas, this covenant is logical—yet implausible in today's short-term, bottom-line, stock-focused reality. Today's glib promises to use training and experience to keep employees marketable will be fulfilled only for the employees the organization has a real interest in—those few who are designated as having high potential.

An executive of one of the Seven Bells whose job was to manage downsizing stated, "The times when we have to let people go are depressing. But," he added brightly, "while we're cutting, we're also hiring. We can't find enough recent graduates of two-year technical colleges." At no time did the idea of sending their old employees to those colleges for new degrees or skill upgrades come up. And this organization speaks loudly of enhancing hireability through continuous learning.

As well-intended as organizations may be when they say they're going to increase their members' employability, I think that commitment will erode and disappear if any such programs are ever begun. The core changes in employment were all triggered by the need to cut costs.[7,8] The end of traditional job security occurred because the tremendous increase in global competition resulted in tremendous cost pressures. There are no villains here. Huge impersonal forces made it a requirement that, among many variables, organizations must also compete on the basis of price.

When organizations cut costs, they cut training. They also cut career counselors, if they ever had them. Peripheral activities like job posting, skills assessment, and tuition reimbursement are susceptible to the budgetary ax and training is more expensive now as fewer and fewer employees are on an assembly line doing the same simple task over and over. The cost of keeping people's skills cutting-edge has really increased because even line workers need increasingly sophisticated and complex skills in order to do their work.

And, basically, if organizations don't perceive employees as long-term members of the organization, then it is unreasonable and irrational to make costly commitments to employees who are viewed as endlessly scanning the employment universe for better opportunities elsewhere.[9] Therefore, I find it unlikely that, in circumstances where employers are under unending pressure to continuously lower costs, those same organizations will be able, much less willing, to undertake the costly efforts of providing training or work assignments that keep people hireable.

Even in the very best of peacetime, organizations worked hard at designing careers only for people who had been designated as fast-track, the best and brightest. Identifying and designating particular assignments as growth opportunities for particular individuals is a resource-intensive activity. Corporations have never made a commitment to everyone to keep their knowledge and skills cutting-edge, because that is expensive. If being competitive requires that costs continuously lessen, then it is very hard to reconcile that with the very expensive efforts that are required to identify, provide, and hone an employee's evolving skill set. Creating "employability" is not going to happen. Promising it is a lie.

Conditional Commitment

We know that people don't perform at their highest levels when they have too little or too much security. Where then, does security lie? Must it reside in the person? Or is it in the organization? Or is it in a combination of the two?

When security lay in the organization, the result was a no-consequence culture. On the other hand, when organizations don't offer any way for people to earn any security, most people will be too anxious. It isn't progress when the old contract of absolute security is replaced by a new contract of zero security. We've seen that even in virtual organizations efficiency dictates the development of long-term relationships and an informal conditional commitment to employees.

A conditional commitment is a set of arrangements in which people are not promised security, but are promised the possibility of earning some kind of security under certain conditions. People are employed contingent on (1) the organization's ability to handle the cost of their employment; (2) having skills that are critical to the business of the business; and (3) demonstrating sustained, outstanding performance. In the aggregate, employment security will increasingly be more a matter of an individual's skills and contribution and proportionately less a matter of organizational success.

The only workable position that is both ethical and practical is for individuals and organizations to be driven by results and, because of that, to succeed. Achieving successfully and significantly ought to be able to earn people some reasonable amount of security (and a share of the profits) when the organization does well.

Conditional security is a significant and positive change because it clearly ends the complacency of a no-consequence culture and simultaneously encourages the development of skills, confidence, and courage because people have to keep earning their position. Contingent security should increase collaboration and, perhaps, cohesion within an organization because jobs exist only when the organization succeeds.

The Advantage of Commitment

For a while I was comfortable with the logic that justified various versions of noncommitment to employees as long as the organization was up-front about its policy. There is a credible argument that organizations need the flexibility of employment arrangements that do not make long-term promises. But I've come realize that it's a grave error to ignore the human element in the workplace.

Succeeding in conditions of increased competitiveness requires a mutual long-term partnership between employees and organizations because that's the underpinning of employee involvement, trust, collaboration, and cohesion. And if success requires commitment *from* employees, organizations must also make some commitment *to* employees, simply because people will not commit to an organization that doesn't make a commitment to them. Commitment requires reciprocity.

Despite the importance of flexibility, organizations still need employees who trust and admire the organization as much as they need employees who are experienced and knowledgeable.[10] Today's reality of ever increasing competition makes employee commitment to the success of the organization more, not less, important than before. Thus, some commitment to employees is more than desirable; it's necessary.

Conditional commitment is both humanitarian and fiscally prudent. In addition to meeting people's need for some security, creating conditional commitment results in greater profits because knowledgeable and motivated people are able to achieve higher levels of performance. The organization benefits from experienced employees' contacts, knowledge, relationships, and skills.

Jim Olson, who was formerly with Hewlett-Packard's Test and Measurement Organization, told me that one of the critical reasons he was able to achieve a very dramatic change in the business of his business was that his employees knew that "The Hewlett-Packard Way" promised that if they were not going to be retained by the new business because their skills were no longer relevant, but their performance was excellent, they would have a chance to move to another part of HP.[11] That sense of fairness and security, Olson said, gave the employees the courage to face change where others might have become too scared and faltered or clung desperately to the jobs they had. Olson said, "The 'Hewlett-Packard way' was very significant. The ultimate fear is you lose your job. Because of the HP way, the ultimate fear is you'd have to work elsewhere or work on something you didn't want to work on. We had to shrink, but there was a safety line so there was no panic." The commitment that is "the HP way" pays off. The people of HP want the company to succeed. As Ned Barnholt observed: "Our culture works in our favor. Our culture of caring for others, of pride, of success, of integrity and trust is very strong and people do superhuman things."[12]

Steve Peltier, CEO of Industrial Computer Source, says all new employees know they're in a tryout period during which they'll be assessed and everyone knows they may not pass.[13] But once that hurdle is over, and assuming performance continues to be outstanding, the corporation does its best to make the employment very long term.

Industrial Computer Source retains flexibility in its labor force by outsourcing and using temps. That means there are three tiers of employees, with different levels of commitment to each tier. The least commitment is to employees of companies that do work that ICS has outsourced. There is an intermediate level of commitment to employees who are hired as temps, because many permanent employees initially came to ICS as temps. And a major commitment exists to job security for permanent employees; the longer they've been with the company, the greater that commitment is.

Societal pendulums typically swing in extremely wide arcs. Thus, the virtually absolute job security that created a psychology and culture of no-consequences has been replaced by the assertion that job security is an anachronistic idea.[14] Job security will not completely vanish. Organizations will not be able to remove all aspects of employment security and then be able to ask employees to become proactive, risk-taking entrepreneurs. The paradox is that the borderless economy requires innovative, creative, autonomous, collaborative, problem-solving, decisive people. People who are too scared to trust will not be able to deliver the cutting-edge solutions that very competitive conditions require.

While absolute job security created mediocrity, conditional security such as we find at Hewlett-Packard and Industrial Computer Source has led to employee commitment and unusually high levels of innovativeness and creativity. Organizations do better when employees are convinced that layoffs aren't management's first solution to cost problems. Fear is the bluntest of management tools.[15]

Commitment:

- Every organization, even virtual ones (and those that rely on temping and outsourcing), create some employment security by choosing to work with people they already know.

- People need to "know the deal" in the employment contract so they're prepared for reality.

- Conditional commitment to long-term employees is an asset to an organization.

CHAPTER

13

Create Critical Conditions: Success

SEVERAL CONSULTANTS HAD RETURNED TO A DIVISION OF A MAJOR corporation with the results of their diagnostic questionnaire. They presented the data at a meeting that included the top 90 managers and executives. People's responses on the survey were extreme: fear, dread, and anxiety were near paralyzing levels. The data said the respondents were certain the organization was being run by executives who were whipping the troops very hard—tyrannical but floundering. Subordinates were convinced the executives didn't know what to do. Morale was terrible.

Organizations in which people are really scared and anxious tend to lose money. With that in mind, one of the consultants asked the general manager, "Is this division losing money?" "No," the general manager said, "we're not losing money. We're making money." The other 89 people turned to him, each face expressing shock. People called out, "Did you say we're not losing money?" "No," he replied, "we're not los-

178

ing money. We've made money every quarter we've been in business. In fact, every quarter we've made more money than we did in the previous one." He was the only one in the entire division who knew it was successful and profitable.

Everyone else who worked in that division was convinced they were all working incredibly hard and were totally unsuccessful. Everyone but the general manager "knew" that quarter after quarter, no matter what they achieved, they were losers in a losing organization.

Whether it's because they are uncomfortable praising others, or they're afraid that people will slack off after being praised, or they feel uncomfortable differentiating between performers and nonperformers, too often managers don't recognize the efforts of those who work hard and successfully. The majority of managers are not forthcoming enough with news of success and praise in the face of achievement.

Even when corporations are doing well, there can still be anxiety in the workplace over job security, income, involuntary early retirements, and the huge increase in contract workers. People's responses to the next recession or fall in the stock market are likely to be more extreme—more anxious, defensive, and panicked—than usual. It's no small thing when management gurus, consultants, managers, and executives ignore the human element in the workplace.

Recognition in No-Consequence Cultures

It isn't surprising that management is very stingy with recognition when there's a lot of fear and pessimism in an organization, because no one feels very celebratory. But organizations with complacent no-consequence cultures do just as badly. No-consequence cultures drown recognition in bureaucracy—in rules, deadlines, nominations, and meetings of the banquet committee. When a manager from First National Bank of Chicago proposed his team for recognition for their exceptional achievements during the last year, the Nomination Committee for Recognition told him he'd missed the deadline. The normal bureaucratic process of getting recognized is so slow that it usually transforms recognition from something that could be joyous into an emotional zero.

Despite the financial success of a unit within IBM, morale was low. People resented the fact that despite their major contributions to the organization's success, they never got recognized for their achievements. This should have been an easy problem to solve. Management just needed to raise its awareness and the consultants could be on their way. "That's easy to fix," IBM was told. "All you need to do is recognize people appropriately and more frequently." The idea got a major thumbs down.

Management responded, "We can't recognize people any more than we do. We simply can't do it; it just backfires. By the time we make recommendations to the nominating committee and those guys decide who's going to be recognized and then people are finally recognized, no one remembers what they did. So everybody ends up ticked off, wondering why some people got recognized and they didn't. We'd just as soon not bother with any of it."

The managers didn't understand that the best accolades are celebratory, spontaneous, and heartfelt. They just didn't "get it" and couldn't give up the bureaucratic recognition process that they themselves had identified as totally destructive in terms of generating a positive recognition outcome. They simply couldn't be spontaneous and joyful.

Since no-consequence cultures Manage-to-Morale, it's common to find that everyone and anything gets rewarded so that the coinage of recognition is debased. Since the goal is to raise morale as high as possible, the proliferation of recognition programs and awards ultimately makes it all meaningless.

One of the seven regional Bells had recognition officers for each unit whose major responsibility was to make certain everybody got the recognition they were entitled to (!).

People could get certificates, on-the-spot awards, monthly awards, quarterly awards, and annual awards. Awards included key chains, coasters, T-shirts, $5 gift certificates, dinners, and trips. Everyone had the right to nominate anyone for an award. One particularly impressive nomination came from a worker who nominated her coworker for showing her how to start her computer. In fact, there was also a program in which employees could nominate themselves for awards. In just one unit, the recognition manager had processed 8800 awards in six months.

Since you can fool very few people for any length of time, it was not surprising to learn that the recognition manager's mail included destroyed awards—smashed coasters, slit strips of leather, torn $5 gift certificates. When the value of recognition is so debased, people get angry because the significance of their real accomplishments cannot be heard above the white noise of the pathologically nondiscriminating, and ultimately cowardly, recognition programs of no-consequence cultures.

Manage-to-Results; Manage-to-Success

It couldn't be simpler: People need and want recognition of their significant accomplishments. The overall goal of Managing-to-Success is to have as many individuals, teams, business units, or projects earning success as possible. Organizations must Manage-to-Success. Success is the only outcome that creates the feeling that the game is worth it. Only success achieves a reality that says we have a future. Only success creates positive, purposeful, focused energy, optimism, and the conviction we can do anything. Only success creates a certainty that there is light at the end of the tunnel and we can get there. Success is the natural—in contrast to a contrived—motivator. Success is what makes people say, "We're on a roll. Nothing scares us. On to the battle! Hey, this is fun!" Successful risk taking is the only way to create confidence in people and in the organization. Morale is highest when there's success and motivation is highest when people's success is celebrated.

Management must find ways to make people feel successful. In order for success to be meaningful, success has to involve achieving measurable and significant stretch goals in the business of the business. Hitting those targets is also the outcome that creates conditions for achieving future success. Wise management finds ways for people to achieve success.[1]

Managing-to-Success means that goals, though difficult, must be achievable. If they're not, the outcome is failure. In the pursuit of breakthrough accomplishments, management is likely to set goals at levels far beyond what can be achieved. While it's a big mistake to set targets too low, it's probably a bigger error to set targets so high that people fail. Consecutive failures are demotivating, disheartening, and just plain scary. In addition, no matter how much was actually achieved, whenever there's a significant gap between what was accomplished and the goal, the focus will always be on the shortfall between the achievement and the target. In other words, when the goal is set too high, the focus will be on the amount of failure rather than the level of achievement. While goals should always be a stretch, they also need to be accomplishable.

Al Derden of Texaco's refining and marketing division says that his division uses stretch targets when setting goals.[2] First, members analyze the gap between their current performance in key processes and where they want to be in three years based on their assessment of industry first quartile performance. For example, if Texaco's current or "baseline" performance is 80 and expected industry first quartile performance in three years is 110, then the gap is 30. "Then we establish our *action plans* to achieve a stretch improvement greater than the gap, generally 150 percent of the gap," says Derden. "In this example, our stretch goal will be 125 in three years. Everything we do will be targeted toward achieving the 125 mark in 36 months. We do this because there is always the potential that competitive reactions and other significant events might occur that might raise the first quartile "benchmark" performance more than we expect, or that all of our action plans may not be as successful as envisioned. This is a simple concept of leading the duck. Without it, we don't stretch our minds, innovations, or performance skills and lessen our opportunity to close the gap or even more important, gain a competitive advantage."[3]

As stretch targets are hit, negative emotions naturally decline and optimism and a sense of confidence about hitting goals and handling risk naturally develop. And, as the goals that are accomplished are a series of targets in which the bar keeps being raised, then what is experienced as a medium level of difficulty will rise in objective terms. What was once impossible becomes difficult, and what was difficult becomes easy. That is, people and units become increasingly comfortable with more and more difficult targets.

Nothing energizes like success. And many and frequent successes are vastly more exciting and motivating than one huge success that took years. That length of time is demotivating. Stripe the field. Norm Schoenfeld says football was boring when it was a touchdown—or nothing.

Employers must reward first downs. They must put stickers on players' helmets for every outstanding action. Some would say that American football is a more exciting game than European soccer because success comes in increments. Unlike in American football, soccer fields aren't broken down by yards and success is either a goal or nothing. American football is vastly more exciting because there are first downs as well as touchdowns. If the goal is to have as many real successes as possible, it is important to break a large task into its smaller components so people experience achieving success more frequently.

The best way to get dramatically improved performance and inject a sense of zest into the workplace is to challenge people by giving them specific, unambiguous, short-term stretch goals. To get people to accomplish more than they ever have, or go beyond what they knew they could do, the challenge needs to be concrete, short-term, difficult, and doable. If done right, in the words of Ronald Ashkenas and Robert Shaffer, that challenging goal "creates a laser-like focus, excitement, and learning."[4] That's Managing-to-Success.

Nothing beats the high, nothing equals the zest, nothing is sweeter than being a winner in a winning organization. "My people came from the old organization because in the first two years we hired almost no one," says Jim Olson, formerly of HP, "and some people's lives got transformed. Some who were retired on the job came to life. I have about a dozen managers who just used to do their jobs but now they're on fire! Their confidence soared as they got products out quickly. We cut the development time from three to five years down to nine months and we produce award-winning products. Win in the market! Kicking butt is the only true morale builder."[5]

When a stretch target is accomplished, that achievement needs to be celebrated! *Celebrate* is a better word than *recognize* or *reward* because celebrate creates a joyous image. Celebrating is very different from the bureaucratic, planned, fit-into-the-calendar banquet of no-consequence cultures. The best organizations celebrate achievements as though they really mean it. They give praise and awards gladly—frequently, generously, publicly, personally, and passionately.[6] Psychologically generous organizations sometimes include employees' families and friends in aspects of the celebration. We celebrate success and we acknowledge winners. That's critical to getting people to feel good about what they're doing and what's happening to them.

An AT&T manager said: "You know, I was on the recognition banquet committee. We had worked for months to arrange a banquet for the people that the nominating committee said should be recognized. I was standing at the door of the dining room where we were holding the banquet and one of the people who was being recognized came up to me and said, 'You know, I would have appreciated a 30-second phone call from the vice president a hell of a lot more than this.' "[7]

The manager continued, "Now I understand the power of what our boss did last week. He called everyone to the cafeteria and said, 'As you all know, we've been writing competitive bids. It's a real pleasure for me to tell you that we've landed three of them. Now I'm going to call out the names of the people on the winning teams.' As the names were called, everybody in the room started clapping and whistling. What a great moment. Next to that the banquet was nothing."

The very best response to people is immediate and spontaneous. People want to know that what they've done is appreciated by those whose respect and admiration is important to them. They want to feel that others are proud of what they've accomplished and are glad for their success. Ritual recognition is usually not much of a real celebration. People flourish when their accomplishments are celebrated in a way they can experience as personal.

For most people that's very important and very motivating. One of the most meaningful gifts I ever received for doing a good job was some shards—pieces of ceramic pots made by an ancient people called the Anasazi. The shards were broken pieces, of no financial value. But the intrinsic value to me was enormous. The people who gave them to me had learned I had a collection of pre-Colombian art. The gift was important to me because it was so thoughtful and so personal. Everyone has his or her Anasazi shards, and it's management's job to find out what that is for each person.

Broaden the Definition of Success

From a motivational point of view, it is always dangerous to have very few things regarded as the only real measure of success. Traditionally, success in organizations has been measured mostly in terms of promotion and the resulting status and financial gain.

Promotions have always been one of the biggest of an organization's carrots. But very few organizations are honest with employees about the extremely small probability they will reach the executive level and not plateau.[8] Over 99 percent of all employees have always reached their highest organizational level decades before they retired. But, because the majority of organizations Manage-to-Morale, most organizations have created a population of employees who are hooked on the idea they are exceptional. As a result, the majority of employees have a hard time accepting the truth that they're not exceptional enough to be competitive in terms of promotion. When organizations link success primarily to promotion, they should expect employees to have a difficult time when promotions stop.

Today, promotions end more than a decade earlier than they did in the early 1980s. Most people now reach their career plateau when they're in their mid- to late thirties. James Rosenbaum, a sociologist at Northwestern University, spent 13 years studying promotion in large industrial companies and found people either make it big in their mid- to late thirties or plateau because the rate of upward mobility declines very severely after that.[9] Imagine: Employees who are fortunate enough to remain in an organization until they retire at 65, will, on average, have been plateaued for the last 30 years of their career. How can these people feel successful?

Most people are managed by other people who have been judged as having a higher potential than they do, and high potential people are fast-track. Fast-track means people remain in grades and in jobs for a far shorter period of time than do people whose potential is average. The result is most people who are older than 35 or 40 end up being managed by people who are significantly younger than they are. That's hard on the ego. It's one reason why angry, older employees often say, "I am more qualified because I have been with the company longer." Psychologically, it's a lot easier to feel angry because younger people were promoted over you than it is to acknowledge that younger people may be judged as more able than you. But, ultimately, many employees are forced, just by the increasing youth of their managers, to feel less and less successful.[10]

Since organizations need their members to feel successful, they also need a broader concept of what constitutes success, and they need additional routes to success other than promotion. Both extrinsic and intrinsic motivators can be powerful. Extrinsic motivators are those rewards that do not come from the process of doing the work, or the content of the work, or the achievements within the work. Extrinsic payoffs include money, promotion, and the corner office with big windows, a thick carpet, and a private bathroom. Extrinsic rewards are always in limited supply.

Intrinsic payoffs are those that come from the process, or the content, or the achievements of the work itself. Intrinsic payoffs involve challenge, responsibility, and significance. Challenge involves having opportunities to learn and do new work, which means it also involves opportunities to handle risk. Responsibility means opportunities to earn increasing degrees of autonomy. Significance involves opportunities to do work of increasing importance. Intrinsic rewards are limited only by a lack of imagination in creating opportunities for people to earn greater challenges, responsibility, and significance.

Our heroes and heroines cannot be limited to the relative few who continue to climb to the top of an organization's ladder. We also have to include people who solve really difficult problems, people who are particularly effective team leaders, people who have demonstrated unusual creativity and innovation, and people who are extremely good at developing the talents of others.

Lyondell is a petrochemical company that was created in 1985 when Arco (Atlantic Richfield) decided to create a new division by combining its huge oil refinery near the Houston ship canal and a nearby petrochemical company. Both of those facilities were Arco's big losers, and Lyondell was expected to fail. Stunningly, in its second year the new corporation was profitable.

What made Lyondell so effective? It has tremendous pay and benefits, pride in the work it does, a culture of openness and fairness, and a tremendous amount of camaraderie. It has recognition programs and profit sharing and bonuses. There's tremendously open communication and people trust the executives. But Lyondell is also notable and upfront about the relative scarcity of promotions.

Lyondell has few promotion opportunities because there are few management positions because most of the work is done through multifunctional teams. That has proved to be a tremendous asset for the company. Since there are many teams, there are many chances for people to become team leaders. In addition, because the teams are multifunctional, people have an enormous number of opportunities to join teams that are doing different kinds of work, so people naturally have opportunities to keep learning and stretching. An important part of Lyondell's success comes from the fact that Lyondell has succeeded in creating opportunities for each employee to keep learning, to become a leader, to contribute to decisions. Lyondell has created multiple ways by which its people can earn the sense of being successful.

Business Success and Psychological Success

If there's no psychological success, you cannot have sustained business success. Business success, defined as profitability, market share, or stock price is a necessary but not sufficient condition for creating psychological success. Psychological success is motivation, enthusiasm, and commitment. But psychological success is a necessary condition for business success. Psychological success is not a luxury, it's a necessity.

The following chart represents the relationship between business and psychological success.

Psychological Success Rests on Emotional Generosity as Well as Business Success

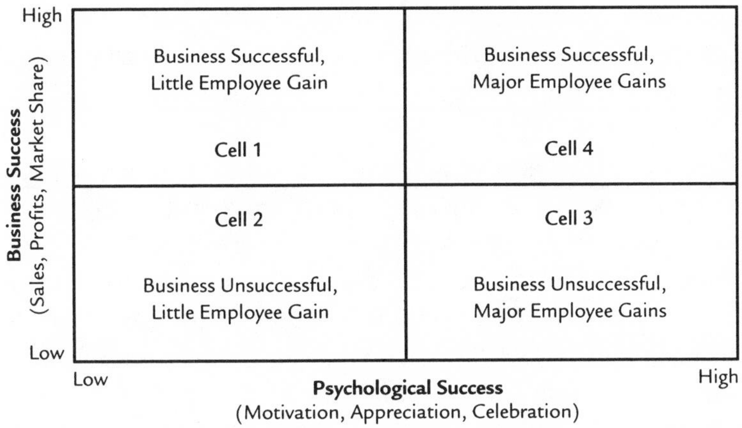
High
Business Success (Sales, Profits, Market Share)
Low
Business Successful, Little Employee Gain
Cell 1
Business Successful, Major Employee Gains
Cell 4
Cell 2
Business Unsuccessful, Little Employee Gain
Cell 3
Business Unsuccessful, Major Employee Gains
Low
Psychological Success (Motivation, Appreciation, Celebration)
High

Cell 1 is extreme when management manages to fear.

The conditions in cell 2 are, of course, worse than they are in cell 1 because there's no business success. Without business success, there's little or no hope. That's a truly defeatist place to be, which is why we often see cell 3. In cell 3, management sets out to artificially create good feelings of camaraderie, appreciation, and celebration *because* the business is in trouble. That's a highly ineffective version of Managing-to-Morale. Warm and fuzzy feelings can be created briefly, but psychological success cannot be maintained in the face of business failure. Both business and psychological success are necessary for the sustained high levels of motivation that are required to achieve long-term business success. That is cell 4.

The business unit being studied was financially successful, but corporate executives above the general manager of the unit refused to let him hire more people. Orders kept piling in and the result was that too few people had to work extraordinarily long hours to try to keep up. Not only were people pushed to the wall by their workload, but the profits they were generating were either being used to shore up other units that had poor financial results or the money was invested in other parts of the large corporation. From white-collar to blue-collar, the employees in the unit we were studying understood the reasons for the business strategy, but they felt bitter. That is cell 1 in the chart. While the business flourishes, the people don't.

I remember visiting a manufacturing company whose business was extraordinarily fast-changing and competitive. Their reality was really very scary. Unfortunately, the management style of the general manager, and therefore of his direct reports, was one of authoritarian, tight-lipped order-giving. There was no joy in Mudville. Our questionnaire data revealed that levels of anxiety, fear, cynicism, mistrust of leadership, doubt about the future, inequity, punishment for failure, and arbitrary use of power were off the scale. We actually couldn't imagine how people could come to work and function at all. How much more effective that organization would have been if management had led to success rather than fear.

While Managing-to-Fear can result in short-term gains in business success, it's a very serious mistake to deliberately increase people's sense of anxiety, dread, and fear as the major management tool. Long-term fear is debilitating and demotivating; people cannot tolerate interminable pain. Managing-to-Fear is a psychological license to increase people's sense of danger far beyond anything that is useful and effective because Managing-to Fear almost always makes people too scared. Managing-to-Fear takes people into paralyzing levels of pessimism, dread, and anxiety. Managing-to-Fear is a bad decision; it results in poor long-term results and should be judged as unethical.

It can never be assumed that business success alone will create psychological success. People who achieve business targets must benefit from the success they created. If there's no personal gain as a result of the business success, people become demotivated over time, and that should be considered psychological failure. In the face of psychological failure, people become significantly less willing to put the organization's needs before their own, less willing to work very hard or very well.

Psychological success is a prerequisite for sustained business success. Without psychological success there won't be an emotional commitment to the organization, its mission, or its leaders. Without psychological success, motivation cannot be sustained. Sustained motivation, effort, and enthusiasm requires the emotional commitment that comes only from psychological success—and that must come from the organization's real success.

Nothing raises motivation and morale more than winning. Organizations must manage to both business and psychological success because the spirit of *Go for it!* naturally reaches its highest levels where there is success—and that becomes self-sustaining.

 Success:

- Effective organizations Manage-to-Success and celebrate it.

- Organizations need to create a range of opportunities so everyone is able to earn the sense of being a winner.

- Sustained business success requires both business and psychological success.

What Matters Most in Managing Today

IN SUMMARY FORM, HERE'S WHAT EXPERIENCED PRACTITIONERS AND I believe really matters.

CONTRIBUTES TO SUCCESS	CONTRIBUTES TO FAILURE
If you can't explain your change process on one page, it's too complex. —STEVE MASON	*Retrofitting an existing culture is tough.* —NORM LORENTZ
This is not rocket science. —NED BARNHOLT	*Despite little sparks of brilliance, we haven't yet affected the whole.* —MARY JANE WILLIER

Urgency

CONTRIBUTES TO SUCCESS	CONTRIBUTES TO FAILURE
• The competition of the marketplace creates focus and motivation.	• The organization is successful, prestigious, praised, and profitable.
• The enemy is clear and the threat is undeniable.	• Nonaccountability is ignored.
	• People don't perceive a need for change.
	• The old paradigm of reality is not challenged.
• People "speak the unspeakable."	• Too many skeptics are waiting for this, too, to go away.
	• Management is too nice to communicate bad news.
	• Politics makes it too dangerous to speak out.
• The lifetime employment contract is ended.	• Human resources techniques are the primary tools to create change.
• Symbols of urgency—outsourcing, downsizing, cost-cutting—are used to destabilize the organization.	
• Urgency has everyone on their toes.	• Generalized anxiety prevails.

Leaders

CONTRIBUTES TO SUCCESS	CONTRIBUTES TO FAILURE
• Are new to their position.	• People who created the status quo remain in power.
• Think like outsiders, though they may be insiders.	

- Continuously challenge assumptions.
- Leadership is required and found at many levels.
- Define the business accurately.
- Know where the organization must go.

- Communicate the mission, values, goals, and rules.
- Communicate effectively.
- Create "meaning" in the work.
- Require business results.

- Are fair—neither kind nor tyrannical.
- Are transparent.

- Are persistent: consistent, disciplined, and focused.
- Are committed to years of hard work.

- Require creative confrontation.
- Decide and act.

- Require alignment.

- Get people emotionally involved.

- Hierarchical power games continue.
- Barriers to progress are not identified.
- Are uncertain what the business of the business is.
- The mission, goals, and values are just words, words, words . . .

- Pursue process improvements.

- Talking and doing are different.
- Buyer's remorse replaces initial enthusiasm.
- Executives keep changing models when change doesn't take root.
- Officers are fearful of fear in the organization.
- Officers are afraid and indecisive.
- Analysis paralysis.
- Allow disagreements to flourish after decisions are made.
- Disagreement is silenced.
- Mistake understanding for motivation.

- Believe creating change is management's key job.

- Accept the need for endless change.

- Are realistic and optimistic.

- See opportunity in change.

- Change management is a topic, a process, a tool or a training course. It is not what management does.

- There's no follow-through action.

- There's repeated downsizing and restructuring with no systems change.

- Deny reality.

Strategy

CONTRIBUTES TO SUCCESS	CONTRIBUTES TO FAILURE
• Is designed to win in the market!	• Focuses on cost cutting.
• Is based on where growth and profit are probable.	• Focuses on a process instead of a business outcome.
• Optimizes the organization's capacities.	• Doesn't achieve a competitive advantage.
• Aligns the organization's interests with the customers'.	
• Is designed to beat competitors.	
• Is specific to different businesses within an organization.	• Is based on short-term financial objectives.
	• Ignores the possibility of mistakes and failure.
• Describes different options with different conditions.	

- Is both short- and long-term.
- Is conceptually simple.
- Is intrinsically exciting.

- Is mundane.

Purpose

CONTRIBUTES TO SUCCESS	CONTRIBUTES TO FAILURE
• Everything moves the rock.	• Activity is "work."
• Achieving business goals is used to focus and/or change the culture.	• The focus is on process.
• There are a limited number of goals.	• Either outcomes are not measured or the wrong ones are measured.
• Measurement is ongoing and generates feedback.	• Goals are fuzzy.
• Barriers, gaps, and outcomes are clear and visible.	
• Management limits the number of change efforts.	• Change efforts are too complex.
	• Too many change efforts.
• Unnecessary work is eliminated.	• There's too much information.
• Simple is seen as best.	
• Incentives and pressures guide people to do the right things.	• Differentiating between people is perceived as unjust.
• There are significant consequences for failure or success.	• Identical outcomes (compensation and rewards), despite differences in contribution, are viewed as ethically fair.

- People who identify a problem solve it.
- Staff produces only what line requires.
- Learning results from solving real problems.

- The bar keeps getting raised.
- People are both challenged and supported.

- Nonperformance is tolerated.
- Staff and line are separate, so staff goals don't focus on what really matters.

- Training is a stand-alone activity with no follow-through.
- The culture spits out "glass eaters"—tough-minded people who buck the system.

Collaboration

CONTRIBUTES TO SUCCESS

- Ideals create cohesion.

- Management assumes collaboration.
- Teams evolve naturally when small groups work together to solve important problems.
- Hoarding is not tolerated.

- Subordinates solve the problems they identify.

CONTRIBUTES TO FAILURE

- Hitting the targets is all that matters.
- Personal fiefdoms persist.

- "Teambuilding" is a process goal.
- There's no necessary cross-divisional or cross-functional collaboration.
- Executives, middle management, and supervisors are in different "realities."
- Middle management and supervisors resist change.
- Relations are adversarial between management and employees.

- Compensation rewards collaboration.

- Compensation rewards individuals and/or separate businesses.

Selection

CONTRIBUTES TO SUCCESS

- People are selected who model the right values.

- Leaders "get" the new values.

- People are first selected and then trained.

- Nonperformers are fired.

- Skills are aligned to tasks.

CONTRIBUTES TO FAILURE

- People who model the wrong values are not removed.

- People select and promote their buddies.

- Training is expected to transform character and personality.

- Contracts protect jobs.

- There's no control over performance issues.

- Seniority outweighs performance.

Methods

CONTRIBUTES TO SUCCESS

- They are intrinsic to the work.

- They are a natural part of the work style.

- They're evaluated in terms of their business outcome.

- There are as few as possible.

CONTRIBUTES TO FAILURE

- They are separate activities from the organization's work.

- They are standardized and purchased as solutions.

- They're evaluated as goals in themselves.

- They are complex.

- They are as simple as possible.

- They feature exotic, graphically dazzling models.

- They are a battleship where a rowboat is needed.

Trust

CONTRIBUTES TO SUCCESS	CONTRIBUTES TO FAILURE
• Management walks with the troops.	• Management gains from employee pain.
• Management walks the talk.	• Management does not do what it says.
• Subordinates are respected.	• Empowerment is a word, not an action.
• Communications tell the truth.	• Management does not acknowledge problems.
• Dialogue is interactive.	• Management tells and does not listen.
• Communications are personal.	• Management assumes it's "heard."

Commitment

CONTRIBUTES TO SUCCESS	CONTRIBUTES TO FAILURE
• Employees have conditional commitment.	• There's no way for employees to earn any security.
• The organization acts responsibly toward its employees.	• The scorecard is unbalanced between employees, shareholders, and management. Employees come last.

- The organization is honest about its commitment to employees.

- Most people want the organization to succeed.

- People have an emotional bond to the organization, its mission, and each other.

- The organization promises employability.

- People are too weary; they've been bruised and battered for too long.

- Stress is greater than people can tolerate.

Success

CONTRIBUTES TO SUCCESS	CONTRIBUTES TO FAILURE
• There's both business and psychological success.	• Efforts are made to create psychological success without business success.
• Success increases the speed of further change.	• There's business, but no psychological success.
• Success is a quantified business target.	• Success is a process outcome and not a business result.
• Stretch goals are achievable.	
• There are individual, team, and organizational goals.	• The focus is on avoiding failure.
• Success is celebrated.	• Recognition is a bureaucratic activity.
• Success is rewarded significantly.	• Every accomplishment, of any size, is rewarded.
• Success creates an emotional high.	
• Success is visible.	• Success is achieved but is invisible.
	• There's skepticism that any success has been achieved.

PART

THREE

Implications for the Future

You Are Your Own Business

IN 1983, I RESIGNED FROM THE UNIVERSITY OF MICHIGAN. MY REASON was simple: I wanted to remain in La Jolla because it made my heart sing. How happy! How romantic! How risky! I can just about remember what it was really like during that first couple of months after I set out on my own. The absence of those small, but steady, monthly checks gained them a sweetness they had never had when I took them for granted. I had gone from being a tenured full professor to a freelance entrepreneur with just one decision. I can never again take a paycheck for granted. My life is exciting, but it's also stressful. When it really is your own business, time is money and you don't waste either. You're always selling and you're always competing. Even when you're very successful, you cannot assume there's a customer tomorrow. You're on your own and the customer is the one in charge. No matter how successful you become, there simply isn't a home plate. There is no such thing as permanently safe.

People are under tremendous pressure to demonstrate and convince potential employers of their value. The new and really fundamental question for employees is, What do you do that makes it worthwhile for employers to hire you instead of outsourcing this activity or eliminating it altogether?

The seriousness of this challenge might be grasped if people realized that:

- The business of health care is the prevention of illness and the cure of sickness.
- The business of academia is the discovery and dissemination of knowledge.
- The business of charities is to provide help that increases people's competencies.
- The business of government is ensuring the people's safety, rights, and liberties.
- The business of corporations is creating profit.

Creating jobs and providing security is never the core business of any organization. While growing jobs and providing conditional security are obviously desirable, that has to be the result of succeeding in the business of the business. Increasing the number of jobs and creating security cannot be the goals of an enterprise because, as goals, they inevitably lead to a culture with no consequences.

You Can't Count on Your Employer

Despite slow but steady economic growth, the nation is uneasy. Although consumer confidence rises as well as falls, people sense a sea change; something fundamental and extraordinary is happening and it threatens their sense of security. In addition, we're blasted by bad news and, accustomed to sensationalism, we're exposed to higher and higher levels of shriek in order to gain our attention. Security we once took for granted is assaulted by blaring headlines of mass layoffs, stagnant wages, outsourced work, and plant closings. Job growth is briefly noted, while job loss is center stage. Bad news generates a prolonged surge of adrenaline; good news a fleeting smile.

Not so long ago, you knew what you could count on. You could count on your spouse, your friends, your extended family, your employer, and your community. Now, high levels of uneasiness have expanded beyond work to other social institutions. In the same way that we highlight job loss over job growth, we have focused on the erosion of morality, the impermanence of family, the decay of neighborhoods, the decline of our schools, and the loss of a sense of community. Despite having the personal experience of an enduring marriage, a rich family life, good friends, and a safe neighborhood, many people feel the existential anchors that create stability and provide identity are gone or in jeopardy. The world became borderless and that ended the conditions that created job, financial, and other kinds of security.

Not long ago, many organizations proudly called themselves families, and the organization-as-family had come to be seen as the ideal organizational culture. But there is a downside to the family at work that is identical to the downside of powerful, benevolent parents at home. When anyone is taken care of for too long, the outcome is prolonged dependence. In fact, the cost of that dependence becomes clear when we ask, What did organizations mean when they asked employees to be loyal? Being loyal means more than taking part of your identity from your membership, it means more than agreeing with the values of the organization, it means more than contributing through excellence to the success of the organization. Loyalty involves a concept of sacrifice: Loyalty means that in exchange for protection, people put the welfare of the organization before their own. That is a heavy price to pay. Dependent employees paid that price gladly because, psychologically, they had no alternative.

The old version of loyalty is dying. Increasing numbers of people are learning that whether they work for an organization or for a temp agency, whether they work on a five-year contract or for themselves, they are their own businesses. As organizations have been forced to maximize their self-interest, they've forced employees to see that survival calls for an appropriate increase in their self-interest. Increasingly, not only are people responsible for keeping themselves valuable as employees, but they're also fools if they don't keep scanning the environment for better opportunities. With continued downsizing, restructuring, and outsourcing, more and more, people's only obligation to an employer is to earn their compensation through the excellence of their performance.

Since it's psychologically and financially uneconomical to take care of employees who might voluntarily or involuntarily leave at any time, parentalism is ending and that's good. Grown-up people need to depend on themselves more and on organizations less.

Andy Grove, CEO of Intel, America's largest manufacturer of semiconductors and the 43rd largest American corporation, says the only thing that can conceivably keep employees safe is the ability to end up where "the invisible hand of the economy wants you to be."[1] Intel originally tried to plan employees' careers, but the corporation gave up: First, the task was too complicated, and second, the corporation felt it was accepting too much responsibility for making decisions that people should make for themselves. Instead of telling people what to do, every quarter Grove gives a two-hour talk about what's happening in the business, and people gain a sense of where the opportunities are increasing or declining. The responsibility for figuring out what that might mean to any individual is left to the individual. Grove says even at Intel, the ideal of providing continuous employment through employee adaptability can't be maintained all the time. And that's why a truly benevolent organization wants its employees to be able to take care of themselves.

No organization was more parental than Ma Bell. It was, therefore, a dramatic challenge to employee assumptions when I heard Ray Smith, CEO of the AT&T spin-off Bell Atlantic, say: "Once in the corporation, the employees' own skills, talent, and personality must bring them to the fore, because the corporation isn't really tracking people." Bell Atlantic's training courses, Smith said, were now in the computers and employees were responsible for learning what was available and mastering the content. Job openings were also in computers and employees were responsible both for knowing what was available and for applying for a position. Mostly, Smith said, employees were responsible for increasing their value to the company. There was nothing in Smith's message about taking care of employees.

Aside from the major tremor of downsizing, AT&T's employees are getting more accustomed to an awful lot of aftershocks. People can be notified at any time that their jobs are at risk.[2] That can mean their unit is cutting the number of people in their area or their discipline, or it may mean that their skills are obsolete, or they had a poor job evaluation compared with their peers. Even if there are no layoffs, and even if their performance evaluations are really good, AT&T employees who are working on a project can never forget that when the project ends—and projects typically last only one to two years—the employee is responsible for finding the next project. If employees can't find another slot within a few months, they're required to leave. Increasing the tension, AT&T's insiders are having to compete for positions not only with each other but also with outsiders. Now, successful AT&T employees are always hustling, striving to get the skills they need to either keep the position they have or win a berth on a new project.

Parentalism is either dead or dying in AT&T and most of the other great American companies. But parentalism is appealing. It makes employers feel they're good, and employees cuddle in it as though it were a down comforter. It will go, but more slowly than it should. In most circumstances, cost will force change.

Tom and Gun Denhart are the founders of Hanna Andersson, an upscale children's clothing line sold by catalog.[3] In 1992, at $40 million in sales, Hanna Andersson had become the largest direct mail marketer of children's clothing in the United States. As the company succeeded and grew, the founders still managed to keep the culture like that of a small family-owned and -operated store. The company was widely admired for its humane practices. It had generous family leave and child care subsidies, participatory management, significant charitable giving, flex time, sick time, and subsidized low-calorie gourmet food at lunch. Hanna Andersson paid half of employees' child care costs. It gave full benefits to seasonal workers and part-timers who worked 30 hours a week. It paid the employees' parking. It distributed cash bonuses, reimbursed people for tuition costs, and shared profits. In effect, every job at the company had tenure. The culture nurtured and employees expected to be taken care of.

In 1993, the good times stopped. While sales had been falling, costs had been rising. The costs of employees' health insurance, of the catalogs, and of mailing the catalogs had all increased. And so had the number of competitors. The competition had gotten very tough and Hanna Andersson's costs were out of line, especially because of corporate generosity. Suddenly the benefits that Hanna had happily given employees (and its cordial relationships with suppliers, which didn't always give Hanna an advantage) were reviewed. With success, those costs had been ignored. But with competition and declining sales, costs had to come down.

Tom and Gun Denhart were committed to achieving two kinds of success, what they called the "double bottom line." One outcome was measured in profits and the other in good work. Companies that have only one primary goal, that of maximizing profits, would be more likely to minimize costs and anticipate competition than Hanna did. According to Tom Denhart, "We became so introspective that we lost sight of what was happening outside the company. Instead of looking out at what was happening in the marketplace, we were all wrapped up in figuring out the best way to run the company."[4] Hanna had so wanted to be a different kind of company, an organization with real soul, that it had lost its eyes. It became a no-consequence organization, and no-consequence cultures always focus inward.

Harder times forced the company to teach its employees that it does not exist simply to employ and protect them. Now, employees contribute to the cost of their health insurance and there's a ceiling on reimbursement for child care. Paid parking, which cost the company $80,000 a year, is gone. In April, 1993, 20 employees, 10 percent of the direct labor force, were laid off. Employees had to learn that there is an enormous difference between what the company can afford when it earns $2 million or $4 million and when it earns no profits.

The right thing to do in good times is not nearly as obvious as it is in hard times. Commenting on the experience of Hanna Andersson, venture capitalist Tom Murphy said: "Like Entitlement, being 'socially responsible' can kill jobs because it's so expensive. They both spring from the same well-spring of using business for noble purpose. Perhaps it is true that no good deed goes unpunished. More likely, institutions have roles and mixing them does not work very well."[5]

While warm and fuzzy may have more obvious appeal, the basic market-driven forces of capitalism, which can feel cruel and appear unfeeling and unfair, are actually what enables organizations, especially corporations, to become and remain vital and successful. The corporation's greatest responsibility to its employees is to succeed. Success in the business of the business is the only source of any kind of employment security.

The primary goal of any organization must be to succeed in its primary mission. While altruism can be an esteemed value within any organization, it cannot be allowed to divert its members from the organization's essential reason for being. *Save our jobs!* cannot be allowed to crowd out *Succeed in the mission! Grow the business!*

Being taken care of will not be part of the new commitment between employees and employers. We are now in a period of transition from parental organizational cultures to conditions that require employees have increasingly high levels of autonomy. This transition period is the hardest phase of all because, while many old securities are gone, the new mechanisms by which people can earn some level of security are generally not yet established.

The end of parentalism is a profound philosophic shift in our ideas about what constitutes ethical behavior on the part of organizations. We're going from believing the best organizations take care of their people to believing the best organizations, like the best families, both nurture and challenge their members, preparing them to be self-reliant and self-initiating. The basic corporate message is *Grow up.* In the long run, that's a good idea. As hard as the transformation will be for some people, it's a move toward something much healthier.

The One-Person Business

All of it—getting a job, keeping the job, keeping skills technologically advanced, deepening knowledge, widening experience, evolving priorities among responsibilities, preparing for retirement, managing life in the face of possible unemployment, getting the best and most useful or relevant education—are increasingly the responsibility of the individual, and responsible individuals will accept that responsibility as theirs. Those who don't will fail both personally and professionally.

Everyone who wants to be employed is under endless pressure to sell the merits of his or her contribution. There is a direct parallel: just as organizations have to continuously revisit the question *What is the business of this business?* in order to optimize opportunity within conditions of endless change, so, too, do individuals have to continuously hone their skills and ask, *What can I do that someone will buy?* Just as organizations face changing customers, so, too, will increasing numbers of people find themselves selling their skills to changing buyers.

Some people will win, and others will lose. People who do the most significant work and are the hardest to replace will get the greatest share of rewards. The people most likely to successfully make the transition and be comfortable with more autonomy will be educated, confident enough to be flexible, highly skilled, and entrepreneurial. The end of parentalism will lead some people to a struggle to remain somewhere in the broad middle class; for others, it will involve an erosion to downward mobility. Those most likely to be losers are people who never completed high school, semiskilled workers in manufacturing, and people who worked for many years in no-consequence organizations.

Losers will include all the people who don't comprehend that now, wherever they work, they're a one-person business. This makes some people feel unconnected, isolated, vulnerable, and tired. Others respond by becoming entrepreneurial, autonomous, and energized. There's more than one way in which the gap between the haves and the have-nots is increasing.

The outcome of draconian change is not predictable. Huge changes always generate massive problems, but for those who are adaptive and entrepreneurial, the same changes generate massive new opportunities. A small percent will be able to generate the guts and outlook of an entrepreneur, and for them, a corporate kick in the pants can result in higher levels of traditional success, of money, status, and power, than they would have achieved if they had remained in the bosom of the organization.

Other people will respond to the new, more Darwinian values of organizations by changing their values and therefore their goals. They will move to kinds of work that are less competitive and less financially rewarding, but that offer great personal satisfaction. Those people are, in their lives, real winners. While financially they may move downward, they gain something else, often more socially valuable and personally relevant.

It's not surprising to find there's now an increased interest in social work and teaching by people who had previously been loyal corporate participants. When people ask themselves *What should I do about my career?* the answer should involve their careers and also their sense of what's worthwhile in their lives. People's definition of success or failure should evolve as a function of what they have achieved or failed to do, as they review their options and values. For example, a person may go from being a corporate vice president with enormous responsibilities to being a high school counselor, shifting from a goal of high-powered and traditional success to a goal of helping humanity on a one-to-one personal basis. The choices are extremely personal, or should be.

The New Qualifications

Being a narrow specialist today can become very dangerous. A continuous process improvement expert is in danger when reengineering grows more popular: An oral surgeon who specializes in implants loses out when pharmaceutical companies grow cells in the jaw bone, or a tax specialist in stone quarries can have no business when the tax code changes. At the same time, a person without a commanding specialty is in danger of not being perceived as especially valuable. But concentrating only on a specialty makes people vulnerable because today any specialty can swiftly become less valuable in the face of changing technologies and expanding knowledge. It's probably a good idea to have both breadth and at least one deep area of specialization. The value of the specialist is obvious; that person is an expert among experts in something of key value. But the leaders of organizations, the people who have general management responsibilities, are people whose experience allows them to grasp all the significant variables. In the flux of change, a wise career strategy is to alternate assignments that increase depth in a core specialty with responsibilities that broaden knowledge of the organization.

While organizations should ask people, *Are you willing to keep on learning?* employees have the right to ask organizations, *Will you let me create opportunities so I keep on stretching?* When success is defined as increasing the complexity of what you understand and do, and a key focus is on doing work of increasing impact, then continuous learning through relevant experience or formal education naturally becomes a lifetime requirement.

Seizing the initiative and learning continuously have become critical for keeping oneself valuable. Jeffrey Schmidt, a managing director at the major outplacement firm of Towers Perrin, says that everyone has to do an exhaustive inventory of his or her skills because "You have to assume that the half-life of the skill set you've got is about three to five years."[6] If the half-life of your skills is three to five years and you're just beginning your career, then the skills you have now will be adequate for about one-tenth of your career. Therefore, everyone has to proactively assess the skills the business will need in the future and make sure they obtain them.

In 1982, the extension program of the prestigious branch of the University of California at Santa Clara, which serves Silicon Valley, had 8000 students.[7] In 1994, there were 30,000 students. This school is doing the right thing exceedingly well. Most of the students are working professionals, many from Silicon Valley companies. For these students, learning and working are continuously intertwined. Some of the course offerings are sponsored by corporations to keep their employees at the cutting edge; other courses are requested by the students. The curriculum of the extension program is totally market driven. These students, and they are now the majority in the nation's community colleges, are mostly older and mostly intermittent learners. They and their teachers know that fast-changing technology makes obsolescence a continuous challenge. It is becoming more and more obvious that people need to hold themselves responsible for ever increasing professionalism, which includes formal education in addition to experience.[8]

Just as people are now responsible for making themselves effective and valuable, employees are also responsible for making their contributions visible. They not only have to add value, they need to make it possible for others to perceive that they did. Therefore, they are responsible for accepting assignments or creating initiatives in which they can demonstrate their value, and they must strategize to make that happen.

Increasingly, employees are responsible for positioning themselves so they're key players and perceived as such. They need to become people whose views are solicited and whose ideas are heard. Thus, employees should strategize to do work that gives them a chance to learn, to do something important or increase their visibility as effective people who make a difference.

People must be tough on themselves. They must really be willing to acquire the knowledge, the skills, and the experiences that are, or in their judgment will be, in high demand. If you are on staff—in administration, human resources, finance, law, or quality—you must force yourself to think like someone who runs a business and must generate profits. You must confront the issue of your value by evaluating yourself as a business partner. And, to the extent it's possible, never accept an assignment, a responsibility, much less a job that doesn't allow you to learn and make a significant and measurable contribution.

Keeping your knowledge cutting-edge has become so important that the decision of whether or not to do so is the choice of keeping yourself valuable or jeopardizing your employability. The people most likely to be let go today are those who will not or cannot adapt to the new realities and learn and change. The more entrenched people are in the old ways of doing and thinking, the more resistant they are to changing, the less valuable they are. Flexibility, adaptability, and a willingness to retrain and even relocate are becoming increasingly critical in terms of maintaining one's employability.

I've just described what you have to *do* when you're your own business. It's also necessary to *be* a certain kind of person. The strongest asset anyone can have in a world of volatile change is the mind-set of an entrepreneur, combined with optimism that comes from confidence in oneself. Being entrepreneurial will be more important than being educated in tomorrow's labor force. Successful people will perceive opportunity where the majority perceive only problems. Someone's problem can always become another person's opportunity. The two-paycheck household, for example, especially one with children, has been the driver creating many businesses. Joan Corwin started Mother Hen's Helpers in 1995.[9] Fifteen dollars pays for a round-trip for children anywhere within a 10-mile radius. Two years after it was started, Mother Hen's Helpers has 1094 customers. Households in which all adults are employed is why all kinds of take-out food sources are proliferating, ranging from the deli case of your local supermarket to the extraordinary growth of Boston Market.

Everyone is responsible for keeping him- or herself ahead of the wave. In Peter Drucker's words, the corporate ladder has disappeared and what's replacing it is more like a tangle of vines to which you bring your own machete.[10] This doesn't mean that people can't plan the kind of work they will do; they can. What they will not be able to do is predict how they will use their knowledge and skills as the rate of change keeps accelerating. On one hand, they'll need specific goals and relevant skills. On the other hand, they had better be proactive, flexible, and very keenly attuned to work's realities.

My son Peter's most recent career move illustrates how the wave is moving faster and going to unpredictable places. Peter has been an investment banker and an operating financial officer in the radio industry. In 1996, Congress further deregulated radio, which made it possible for owners to have multiple stations in the same geographic area. This legislative change resulted in a boom in acquisitions and mergers as owners sought to gain advantages of scale that had never been available to them before. The industry began to be transformed from multiple small operations to far fewer and much larger players. Large radio groups require much more sophisticated finance than do individual mom-and-pop stations.

The regulatory changes created a major opportunity for Peter because he had the experience to provide sophisticated financial advice and the financial connections to raise money in an industry he knew. That led him to join a very successful radio broker firm, his task being the creation of a financial arm for the firm's radio clients.

Within the first few months after Peter joined the radio brokers, they found that while there were opportunities to provide financial assistance to their radio clients—just as they had expected—there were as many unexpected opportunities in the crossovers between technologies. While legislative change had created opportunities in radio, the accelerating fusion between computers, the Internet, satellite transmissions, TV, telecommunications, radio, and print is creating equal or even greater opportunities. The firm is talking to people who do long-distance teaching via satellites, to people who create material for children that is accessible in all of the media, to people who want to do interactive talk shows on the Internet . . . no one knows where this is going to end up.

The most reasonable thing to do is to create as many opportunities as possible in which things might arise that might be converted to opportunity. Being flexible enough to perceive a range of opportunities as they arise—either by happenstance or because you created them—is good preparation for these less predictable times.

Michael Driver, a professor of management at the University of Southern California, says, "We used to want people who were very focused, structured, analytical, and action oriented."[11] He means that until fairly recently, employers preferred people who made decisions by sticking to the hard data, crunching numbers, and going with the quantitative outcome. But, Driver says, as we move into the Information Age we need people who have "adaptive, multi-focused thinking." In other words, in a period of continuous change, we need people who have an integrative problem solving style so they're able to use all kinds of information, both quantitative and qualitative, from multiple, diverse sources.

Put more simply, fluid conditions require fluid mental processes. Increasingly, problem solving will require people whose minds are adaptive, who can create a coherent reality out of a stream of ongoing bits of data. People who are more likely to be effective in the midst of change will be those whose minds grasp, analyze, intuit, and synthesize so the result is a gestalt; the whole of these people's grasp is immensely greater than the sum of the parts.

The most effective workers in the future will not only synthesize ideas, they will also bring people together, creating something greater than the sum of individuals. They will have the capacity to create a gestalt of individuals, forging people together as a seamless team for as long as they work together. When teamwork becomes the preferred way to organize work and it involves continuously changing combinations of people, being able to easily win other people's trust and collaboration is an enormous advantage. The liability of not having those qualities is obvious.

Peter Drucker says the subjective competencies will be critical.[12] Effective people will be empathic, a critical competence for interactions with others. A parallel competency will be really knowing yourself as a precondition for being comfortable with yourself. And confidence, of course, is probably the most critical of the personal competencies because it means you're liberated from inhibiting fears.

Successful people, in the new reality, will like pressure and remain steady when things are confused. They will have to be comfortable with a high degree of ambiguity, uncertainty, and incomplete data because decisions in a fast-paced economy have to be made long before all the data can be gathered and comprehensive analyses completed. In a fluid, less predictable world, people have to be able to think on their feet and not expect to, or need to, operate by the book because the book will always be out of date.

When we all just received monthly paychecks and the benefits that came with them, it felt like we could afford to be passive about our careers and basically just do what organizations, in the form of our managers, told us to do. Today, people have to continuously assess their status in terms of their value at work and they must be psychologically prepared to change where they live or what they do as opportunity declines or increases. The loss of security needs to become the motivator for proactive initiation for yourself. Just as organizations need a sense of urgency in order to change, so, too, is a reasonable amount of fear an asset to individuals. People must learn to use their fear of economic insecurity to make themselves do what they need to do in order to increase their value, even if it involves disruption, dislocation, and more hard work.

International Survey Research (ISR) polled 100,000 managers in 1995.[13] Thirty-seven percent of those polled said they were frequently concerned about being laid off. That is the highest anxiety level ISR has recorded in decades. Forty percent of the managers said they could not count on keeping their jobs even if they did perform well. Nearly half of those polled were seriously worried about the futures of their companies. It's as though the psychological midlife crisis of the big 5-0 has become a more realistic crisis of finance, value, and self-esteem for many more middle-aged people than it used to be. The most important job anyone has is keeping him- or herself valuable. The thing is, that's *your* job.

You are your own business means:

- You add significant value to your customer or you're history.
- You are responsible for having relevant skills and knowledge, just as you are responsible for being flexible, collaborative, insightful, and decisive.
- There is no comfort zone of parental protections.

CHAPTER

16

Education

Results Matter

The public schools are failing our children. America's competitiveness is being jeopardized by our children's soaring ignorance in comparison with students from most other nations. In 1997, about 40 percent of American fourth-graders didn't reach minimum standards on the National Assessment of Educational Progress, a reading test; and in 1996, 55 percent of eighth-graders didn't achieve an international average score in math in the Third International Math and Science Study.[1] In a comparison with students in 41 nations, our eighth-graders ranked in the middle of the pack in math and science, between Romania and Bulgaria.[2] Three factors are crucial in terms of contributing to the deterioration of the schools:

1. The public schools have forgotten that the business of the business is to educate. In a misguided effort to be

humane and redress the awful deficiencies in some kids'
lives, the schools have become social work agencies, police
stations, therapy centers, and so forth. The most effective
schools stick to their primary responsibility, which is educating. They teach a core curriculum that lends itself to creating standards of performance and measurements of
achievement. In the most effective schools, no child is perceived as a victim who is exonerated from having to learn.
Instead, all of the children are expected to work to a high
level of performance. The best schools, like the best corporations, Manage-to-Success.

The American curriculum typically includes many soft,
touchy-feely self-esteem and personal relevance courses.
Nations whose students perform better on academic tests
stick far more closely to the basics. While no one disputes
the advantage of student creativity, creativity must extend
from a mastery of basic knowledge. In addition, effective
systems of education don't make excuses for student nonperformance. Instead, they make high demands on every
child proportionate to the child's ability. Doing otherwise,
either because it's assumed the kid can't learn or the goal is
to make learning "fun," deprives children of the greatest
thrill—which is to master something that used to seem
hard. *That's* fun! in school.

2. The public school system is effectively a monopoly and,
like any institution not disciplined by a competitive marketplace, it has become a bastion of nonaccountability with an
enormous bureaucracy. Without powerful guidelines of right
and wrong, without the cohesion created by strong ethics
and a sense of mission, the educational establishment is primarily self-serving. Thus, despite the efforts of individual
teachers and principals, the system ignores its customers.

Like any other monopoly, the seeds of failure of the public education system lie in its contempt for its customers.
Without the discipline of the market, a no-consequence culture develops and the system serves itself rather than the

students, their parents, the community, and ultimately the nation.

3. The teacher unions are much too powerful and have chosen to lead the resistance to constructive change rather than to lead the innovations the system must have if it's to regain its former effectiveness.

The two teacher unions, the American Federation of Teachers (AFT) and the nation's largest union, the National Education Association (NEA), have policies and practices that contribute directly to the academic failure. Between tenure and seniority rules, principals do not have control over teachers because the unions have actively resisted reforms of a system in which tenure and seniority protect teachers who are poor performers. Tenure makes getting rid of poor teachers so expensive that most school systems give up and, instead of firing such teachers, just try to get them transferred anywhere else.

State and local licensing systems for becoming a teacher generally require that applicants take the correct college courses, but, unlike other professionals, teachers don't have to demonstrate that they know the subject they're teaching or that they are effective teachers of it. This profession has attracted and accepted too many people to colleges of education who "by and large . . . wouldn't be admitted to college in other countries," according to the late Albert Shanker, once AFT president.[3] In fact, an appalling number of graduates from colleges of education have recently failed basic literacy tests. In 1994–1995, California administered about 65,000 such exams to teachers; 20 percent who took the test failed. The teachers' unions never made tough standards a priority in licensing and employing teachers.

The unions have enforced a single salary schedule that pays teachers strictly on the basis of seniority and number of college courses completed. Differences in performance have nothing whatsoever to do with teacher's pay, and the college courses teachers are rewarded for having taken do not have to be linked to what they teach. There is nothing in the reward system to encourage teachers to shine.

Dumbing Down

The public school establishment makes two horrendous and basic errors. One is resisting teacher accountability for student performance and the other is managing to student morale. Army General Tom Kelley says the army has six-week courses in which non-English-speaking recruits learn enough English to manage their responsibilities. "When students fail," Kelley says, "their teachers are fired."[4]

The general rule is, if you don't measure something, people don't pay attention to it. That's why it's necessary to have achievement tests that can assess student knowledge in a relatively objective way. Without measurement and repeated measurement, it becomes very difficult to require teacher accountability for student learning and to differentiate between teachers on the basis of their effectiveness.

Getting schools to Manage-to-Success requires that "success" be able to be measured quantitatively. Sustained, fundamental change, especially in terms of becoming results-driven, never happens without repeated measurements of goals in the business of the business. This is a serious problem for the mess that is public education: Education will not be able to define its goals until it has reached agreement on what would be regarded as appropriate levels of learning for each grade. To designate appropriate levels of learning, there must first be agreement on what the core curriculum of each grade should be. While there can be choices about electives, the core curriculum should be a constant because it's supposed to be what every person needs to know. It is the educational foundation. With a basic curriculum and designated appropriate levels of learning for every grade, it's possible to create standards of pupil and teacher performance. More specifically, it's possible to create standard tests that measure levels of learning that are viewed as both necessary and significant.

The teachers' unions resist standardized tests, saying they force teachers to teach to the test. There's nothing wrong with that if the test measures what's important. Not measuring knowledge and mastery because "it reduces creativity" is a foolish argument that reinforces fuzzy thinking. Even in the faddish world of K through 12 education, there should be agreement about the core of what children should know.

When I was in high school in New York State, there were state exams in every major subject that students had to pass in order to graduate. That meant there was agreement among educators as to what constituted the important subject matter of a course. Today, the increased power of political correctness, in addition to hotly contested theories of education, has diluted consensus about what content should constitute the core of any academic curriculum. If there isn't clarity about what people ought to know, then it becomes impossible to create standards against which performance can be measured. The absence of learning standards contributes directly to the lowering of teaching standards. That, combined with a goal of student self-esteem, ultimately led to low teacher expectations of what students should and could do. Low expectations are always met.

Academically speaking, we're killing our kids with kindness. While we spend more per primary and secondary school student than any other country, our kids do very poorly in comparison with kids in other countries. What accounts for this outcome? We have more administrators and support staff that don't teach than any other country; and nations that have strong curriculums and high and uncompromising standards have students who learn more and test better.

The education establishment decided its real goal was to have students feel good about themselves. They sought to achieve that by diminishing competition, inflating grades, and praising kids in the absence of achievement. That, in combination with a lack of academic standards, led to a dumbing down of requirements for student as well as teacher performance. Combined, these practices deprive our children of the real guts of self esteem, which is the mastery of new tasks.

When education manages-to-morale, it raises the goal of student self-esteem above that of achievement. This leads easily enough to teacher guidelines that students should not be told that they're doing something incorrectly or that their information is inadequate, because that would injure the student's level of esteem. That view was combined with the influential education doctrine of constructivism, a theory that contends that people have their own ways of constructing knowledge or adding to what they already know. Constructivism led to a conclusion that there are no better *ways* to learn, and ultimately, that there are no better *things* to learn. Thus, educators have abdicated their primary responsibility, which is to teach a curriculum that prepares students to learn how to learn and gives them the tools to do so. Instead, our public school system is producing students who consistently score near the top of the scale in the international comparisons of students' own evaluations of their academic competence— while they score near the bottom on achievement.[5]

Schools cannot have goals of generating self-esteem or providing opportunities for fun. These goals lead to a proliferation of sheer froth in the curriculum and an evasion of the need for mastery. That's a bad life lesson. Naturally, we want children to enjoy school. But we want them to view school as a place where they work hard and they stay until they get it. That's preparation for succeeding in a demanding, competitive world.

It was the failure of the plausible but futile efforts to first change a corporation's culture in order to improve business results that got me to see we had the logic wrong. To get better business results, you have to start with a focus on improving business outcomes, and that process is the instrument that creates change in the culture. In the same way, schools must refocus on their real mission and responsibility, which is to educate. Other positive outcomes like confidence, high self-esteem, self-discipline, optimism, enjoying challenges, autonomy, logic, the ability to conceptualize, articulateness, and so on, will develop in students as the result of their achieving significant success.

I have never known a child to be fooled for long by a ritual pat on the head and a cheerful "Good job!" when they've done a lousy job. Like any other institution, education will not be able to get the positive results it wants in children, nor will it be able to create and sustain children's motivation to learn, until it manages-to-success and all kids achieve more success than they thought they could.

Helen Carithers and Melanie Krieger are directors of programs within their high schools that are designed to bring out the best in the best students.[6] Students are expected and encouraged to excel. Carithers and Krieger have created cultures of high expectations and high achievement. They've found the most important element in increasing a student's academic success is having a teacher who has high expectations for the students. Students learn when they are challenged as well as encouraged by their teachers. One hundred percent of the graduates of each program go on to four-year colleges. Carithers' students, who are as successful as Krieger's, are black, while Krieger's students are white. When kids become comfortable with their ability to achieve, both teachers say, it becomes a natural thing to do your best.

John Murphy is a school superintendent.[7] When he took over the Prince Georges County school system in Maryland, Columbia Park Elementary School was typical of the district's worst problems. Student math and reading test scores were among the lowest in the district. Parents experienced many teachers as indifferent or hostile, and vandalism, drugs, and graffiti invaded and plagued the school. Murphy found the kids' poor performance was blamed on their poverty, their race, and the assumption of parental neglect. He countered those assumptions with the belief that "All children can learn and we push high expectations."

Murphy brought in a new principal who raised demands: stricter discipline, harder books, higher test scores. But for sticks to be effective there must also be carrots. Ms. Green, the new principal, rewarded kids for everything they did well. The school is now strict and structured, the kids are pushed hard in the classroom, their test scores have risen very significantly—and they are excited about learning.

School Reform

Calls for major school reform began in the early 1980s. Those reforms normally include tougher standards for a teaching license, pay based on performance, more powerful control over teaching standards so incompetent teachers can be fired, some modification of teachers' tenure, and teacher accountability tied to some form of standardized tests.

Albert Shanker, the AFT's president until his death in 1996, was among America's most militant teachers in the 1960s, and he led the movement that created hard-edged unionism in the public schools. But in 1996, in the face of the public's resentment about the practices of the teachers' unions, Shanker called for the unions to focus on standards of teacher quality. He called for higher entrance standards for teachers, pay related to the quality of performance, and a simplification of due process protections. Increasingly, other union leaders share Shanker's view: "Unless we restore the public's faith in what we do, public education is going to collapse. A lot of our leaders believe that we're close to the end of public education. They never did before."[8]

The public's confidence in the public school system has declined enormously. And the intransigence of the unions, especially the NEA, in reforming its practices has led to the proliferation of variations on school choice so parents have greater control over which schools their children attend. The failure of the public school system is leading to the growth of alternative, competitive education systems that, in the long run, will break the public school monopoly and the power of the teachers' unions. The predictable outcome of the unions' resistance to constructive change, especially in regards to increased teacher accountability and improved student performance, will result in the creation of significant alternatives to a deteriorated public school system.

Parents are very aware of the ever increasing competition and performance requirements their children face. So they are increasingly angry about the failure of the schools to give their children the advantage of an outstanding education despite the money that's been poured into the system. As with any other sector in the boundaryless economy, the failure of the public school monopoly will lead to its destruction. Either the teachers' unions will lead the necessary changes or they will be left small, with little power.

Teachers, administrators, and parents who want reform are proposing new forms of public schools, one of which is charter schools.[9] While the laws vary between the states, charter school laws usually allow parents, teachers, and other interested people to set up schools if they win approval from the state or the local school district. The state pays the charter school the same amount of money per student that it does the regular public schools. In turn, charter schools are required to deliver specific academic results. Under this system, the state waives most union rules and regulations.

Despite union opposition, 25 states and the District of Columbia had approved charter schools by 1996.[10] Since 1993, about 500 charter schools have opened, and in December 1996 *The Wall Street Journal* reported that President Clinton's 1997 budget will ask for funding for 3000 charter schools by the year 2000.[11,12]

Proponents of charter schools see them as supplying necessary marketplace competition to existing schools for students and thus for funding. While the amount of competition created by the charter schools is still too small to achieve a systemwide improvement, one can hope that, with more alternatives in the form of vouchers, state aid, private schools, religious schools, charter schools, and any other innovation that might come along, the dynamics of capitalism will prevail in education just as in the marketplace. With sufficient competition, schools that are not selected by the parent-student customer would and should close.

Advocates of school choice want parents to be able to choose the schools their children attend. While the NEA says, "Giving students vouchers to help them attend any school they like is giving them a ticket to nowhere," alternative schools have often proved extremely effective, especially in terms of teaching a core curriculum.[13] Catholic schools, for example, have demonstrated that the neediest kids are educable and spending money isn't the answer.[14] Cardinal John J. O'Connor has repeatedly made New York City an extraordinary offer: He's asked the city to send him kids from the lowest-performing 5 percent in the public schools, and he has promised to put them in Catholic schools, where they will succeed. The city has not responded.

In 1993, the New York State Department of Education found that Catholic schools outscored New York City's public schools with the same percent of minority student enrollment. The success of the Catholic schools and the implications of that success are far less visible than they should be. In part, that's probably because Americans want to keep religion and aspects of the state separate. But I believe the relative invisibility of the success of the Catholic schools with the most disadvantaged children results from the power of the teachers' unions, who fiercely oppose any threat to their monopoly.

Catholic schools are disciplined and orderly, and for many children that's their only haven of security, safety, and predictability. Parochial schools have one major goal, that of educating children, and the children are engaged in mastering the content of the curriculum. The curriculum is the old-fashioned basics of English, math, history, science, and language. Grammar, spelling, and vocabulary are regarded as critical. Kids do homework. It's the best American story: students are told, and they come to believe, that whatever their life situation is now, if they work hard and study, they can succeed. Poor, black and Hispanic, inner-city, disadvantaged students are far likelier to take advanced academic courses if they go to Catholic rather than public schools.[15]

Public schools are mired in pity for the less-advantaged and make the mistake of being "kind." They understand and forgive student nonperformance. Religious schools seem to have the same high academic expectation for every student—whatever their race, class, ethnicity, or family circumstance.

The best schools Manage-to-Success. Many religious schools reflect that view because they never deviated from emphasizing mastery—of a core content that is the traditional liberal arts curriculum of reading, writing, math, history, and science. Many, like Zion Lutheran Academy in Fort Wayne, Indiana, draw from the same inner-city population as do the public schools.[16] At Zion, more than half of the children come from one-parent families and more than half come from families in which a family member has committed a serious crime within the past five years. Nonetheless, the school's kindergarten through eighth-grade students score in the 60th percentile on standardized tests.

Reverend Joel Brondos is the school's headmaster. He says: "Too often, the best that has been thought and said is not provided to the types of kids who come to our academy and similar schools. Our country has gotten into the mindset that disadvantaged kids should go to a school 'that isn't too tough.' We are working to reverse that mindset. If the standards are high, kids will meet them. The goal of education at Zion is to push students to enlarge their minds, cultivate civic virtue, and develop their full human potential. We play up to the best in them, not down to the worst."

High expectations and requirements for performance, combined with caring and discipline, result in lower dropout rates for Catholic schools (1.3 percent) than public schools (7.6 percent). A major federal report, the National Educational Longitudinal Survey, found a truly remarkable difference in the educational expectations of kids who went to public schools and those who went to Catholic institutions. Only 34 percent of the students who went to public school expected to earn a graduate degree, while that figure was 59 percent for those who'd gone to Catholic schools. And, just as the Catholic schools get kids to succeed in reading, writing, and math, they also succeed in keeping kids in school, warding off delinquency, and preventing teen pregnancy.

In increasing numbers, middle-class parents are sending their children to private schools.[17] They're doing that despite the financial sacrifices involved because the parents are determined to give their kids the best education they can provide. Public Agenda, an independent think tank, polled parents nationwide in 1995. Parents ranked the public schools higher than the private schools in terms of serving kids who have special needs and in teaching kids how to get along with people who come from diverse backgrounds. They ranked the private schools higher in the other 11 of 13 categories, which included preparing students for college. Many believe the schools don't challenge their children enough, don't focus on the basics, and don't provide an adequate technological education; and they believe that because of legislation, their healthy children get far less attention from teachers than their mainstreamed classmates with special needs.

The combination of the wrong priorities, goals, and values, education's central bureaucracy, and the teachers' unions has managed to destroy a magnificent public system of education. By resisting accountability for performance, lowering expectations of student performance, diluting the curriculum, "understanding" nonperformance, embracing political correctness, and viewing rights as more important than responsibilities, those involved have jeopardized their students' futures.

There's no question that we must have a school system that prepares our children to compete. It's best if, to the largest extent, it's our public school system. Historically, the public schools made Americans of us all as they opened the doors of learning and upward mobility for the great majority. An excellent public school system makes the playing field level for everyone. In addition, we are a nation of immigrants from all over the world and we need to spend time with each other in order to understand, relate, bond, and form a nation. The public school system should be an exciting place in which this begins.

When my brother and I were growing up in New York City we went to public schools that could compete with any private school. We went to a school within a school in grammar school and then to the Bronx High School of Science. Those programs were open to anyone on the basis of achievement. In those days, The City College of New York, which was also open to anyone on the basis of accomplishment, was called "The Poor Man's Harvard." The public school system was responsive to its customers, innovative in driving for higher standards of learning, and enabling to its constituency, who saw it as their lever to enter and succeed within the larger community.

Shame! on all the components of the education system that fail our children and perpetuate a bureaucratic, nonaccountable institution. The education establishment must change its views and practices and become results-driven. The fuzzy must become specific. There must be significant, positive consequences for students who learn and teachers who educate, and significant negative outcomes for the reverse. If this doesn't happen, in the face of education's jeopardizing the future of the country, the country will dismantle the public school system and create something more effective. The education bureaucracy, including the members of the teachers' unions, has everything to lose if it doesn't transform the entire system. There's a borderless economy in education, too.

Education:

- Like industry, must Manage-to-Results.
- Real self-esteem is the result of mastering challenge.
- Managing-to-Morale and dumbing down the curriculum is a disservice to all students and a tragic error for the neediest.

17

Presumption of Rights, Fear, and the Loss of Ethics

WE HAVE FALLEN FAR FROM OUR PURITAN ROOTS OF AN ETHIC BASED on work, self-reliance, thrift, and self-discipline. The nation is appalled. Rights supersede responsibility and self-interest eclipses duty and community. Our culture is in disorder.

At one time, morality was an absolute. Those of us who were born and raised in the 1930s, 1940s, and 1950s were taught that there were very strict rules of right and wrong. That same message was repeated at home in the family, in school, in church, and in the neighborhood. Everyone was pretty certain they knew what was right or wrong. No one was confused about, and nobody debated, morality.

The experience of people who were born and grew up in the late 1950s, 1960s, 1970s, and 1980s was very different. The social movements of the time, especially those in the decade from 1965 to 1975, challenged many widespread assumptions. The change in values was initiated by young, upper middle-class baby boomers, many of whom were in college. Perched metaphorically atop the shoulders of their hardworking parents, the leaders of the movement against tradition felt free to reject traditional morals and lifestyles.[1] They rejected the rules of the nation: Young men refused to fight in the Vietnam War as their fathers had fought in World War II and Korea, and women refused to center their lives on raising children the way their mothers had. They rejected the past and they rejected adults as sources of knowledge and wisdom. I remember walking into class on the first day of semester in the late 1960s in Ann Arbor, Michigan, and before I could introduce myself a student yelled out, "Hey, teach, what the hell do you think you know that we would be interested in?"

The boomers succeeded in challenging the very idea of absolute values, which led to the creation of moral ambiguity. Many traditional beliefs and practices that we had been certain about came to be seen as arbitrary. What had been absolute dogma came to be perceived as complex, situational, and relative. Morality had become debatable. Where people were once certain they knew right from wrong, now they asked questions: Is the Vietnam War moral or criminal? Is abortion moral or murder? Is monogamy moral or an arbitrary convention?

Over the past 30 years, certainty about morality has been replaced by debatable relativism—which simply means we say, "Ah, it depends upon your point of view"—and in this way the nation has lost its certainty about what was moral. Relativism has replaced moral authority and destroyed traditional guidelines of right and wrong.[2]

When there is no certainty about right or wrong, behavior is neither rewarded because it is moral or right nor punished because it is dishonest or immoral. As a result, there isn't a clear relationship between the ethical rules and what people do, or how people behave and what happens to them. Even more profoundly, the distinction between right and wrong, between honest and dishonest, ethical and unethical, gets blurred.[3] Over time, things that are blurred can be lost.

The transition from Kennedy's Camelot to LBJ's Vietnam nightmare began a fundamental loss in respect for the presidency and politics in general. In the 1970s and 1980s and 1990s the nation's political and financial leaders sank to terrible and highly publicized ethical lows. Those were decades of horrendous economic and political corruption. That period produced Watergate and the resignation of a disgraced President Nixon, the Iran-Contra scandal that hovered around Presidents Reagan and Bush, the Keating Five, the forced resignation of Speaker of the House Jim Wright, the BCCI, Gary Hart, Mike Milken, HUD Secretary Samuel Pierce, Mayor Marion Barry of Washington, DC, and the ethical pall that has settled over the Clinton White House . . . it's an unspeakably long list.

What a moral climate our leaders created! In addition to a general climate of moral relativism, we've had decades of media images showing people in power and people with power being models of despicable behavior. When the nation's leaders behave in manifestly unprincipled and unethical ways, their behavior contributes to weakening the power of an absolute morality.

In 1996, 87 percent of Americans said they believed the decline in our moral values had created a serious problem.[4] The clearest worries are specific and have to do with the family: concerns about teenage pregnancies, the increase in family instability, and growing fears that the two-paycheck household has had important negative effects on young children. But Americans, says Daniel Yankelovich, also have a more basic, more fundamental concern than a list of specific issues. We are worried because we sense a loss of moral virtues—a loss of respect for other people. We are upset that humane concern for others has been replaced by selfishness.

While it is clear that huge variables involving major social change underlie a decline in moral behavior and the guiding power of morality, the loss of ethics can be seen from a more psychological view. The nation's culture moved to one of Entitlement, a presumption of rights including that of being owed happiness and the good life. Entitlement encouraged increasing numbers of people to feel they were victims, as did being shoved from the womb of The Comfort Zone into the harshness of risk of the borderless economy. During this period, "Don't blame the victim" was widely accepted and "victims" were exonerated from responsibility for choices they made and actions they took. A psychology of Entitlement and victimization, feelings of resentment and fear, and exoneration from personal responsibility lend themselves to cheating, behaving immorally, and breaking ethical rules.

Distorting the Rules

As the new morality loosened the tie between behavior and outcome, cultures of no-consequences loosened the tie between what happens to people as a result of what they do or don't achieve. The psychology of being owed arises out of conditions in which there aren't significant punishments when people don't perform or rewards when they do. When people are not held responsible for their behavior, over time, it gets easier to explain the lack of performance: *No one else is doing much, so why should I? Since no one complained, I guess it wasn't too important in the first place. Everyone works this way.*

In a no-consequence culture, the rationalization for unethical behavior is *You owe me more than you gave me. Since I was shortchanged, I'm entitled to make up the difference. That raise (or bonus or prize) should be mine, so I have a right to get it by whatever means.*

Large organizations, especially, have been pushing people hard, laying off thousands, raising the bar, taking away the protections of a no-consequence culture. Naturally, many people feel vulnerable and frightened. Frightened people try to protect themselves any way they can. When people are desperate to improve their position, some will find ethics irrelevant in terms of guiding what they do.

In order to make decisions based on ethical grounds, one has to be able to de-center—to view consequences either from the point of view of others or in terms of abstract principles. People are not able to de-center when they feel greedy, resentful, or scared. When confidence is low, people are defensive, self-absorbed, and self-protective. That's especially true when people think of others only in terms of the extent to which they are a competitive threat. This lends itself to discarding traditional restrictions on behavior, especially when important outcomes are on the line. When people believe they've been cheated and others have an advantage over them, they can feel free to ignore morality in terms of what they choose to do.

The probability of unethical behavior is highest when a psychology of being owed has given way to anxiety and people are convinced they've been betrayed and victimized. When employees are forced out of no-consequence cultures, for example, some will say: "After years of loyalty from me, there is no loyalty to me. This organization, which got the best years of my life, doesn't care about me at all. Now I better take damned good care of me because no one else is going to do it. I'm hurt and angry. It's okay if I cheat because I was cheated. I don't have to play by the rules because I'm only getting back what I've already paid for."

Resentment is an integral part of being a victim. Naturally, people who believe they've been victimized resent it and feel entitled to whatever they can get, by whatever means are at hand. As victimization increases feelings of helplessness, people try to gain a sense of power. Revenge can give people a feeling that they have real power, that they're the ones in control. It's not hard to imagine the glee and triumph victims feel when they turn the table. Then victims can say, "You know what? I cheated. And I beat you. Now, who's the better one? I *won!*"

A few years ago, during a period of major downsizing, the phone company BellSouth[5] discovered it had a serious ethical problem. The company had created a special sales program within a specific time period. People were told to get out and sell the company's new products, and that when they made sales, they'd get a special bonus. BellSouth discovered that some people wrote up totally phony orders which they canceled just before delivery was supposed to take place. Surely, some BellSouth employees, who had taken lifetime job security for granted, felt betrayed. People who took the security of no-consequence cultures most for granted may feel most vindicated in their drive to turn the tables.

Recently a plaintiff sued his employer, a company long immersed in a no-consequence culture, because he hadn't been promoted to the level he was convinced he was owed. The plaintiff, Alan Smyth,[6] believed he was owed a promotion because he had been with the organization a long time. He said, "I don't see how a company could neglect to give me a promotion after I've been with them almost 20 years. When the company says people are our number one resource, they owe me satisfaction." He hoped that by suing his employer he would gain millions of dollars and a promotion that would take him three levels higher than the one where he had been for 17 years.[7] Psychologically unable to perceive he was an average performer with limited potential, Smyth was outraged by the organization's "betrayal" of his long service. He was convinced he was owed and because he'd been "victimized," he was entitled to vengeance in the court and a level of success he had never earned.

The Expanding Category of *Victim*

The Declaration of Independence declares that everyone has the right to life, liberty, and the pursuit of happiness. The number of rights we believe we are entitled to has ballooned hugely from those few: rights have expanded to include "rights for smokers, parents, taxpayers, consumers, and animals."[8] Much of today's national debate is articulated in terms of rights—the right to life, the right to die, the right to choose, the right to work, the right to privacy, and the right to be personally free to make an idiosyncratic life choice. We're also owed the right to be supported when we do not work, and a right to be compensated because life has dealt with us unfairly. Today rights, or what we are owed, far eclipse responsibility in our mental hierarchy of what's important.

The civil rights movement, especially, created an enormous increase in "victims." Native Americans and African Americans have unique and painful histories in America. There seems little justification for expanding the considerations given those groups to others, especially to recent immigrants who entered the country because they chose to. Over time, with the expansion of rights, the number of protected groups proliferated and more and more people became victims.[9] As it became profitable to be a victim (as well as litigate for victims), inevitably, the category of *victim* expanded greatly: parents sue physicians when infants are not perfect, as though everyone is entitled to a perfect baby; consumers sue manufacturers when they misuse products, as though they were entitled to perfect safety despite themselves; children sue parents because their home lives are not exemplary, as though everyone is entitled to a Norman Rockwell kind of childhood. Over the past 30 years, many people have come to believe they have the right to—were entitled to—the good life. A sense of being owed is a fundamental prerequisite for feeling victimized.

We categorize victims as people who are not responsible for what they do because we have separated the status of being a victim from intention, accountability, or responsibility. Because we unwittingly concluded that victims had limited or no personal control, we exempted victims from the usual standards of behavior and the rules that are supposed to govern everyone else. In the last few decades, as we paid an enormous amount of attention to the idea that we mustn't blame the victim, we paid a lot less to the flip side of the coin, which is, "Don't blame me, I'm a victim."

Basically, we said, "We can't blame victims for what they do because they are victims."

People can be victims of many things—racism, sexism, ageism, favoritism, birth defects, accidents, and so on. The source of the victimization isn't as important as the result. Lawyers, politicians, social activists, and especially the post-World War II social sciences reinforced the idea that we can't blame the victim. Beginning in the 1960s, a victim's antisocial or nonproductive behavior was explained as being caused by social conditions, by the victim's personal history, by the system. More specifically, the social sciences medicalized morality. When psychology or psychiatry explain heinous behavior—cruel murder, violent wife beating, deadly arson—as the result of a personality disorder or childhood trauma, the behavior is attributed to a cause outside of the control of the perpetrator in the same way that pneumonia is caused by a virus or bacteria outside of the control of the sick person. We don't blame people for getting pneumonia.[10]

When the explanation for immoral behavior was attributed to factors that impacted the person and that the person hadn't initiated and presumably couldn't control, we stopped blaming people for what they did as long as a case could be made for their being victims. In fact, the more awful the behavior, the more terrible its consequences, the more likely it became that the person (or group) was exonerated from responsibility for acting despicably. The fact of awfulness became the justification for irresponsibility.

Immorality is excused when people believe that victims cannot be held responsible for what they do. If social conditions or your history or the system are to blame, then the moral imperative of being good, or doing good, is lost. As victims, people were freed from blame because society substituted understanding for moral judgments. Americans have generally been backing away from making moral judgments about people. Instead of judging behavior, we have become far more comfortable understanding and explaining it. When there are no moral judgments about behavior, there is no longer a link between behavior and the issue of whether it is right or wrong.

Two examples of outrageous acts which Americans preferred to understand rather than judge were the Bobbitt case and that of the Menendez brothers. The following observations about our responses to those cases were made by Heather Richardson, a director of the Council on Culture & Community and a fellow at the Progress and Freedom Foundation.[11]

> Many approve of Friday's decision by a jury that Lorena Bobbitt was not guilty of dismembering her husband. They argue that the news represents a rough kind of "tit for tat" justice. Yet the Bobbitt jury's judgment that Mrs. Bobbitt had acted while "temporarily insane" is a deeply problematic one. The verdict reflects a widening cultural divide that is slowly delegitimizing any traditional sense of justice in this country . . .
>
> Think for a moment about the Bobbitt case . . . and the Menendez brothers' trial for murdering their parents. Assume that in fact what the defense in each case has argued is true. That Lorena Bobbitt was indeed "the pathetic victim of physical abuse, humiliation, and sexual torment." That the Menendez brothers were abused by their parents and so deserve freedom.
>
> Such abuse is heinous. But with regard to the question of guilt, the resounding answer in these cases still has to be: So what? This is not a callous answer. Of course we sympathize. Of course other legal and social steps (e.g. leaving home, suing, seeking court injunctions, getting a divorce) are eminently important. That's the point of a civil society: There are civilized procedures for dealing with our problems and with each other. American juries are being told that the individual is not responsible for his own actions.

Victimization separates rights from responsibilities. It allows people to focus on their rights or what is owed to them while it minimizes their responsibility. Victimization creates the assumption that one is owed compensation because one has been victimized and simultaneously one is exonerated from responsibility for one's behavior because of the victimization. As a victim, it's always someone else's or something else's fault. People who believe they're victimized do not believe they are responsible for whatever they become, and they believe they should escape blame for what they do.

One group that was especially affected by the new notion of victimization was inner-city African-Americans. In the 1960s it became fashionable to argue that this group was disadvantaged because it had been abused by the majority culture. Then it followed that these victims did not have to comply with the rules of the mainstream culture because it was that culture that had made them victims. Actually, it went further than that: The counterculture mainstream put its culture down and romanticized the culture of the ghetto. The values and aspects of the black inner-city culture that were deviant from the mainstream culture were extolled by the young, white boomer majority.

Myron Magnet says the values and policies of the 1960s had terrible consequences for the people they were intended to help.[12] The affluent and educated baby boomers radically remade the American culture, turning it inside out and upside down. The old values of hard work, delayed gratification, sex within marriage, and public decorum were taunted. In a period when middle-class whites were experimenting sexually and with drugs, it became politically incorrect to say that using and dealing drugs is wrong or that dropping out of school or being an unwed teenage mother condemns you to a life of downward mobility. The most important value became the pursuit of personal expressiveness. This new set of values encouraged behavior that our most privileged children may ultimately survive, but that, when practiced by the poor, imprisons them forever in poverty. When the affluent and the baby boomers repudiated the values that enable people to succeed, while praising behaviors that preclude success and simultaneously

telling people they were victims and, as such, not responsible for their behavior, these factors combined to create a
self-fulfilling prophesy of victimized poverty.

When people are told they can't succeed on their own—
and their experience bears that out—they come to believe it.
Magnet tells us that between 1980 and 1987 over 18 million
new jobs were created. Nonetheless, spending on means-
tested programs rose 44 percent. Magnet asks why, in the face
of this extraordinary increase in jobs, poor people didn't seize
the opportunity to work and raise themselves out of poverty
in the traditional American way. His answer is that poverty is
less a matter of economics and more a matter of culture and
psychology. Magnet believes the poor who remain poor don't
grasp their opportunities but instead believe in a set of self-
defeating values and make self-defeating life choices.

"Victimization," with its exoneration of personal responsibility, ended up robbing people of the self-respect it was
intended to supply. That's the law of unintended consequences writ large. Self-esteem comes about only when people achieve and behave in ways that meet a standard of
excellence they respect. *No institution can confer self-
respect on an individual or a group. Self-respect and pride
have to be earned.*

In addition to laws and a powerful ethical code, a fair judi-
ciary and an honest law enforcement system, ethical behavior also requires conditions in which people develop
confidence by achieving outcomes that are important to
them. Confident people are likely to have achieved some
amount of success and are less likely than angry, scared victims to break ethical rules in order to gain more success. We
know how people become confident: they must earn what
they get; their performance must be judged; what happens
to them must reflect what they do; and most of the time,
their hard work must result in success.

Confidence is a prerequisite for people to be willing to be
held accountable for what they do and to care about others.
Success in the face of risk is the only way people gain confi-

dence and a sense of their own efficacy. Confidence and efficacy are the opposite of feeling frightened and victimized. We have to change a narcissistic culture of victimization to a culture of achieving, in a nation of laws, with a powerful moral code, with opportunities for everyone to achieve a measure of success. That will restore a civil society.

Restoring a Civil Society

As a nation, we have lost the steering rudder of a clear sense of right and wrong. The outcome is violent and tragic. It is clear that we need a culture based on responsibilities rather than rights, and we need the reestablishment of absolute rather than relative rules of conduct. We need a morality that is so powerful that the automatic response to a breach in ethics would be: *I don't do that. It's wrong.*

A few years ago I was at a Coast Guard meeting where an officer retold a tale that everyone knew. The man said: "We had a young officer in New London who was so good he was clearly on his way up. One day, the guy went to the supermarket. On his way into the store he noticed a shopping cart that was standing by itself, empty, except for a bag of charcoal briquettes on the lower shelf, underneath the basket. When the guy finished shopping he paid for his stuff and walked out the door. He noticed the cart was still there, unattended, the charcoal right where it had been before.

"He probably said to himself, 'I guess whoever bought it missed the charcoal when they put their stuff in the car. It sure looks like they haven't missed it because it's still here. Since someone paid for it, it wouldn't be right for the store to get it back. What the hell, I'll take it.'

The officer continued: "So our guy picked up the bag of briquettes and put it in the trunk of his car. That's when the store's security guards got him. They were working on pilferage. He'd been set up. He was also discharged from the Coast Guard. Do you realize that guy was disgraced and fired for five bucks!"

While this story is true, it doesn't really matter whether it's true or not. The really important thing is this tale was a piece of Coast Guard folklore and everyone in the Coast Guard knew the story, the message of which is inescapable. That makes it hard to imagine a member of the Coast Guard crossing a moral line without thinking about it.

We need to reinstate a moral stance that guides people's decisions. Society decays when it loses the certainty of its values or its values are no longer the basis for judgments about what is or is not okay to do. The loss of America's traditional values is clearly related to the social pathologies of increasing rates of crime, especially violent crime, crime committed by juveniles, illegitimacy, alcohol and drug abuse, falling scores on standardized tests, divorce, and a general breakdown of the family.[13]

Societies that are based on, and uphold, justice can be compassionate without ignoring the need to hold everyone responsible for their choices and their actions. We can feel pity for victims and we have a responsibility to help them. But it is not a help to society or individuals to exonerate anyone, including victims, from being responsible and accountable for what they do. No society can afford a form of compassion in which people are allowed to define freedom as being free from the personal responsibility of knowing the right thing to do—and doing it.

The historian Gertrude Himmelfarb says we are beginning to learn that most social problems are also moral problems.[14] Without morality, society is not civil. This is a new phenomenon. Before the 1960s, nobody talked about personal responsibility. It wasn't an issue. It wasn't an issue because the basic assumption, which everyone shared, was that people are responsible for their behavior. Since there were generally accepted standards of right and wrong, and the ground rule was that everyone was responsible for how they behave, people were comfortable judging behavior. It was psychologically easy and felt morally correct to criticize people whose behavior was bad.

Society can only afford rights when they are balanced by responsibilities.[15] Without a strong sense of responsibility, rights justify selfishness, putting one's own self before anyone else irrespective of the consequences. The awful result of three decades of putting rights before responsibilities is creating a groundswell movement in America to ensure responsible behavior by diminishing some rights.[16]

The founders of this nation created a political order in which they were realistic about human beings.[17] Their system was based on the assumption that self-interest is a given and virtue must be developed. President Woodrow Wilson said the basis of our republic is that every man must take care of himself. No one should look to the government to take care of him or her. That point of view both assumes that individuals are intelligent and independent and simultaneously elicits intelligence and creates greater independence.

Beginning in the 1960s, our government became destructive to the personal characteristics that individuals need and the nation requires for responsible self-government, because government policies grew to foster dependence on government. By trying to be kind, by proliferating rights and creating numerous victims, government policies have set individuals and disparate groups against each other in a race for private advantage. Nations cannot survive when the majority of citizens feel entitled and have forgotten their responsibility to the civic good.

Great swings in a nation's values are always a dramatic reversal of historic positions. The costs of such reversals take time to manifest themselves. The costs of the reversal from moral certainty to ambiguity are now so obvious that even boomers are praising personal responsibility. People need the structure, the guideposts of rules and laws based on clear moral beliefs. People need to know what's right and what's wrong.

Societies never return to their past. Norman Rockwell's *Saturday Evening Post* covers were nostalgic fantasies even when they were first published. Our task is to develop appropriate and certain moral ethics for now and for the future. This is a psychological and not a political statement. People and their societies need the structure of powerful and unambiguous values. Nations need the clear guidance of ethical rules that apply to and can be accepted by everyone. People need that clarity in order to achieve ethical and worthwhile lives.

The view that individuals are free to choose a lifestyle and construct a self that is unencumbered by other people's rules or values leaves people existentially lonely. A preoccupation with rights without responsibility leaves people without bonds or belonging. For life to have meaning, people need to feel virtuous. For citizens to know they've made a contribution, they need criteria of what's worthy. Without values, we are unable to earn a sense of being good. Community needs civility, because without it there's only narcissism. Community requires morality. Without community, we are alone. Thus, the amoral free life is lonely, meaningless, and without virtue.

Societies are in danger when:

- Absolute morality becomes relative and debatable.
- They create an enormous number of "victims" who are not responsible for what they do.
- Rights matter more than responsibilities.

The International Experience

THE GREAT SOCIAL EXPERIMENTS—SOVIET AND CHINESE COMMUNISM, European socialism, and the kibbutzim of Israel, all of which were designed to create a more equitable society and more humane human beings—failed. Societies do not change basic human nature. Unfortunately, the "kindness" of the state that gives and does not require responsibility produces the people who are the least civil. Grievously, the most generous societies pander to and foster the worst of human proclivities: selfishness, greed, dependence, scorn for the greater good, and fear of fear, which translates into cowardice.

The critical reader may rightfully ask if the majority of what has been described is largely peculiar to the American society and the American psyche. The answer is no. No-consequence cultures are a worldwide phenomenon, and the similarity of their practices far outweighs any differences between nations. In this chapter I'll briefly describe the experiences of Britain, Canada, France, Germany, Japan,

Spain, and Sweden with what's been called "the Swedish disease"—though clearly, the phenomenon is not limited to Sweden.

Around the world, a no-consequence culture rests on these deeply held values:

- People are entitled to a good life.

- Redistributing resources from the well-off to the less affluent is desirable and the state is best able to do that.

- Equal outcomes in lifestyle, education, salary, and benefits are morally correct.

- The psychological and economic security created by a no-consequence culture is a desirable outcome of socially responsible policies.

- The purpose of business is first to provide jobs and benefits, second, products and services and third, profits.

Japan

In 1997, the Nikkei stock average had fallen 20 percent from its 1996 high, and many believe the fall reflects the impact of a borderless economy on Japan's overprotected and over-regulated domestic economy.[1] Japan has a two-tier economy: one part is composed of dynamic, highly competitive multinational businesses and the other is made up of expensive, noncompetitive domestic businesses that depend on the protection of trade barriers for their survival. Those protections have slowly begun to disappear.

In 30 years, Japan accomplished an economic miracle.[2] It went from the ruins of its post-World War II economy to become an economic superpower. The economic bubble burst in 1991 and the nation's minimal recovery has made it clear that practices that had seemed to serve Japan as assets are now working to its disadvantage. Specifically, the high trade barriers that protected Japanese companies from competition inevitably led those companies to become noncompetitive—less innovative and less cost efficient.

The most visible part of the Japanese economy is composed of those industries that are exported: autos, electronics, semiconductors, and telecommunications. Those companies are truly successful in global competition. But about 80 percent of the Japanese economy is not international. Those companies operate almost entirely within the boundaries of Japan's very insular home market. Without pressure from competitors to bring costs down, costs don't come down. Thus, much of Japan's domestic service economy tolerates levels of unproductive employment that are extraordinarily high relative to other countries. Even where automated equipment has been introduced, it is common to find employees next to the automated equipment performing redundant functions.

In addition, Article 27 of Japan's postwar Constitution says, "All people shall have the right and obligation to work."[3] While most of Japan's smaller companies never interpreted Article 27 as a commitment to lifelong employment, the large blue-chip companies did. Japanese salarymen were protected by a system of slow promotions and dependable wage increases based solely on seniority. While that reinforced mutual loyalty between employers and employees, it contributed to a no-consequence culture and limited a company's ability to control employment costs.

The no-consequence culture has become a critical cost during Japan's current recession. Robert Feldman, an economist who works for Salomon Brothers in Tokyo, estimated in 1995 that 6.5 million office workers could be laid off without jeopardizing productivity.[4] Shintaro Hori, a director and vice president of Bain and Company in Japan, believes that while white-collar inefficiency is a problem around the world, it is especially severe for Japanese companies.[5] It is bad enough, he thinks, that it directly impacts the competitiveness of many Japanese companies both within Japan and overseas. Increasingly, even Japan's very efficient manufacturing operations are learning they can't afford the tremendous overhead of unnecessary employees.

Koichi Hori is the director of the Boston Consulting Group's office in Tokyo. He says one of the most important reasons why the price of everything in Japan is so high is that, in addition to vast numbers of government bureaucracies and a profusion of regulations, there are so many unnecessary jobs and processes in the economy.[6] Worker productivity is low across all of Japan's service industries including retail banking, general merchandising, restaurants, airlines, and telecommunications. The cost of low white-collar productivity is subsidized by Japanese consumers when they pay very high prices.

To a significant degree, Japan's desire to artificially increase employment rates has led to low productivity, the "hollowing out" of the economy, and a dreadfully high cost of living. In the long run, there will be significant personal pain and corporate downsizing.

The Japan Productivity Center published a study on worldwide productivity in 1992. At that time the center concluded that if Japan were to reach aggregate U.S. productivity levels, Japan's manufacturing companies would have to cut 39 percent of their employees. Basically, blue-collar high productivity in manufacturing has subsidized white-collar mediocre productivity and, in the aggregate, has raised costs. Ultimately, as blue-collar productivity levels off, the long-term effect is reduced or nonexistent company profits. The response has been outsourcing and downsizing. Thousands of industrial jobs have moved from Japan to China, Southeast Asia, Europe, and the United States.[7] Joblessness among the young, including university graduates, is growing more quickly than in any other demographic group because of hiring freezes. At the other end of the age spectrum, older employees are being induced to leave with early retirement packages.

In May of 1995, Japan's number one car company, Toyota Motor Corporation, reported that it was considering the possibility of closing factories and laying off workers in Japan.[8] At the same time, Toyota also announced plans to increase capacity or said it had completed additions to capacity in seven countries outside of Japan. Between 1994 and 1996, Japan's top corporations increased their overseas production by an average of more than 20 percent because Japanese wages are now among the highest in the world.[9] Like the United States, but more slowly, Japan is moving toward a more flexible labor force. Outplacement has become a business in Japan and Japanese companies are starting to use contract labor in lieu of permanent lifetime employees.[10]

The core problems of having too much manufacturing capacity within Japan, with high costs and low levels of white collar productivity, remain significant problems. High costs within the nation have forced and will continue to force job cuts and a shift of production overseas. Japanese anxiety about job insecurity is growing as large Japanese corporations are slowly drawing back from guaranteed lifetime employment, annual raises, and automatic promotions.

Canada

In the 1970s and 1980s, Canada's government spending, especially social welfare spending, pushed Canadian taxes skyward. The top income tax rate of 53.2 percent started at an income of $49,000. There were also an 8 percent provincial sales tax, a 7 percent federal goods and service tax, and extremely high property taxes. Since 1990, average pretax family incomes fell largely because the crushing tax rates hobbled the economy. As exorbitant taxes drained money from the private sector, government revenues fell, which contributed to a high budget deficit and very high interest rates, which further flattened the economy.

As tax revenues fell, public-sector services declined, especially in the state-controlled health system. Between 1992 and 1993, Canada had a significant increase in infant and adult deaths that was blamed on shortages in the health system. As Canada's single-payer health care system's costs kept skyrocketing, the nation's health care service delivery, availability, and choices became increasingly limited. Since single-payer systems eliminate any responsibility for payment on the part of the consumer, demand always ends up outstripping supply. Whenever patients are left out of the loop of responsibility, the health care system will always have ever increasing costs. The long-term outcome is persistent upward pressure on resources with eventual rationing of what can be provided.

In 1995, 1.3 million of Ontario's 10 million people received welfare. That figure had increased every year for the past 20 years, during economic booms as well as busts. In addition to welfare, hundreds of thousands of people in Ontario also received benefits from the federal unemployment insurance program and Ontario's workers' compensation plan. It is not surprising that the number of people on welfare kept increasing, because a family of three would have to have an income of about $20,000 to match the after-tax value of the welfare income the province provided.

Ralph Klein, Canada's pioneer of deficit cutting and downsizing in government, was first elected as Alberta's premier in 1993 with 45 percent of the vote.[11] After four years of aggressive cost cutting and reduced services—Klein eliminated hundreds of millions of dollars from education, welfare, the environment, and health; fired thousands of government workers or cut their pay; reduced welfare payments and old age benefits; and closed hospitals—polls put his Progressive Conservative Party as leading with 67 percent of the electorate in 1997. Alberta's budget deficit is gone. With costs lower and oil and gas revenues higher, in 1997 the province achieved its third budget surplus. As a result, Klein can now afford to significantly increase the budgets for health and education.

With the exception of British Columbia, Canada's other provincial premiers and the national government have followed Ralph Klein's lead. In 1995, Ontario voted for Mike Harris, a Conservative Party leader who promised tax cuts, matching cuts in spending, workfare to replace welfare, privatization of government-owned businesses, and the repeal of Ontario's pro-union labor code and affirmative action law.[12] The voters said the Ontario public sector had forfeited the public's trust.

Mike Harris's "Common Sense Revolution" was a response to the public's anger about being overgoverned, overtaxed, and ripped off by people who cheated on welfare.[13] The Conservative program promised to cut Ontario's income tax by 30 percent, cut welfare payments by 20 percent, and lay off 15,000 government workers. When Harris moved to keep his promise, Ontario's liberal voters increasingly opposed any government reductions in spending. In addition to the poor- and welfare-related programs, many in Ontario want to see their middle-class benefits in education and health care preserved. In March, 1996, a strike by 55,000 civil servants took more than half of Ontario's public work force off the job.[14] Strikers were protesting the planned cuts in government jobs and government social spending.

Canada is much more generous than the United States, and the outcome is that the Canadian unemployment rate in the first three quarters of 1996 averaged 9.6 percent, while the American average was 5.4 percent.[15] Unemployment is high in Canada despite the slow but real economic growth of 1.5 percent a year from 1989 to 1996. In addition to national differences in how unemployment rates are calculated, the largest reason for Canada's high unemployment rate is that benefits are generous, last a long time, and are easy to qualify for. That's a good reason for people to elect not to work and to be very choosy about what jobs they'll accept.

In 1972, Pierre Trudeau's government greatly increased unemployment benefits and their duration, while decreasing the period one had to work in order to qualify for the benefit. One calculation of the potential total value of an unemployment subsidy is to take the percentage of the earnings replaced by the benefit (i.e., 58 percent) and figure in the numbers of weeks one has to work in order to qualify for 52 weeks of benefits (i.e., 13 weeks). That unemployment benefit would equal 232 percent of what one had actually earned. In 1972, Canada's unemployment benefit value rose from 43 percent to 242 percent. Fiscal reform brought that figure down to 72 percent in 1994, but that remains well above the U.S. average of 33 percent. In Canada, 72.3 percent of people who were unemployed received unemployment benefits in 1994; in the United States the figure was 34.3 percent. Under Reagan, the United States made it harder to enjoy not working: on average, people have to work 32 weeks for 19 weeks of benefits and those payments are now taxed like any other kind of taxable income. When jobs are available, people's choice to work or not follows rational rules of how comfortable government has made it to be supported by other people's taxes.

In 1995, despite voters' objections, Paul Martin, Canada's finance minister and a member of The Liberal Party, delivered a very tough budget plan to reduce Canada's budget deficit from 5.3 percent of the GDP in 1994 to 1.2 percent in 1997.[16] In order to bring the country back from the brink of financial disaster, Martin called for cutting programs rather than increasing taxes. With growing deficits and rising interest rates, a softening dollar and a miserable stock market, a left-wing government became as fiscally conservative as one on the right.

Paul Martin and Canadian prime minister Jean Chrétien swiftly achieved fiscal virtue. They cut the federal budget deficit from 5.9 percent of the GDP in 1993 to 1.1 percent in 1979.[17] Canada's economy has moved from stagnation in 1995 to growth in 1997. While unemployment remains high at 9 percent, it is down 1 percent from a year ago. From 1995 to 1997, Canada's economy grew by about one-half million jobs.

Although Jean Chrétien and Paul Martin slashed public spending, they were reelected in 1997.

Britain

Of all the countries of Europe, Britain has the least amount of government intervention and, after 18 years of Tory leadership, Britain's values more closely resemble those of the United States than those of other European countries. But that's only a relative statement.

Fifty years after W. H. Beveridge drew up his plan for a modern welfare state, Britain has a far more generous and abused welfare system than the United States and the professional welfare class is about 1 million people strong. The expectation of rights is reinforced by the various claim forms for social benefits, which all ask, "Are you claiming for this? Are you obtaining that? Know your rights." Many in Britain now believe that people should not be required to work if society doesn't give them a job they like.[18] The belief of the British middle class that it is owed has gained power because Beveridge's plan to create a fairer Britain was perverted into a giant mechanism for buying votes.

Britain has a long history of no-consequence culture. Right after the close of World War II, Clement Attlee's Labour Party made huge investments in social services despite the fact that the country was broke. The government established the National Health Service and built enormous public housing tracts. It also created a more subtle kind of welfare by nationalizing industries that then employed many more people than was necessary. Not accidentally, the nationalized industries conscientiously ignored any technological innovations that would make work more efficient and could result in layoffs. By 1979, after more than 30 years of the Labour Party's generous social programs, chronic inflation had risen to 22 percent, unemployment was 15 percent, productivity was very low, and, as no-consequence cultures are always greedy, there was continuous labor unrest and frequent strikes.[19]

In 1979, with Britain's economy in severe decline, newly elected prime minister Margaret Thatcher initiated draconian measures to stop the country's financial deterioration, which had become accepted as inevitable by the country's citizens.[20] She instituted huge cuts in taxes and government spending—top income tax rates fell from 83 percent to 40 percent—reduced subsidies, and created a tighter monetary policy. Thatcher set out to break the back of the trade unions and privatize Britain's industry, and she achieved much on both counts. In the nearly 12 years she led the nation, about 100 companies were privatized, were rejuvenated, and became competitive.

Since 1979, Britain's productivity has climbed an average of 4.5 percent a year. The economy has flourished as a result of significant deregulation and the elimination of bureaucratic obstacles to entrepreneurial activity. Like the United States, Britain has experienced the elimination of hundreds of thousands of jobs in coal, steel, automobiles, and banking. But while layoffs continue, about 100,000 jobs are added to the economy every three months, though many are low paying.[21]

Eighteen years of Conservative Party rule has resulted in a British workforce that is far more flexible than it used to be. Workers' rights and unions were weakened when the government banned secondary strikes and closed shops. It became easier for employers to hire and fire people. Minimum wages were eliminated and unemployment and other benefits were cut in order to make the dole less attractive. At the same time, the government increased requirements that the unemployed seek jobs. As a result, workers lost their militancy and the number of strikes declined enormously.

But while Britain's economy improved tremendously, the mood of the nation was not happy. After 18 years of Tory rule, the Labour Party, with Tony Blair as prime minister, swept into office in the 1997 general election. With Labour the majority, drawn largely from a constituency of trade unions and the public sector, it will be interesting to see whether or not the party rejects continued austerity and increases public spending.[22] Since increased public spending would result in a rise in the budget deficit, the Labour Party would likely raise taxes. Higher rates of public spending, higher taxes and interest rates, and increased government control and red tape, would combine to drive up the cost of doing business in Britain.[23] In the first year of Blair's leadership, none of that has happened.

Despite pressure from organized labor, Blair insists that success today requires a flexible economy. He means the economy cannot be hobbled by excessive regulation or social legislation. He presented this message, which is an acceptance of Margaret Thatcher's legacy, in a speech to trade unionists, many of whom would interpret a flexible economy to mean job insecurity.[24] In speeches Blair has said that the new economy has far more competition for markets and capital resources than the old one did, and that requires that both firms and employees be nimble.[25] Blair also wants to modernize the welfare state and may privatize it. Unlike Bill Clinton, he has said he wants to trim the role of the state. He sees education as an enlarged responsibility for government, but overall, he has said, government's future role is to organize and regulate social provision, but not provide it.

On the other hand, Blair has said he will reinstate a minimum wage, he will try to force more companies to recognize trade unions, and he has signed Europe's "social charter." In contrast with Blair's stated goal of a flexible economy, the charter is being used by other nations to increase job protection, the reverse of flexibility.[26] A potential problem is the conflict between continued fiscal prudence and meeting the wage gain expectations of organized labor. Public-sector pay, including that of unionized doctors, nurses, dentists, and teachers, accounts for one-third of the government budget.[27] It is too early to know whether there really is a new Labour Party.

France

France has some of the highest government spending, taxes, and unemployment rates of any nation in Western Europe. In France, more than one in five people younger than 25 were unemployed in 1994. In March 1994, the streets of Paris and other French cities were clogged by tens of thousands of workers and students who were protesting new government measures that were intended to cut the unemployment of young people.[28] The new rules would have allowed companies to pay young people 20 percent less than the standard industry wage in exchange for teaching young workers professional skills.

Edmond Alphandery, then France's Minister of Economics, is convinced that France's high unemployment rate requires greater labor flexibility, better job training, and lower costs. He's trying to reduce the high cost of hiring unskilled workers and, in that way, encourage the return of low-wage jobs in the service sector, such as jobs for janitors and gasoline pump attendants. The high cost of labor is the reason why those jobs have largely disappeared. But many people in France (as well as the rest of continental Europe) strongly believe that the low-wage jobs that have been created in the United States and Britain are unacceptable, even if those jobs reduce unemployment. Alphandery has found that changing France's rigid labor laws is immensely difficult.

The mind-set in France is well exemplified by employees of the French state railway.[29] Francis Dianoux's grandfather worked for the railroad and so did his father, and so naturally M. Dianoux became a railway worker too. He lives in railway-built housing and plays on the railway soccer team. He enjoys marvelous fringe benefits: A job, guaranteed for life; retirement at the age of 55; free railroad trips; and five and a half weeks of vacation a year. That this is expensive is of no interest to him: He says, "We are not a company; we're a public service. The idea that this is a company that must make profits doesn't even occur to us. Sure we lose money, but that doesn't bother me. Does the Army make money?"[30]

EU rules will eventually permit foreign trains to run on the French tracks, and those trains will compete with France's state railway, SNCF. Despite $10 billion a year in subsidies, the state railroad lost about $2.4 billion in 1995. Though the pressure is growing for increased productivity in anticipation of competition, the railway's workers are resisting any change. Bus lines that could compete with the railroad are banned by law. Money-losing lines are not closed down, though the railroad needs to close about 20,000 miles of track. The unions are refusing to downsize, though some analysts believe the railroad should cut its workforce of 180,000 in half. In December of 1995, the country endured 24 days of crippling strikes as unions protested cuts in public-sector jobs. In France, the public sector has continued to expand and that sector wants to manage its "business" as if the boundaryless economy didn't exist.

France has some of the highest government spending rates, taxes, and welfare programs—and some of the slowest growth—of any country in Europe. To Americans, France's benefits and subsidies are nothing short of astonishing. Benefits include paid yearly holidays and transportation to resorts; subsidized housekeepers for people who need help coping with household tasks; free school from day care to university; subsidized meals from day care through high school; home care for older people; help with moving expenses; and subsidized apartments, dishwashers, and washing machines. In the greater Paris region, employers are required to pay half the cost of commuting for their employees. Building owners cannot evict tenants who don't pay their rent from apartments during the winter. High-stress jobs, in fields like medicine and journalism (!?), receive tax breaks and the mandatory five weeks of vacation is extended to nine. All office employees have the right to a window from which they can see either sunset or sunrise.

The French justify their resistance to change by saying they want people to matter more than profit.[31] But that's largely a rationalization for insisting the government continue France's extremely generous medical, social welfare, and lifestyle supports and benefit payments despite the fact that these subsidies increase unemployment as they depress the economy.

In 1997, France's unemployment rate rose to 12.8 percent from 11.5 percent in 1995. The unemployment rate of people under the age of 27 had increased from one in five to one in four.[32] Laws restricting companies' freedom to hire and fire employees continue to be the norm. Lionel Jospin, the country's new Socialist prime minister, declared reducing unemployment was his priority of priorities. Jospin's plans call for 350,000 jobs to be created at some future time in the private sector, and for another 350,000 to be created over the next two and a half years in the public sector. Jobs will be created in the health service, education, welfare, culture, the environment, security, transportation, and housing. The government will underwrite 80 percent of the cost of these public sector jobs, which will give people ages 18 to 25 five-year contracts and a wage of at least $1,122 a month, France's minimum. The other 20 percent of costs will be paid by the employer: those employers are part of the public sector—the central government, local authorities, public services, and state-subsidized local community outfits. It doesn't sound like taxes will be coming down any time soon. In fact, Jospin has increased the taxes on companies with sales of more than $8.3 million from 36.6 percent to nearly 42 percent, and the rate on corporate capital gains soared from 19 to 42 percent.[33] Who would want to own a company in France?

Jospin is also proposing reducing the work week from 39 hours to 35—without a loss of pay.[34] It is hard to see how this proposed increase in labor costs and reduced productivity will result in additional jobs. It is clear that France needs to do something dramatic if it is to get its obstinately high unemployment rate down. Jospin has said that even if the economy were to expand at an annual rate of 3 percent from 1997 to 2002, which is a significant increase over the 1 percent of the recent past, the 3.2 million unemployed would be unlikely to decline by more than 70,000 a year. The choice of reforming the basic reasons why labor costs and therefore unemployment are so high does not appear to be on Jospin's mind. There is no hint of encouraging more part-time work, reducing the minimum wage, making it less expensive to fire workers, or cutting generous unemployment and welfare benefits. That decision is guided by the French desire to maintain the perks and protections gained by the majority and ignore the fact that that pleasant life creates a chronically high unemployment rate.

Germany

With unification, West Germany imported one of the world's strongest Entitlement cultures, which strengthened the one it already had. In February 1997, 12.2 percent or 4.7 million people in the world's third largest economy were unemployed.[35] Germany's labor costs are the highest in the world. In 1996, average wages and benefits for a German manufacturing worker were $30 an hour, compared with $17 in the United States.[36] Christmas bonuses in the auto and engineering sectors often equal a month's pay. Workers collect a 50 percent wage premium when they're on their annual six-week vacation. German workers are guaranteed six weeks of sick days.[37] In addition, Germany's workers have the longest vacations (40 days) and the shortest work week in the industrialized world.[38] Restrictive union work rules that curtail work hours keep German machines running an average 20 percent fewer hours than in the rest of Western Europe. German workers earn more pay and benefits for less work than any other workers in the world.

The cost of social welfare benefits, including state pensions, and unemployment and health care benefits are financed through payroll deductions with employers and employees splitting the cost. But, as Germany's high labor cost has resulted in jobs migrating to lower cost economies, a declining number of workers are carrying the economic load for an increasing number of jobless or retired people. The result, of course, is very high taxes.

The German welfare system is so gold-plated that it costs employers $.85 in social security and health insurance taxes for every dollar of wages and the already hefty social security taxes are increasing.[39] That's a heavier burden than one finds even in Sweden.[40] In 1995, Germany had the highest personal income tax rate in the industrial world—57 percent.[41] Germany's Entitlement programs also include $100 billion in subsidies for smokestack industries like coal mining and shipbuilding. As the government shelters certain industries, like the state-owned telecommunications company and the suppliers to that industry, from most foreign competition, there's a lack of innovation in that industry and related ones.

German companies have private retraining programs and the German government has a multibillion-dollar retraining program.[42] Yet the outcome of this system is questionable. Retraining is really part of the vast social benefits package that kills jobs because it makes German labor so extraordinarily expensive. Companies are retraining workers only because the cost of laying them off is so high. Volkswagen alone is retraining 30,000 basically superfluous employees. The government has elected to ignore the cost to the company of keeping an unnecessary 30,000 people busy for two years.

Firing workers in Germany is very expensive.[43] When American workers are fired or laid off, the average severance pay is one week's pay for every year of service. German workers get one month of pay for every year they've been employed. They may also take as long as seven months to leave their jobs and find others, compared with one month in the United States. The high cost of Germany's termination benefits, which also includes relocation services, is an additional reason why employers don't want to hire.

The unemployment figure in Eastern Germany is about 20 percent.[44] As Eastern Germany's labor costs are rapidly approaching those of West Germany, in the coming years a large number of unemployable East Germans will burden West Germany's already overloaded welfare system. People are doing business in East Germany because of the subsidies government offers. The result, however, still leaves East Germany noncompetitive. In Berlin, for example, unemployment in 1995 was 20 percent. That was true despite the fact that there was an enormous amount of construction going on. The government says there were 150,000 construction sites in and around Berlin, but 16,000 construction workers in the city were jobless. In addition to 40,000 illegal workers, companies from nations inside the European union whose labor costs are lower, like Britain, came to Berlin legally to work for just over half the pay East Germans get.

While the German government has been too slow in making the changes that are required to make the nation competitive, German corporations have been taking things into their own hands. Continental Tire, for example, which makes high-speed tires for Germany's luxury cars, moved low-tech production abroad.[45] About a quarter of the company's production went to Portugal and the eastern European countries of the Czech Republic, Slovenia, and Poland. It worked with its unions to reduce excessively generous benefits. It adapted American and Japanese management techniques including total quality management, lean production, and teams. The workforce was cut by 20 percent or 10,000 employees, with at least 2,000 more jobs scheduled to be eliminated.

In January 1996, the German government announced plans to simplify and slash taxes, cut excessive welfare, reduce burdensome regulations, and make huge cuts in government spending in order to regain a prosperous economy and a competitive country. Chancellor Helmut Kohl plans to reduce or eliminate a wide range of taxes on households and business and cut back Germany's welfare system.[46] Kohl wants to support entrepreneurial start-ups, cut taxes, and cut social welfare spending by reducing social welfare benefits by the year 2000 to under 40 percent of an employee's gross income. There will be fewer early retirements and less generous pension payments, and unemployment benefits will be limited to one year for people younger than 45. Kohl wants a civil service pay freeze for one to two years. He is asking for a reduction of employer-paid sick leave from 100 percent of average earnings to 80 percent of base pay. He wants a radical overhaul of taxes so the top income tax rates would be reduced from 57 to 40 percent. While Chancellor Kohl has plans to cut the tax rates, he won't implement them until 1999.[47]

Germany's business leaders have given Chancellor Helmut Kohl a very clear message that major changes are imperative and are needed swiftly: The social contract between workers, the government, and industry is failing the nation. Small, middle-size, and giant German companies, including Daimler-Benz AG, the largest of all, have been forced by global pressures to slash their costs, lay off workers, and move production to lower-cost countries. They're moving to places where materials are cheaper, wages are lower, skills are high, and markets are growing.[48] The 1992–1993 recession especially forced many German corporations to the belated realization that because they had the world's highest labor costs, most restrictive work rules, and highest social welfare costs, their survival depended on expanding aggressively abroad.[49] German workers are now competing for jobs with Russian, Polish, Chinese, Malaysian, and even American workers. German investment money and German manufacturers are hollowing out their businesses in Germany and expanding production overseas.[50] The German model of designing in

Germany, manufacturing in Germany, and exporting from Germany is no longer viable.

Kohl appears to be trying to abandon the consensus style of politics that created social harmony among labor, management, and government. Like organizations with no-consequence cultures, nations with no-consequence cultures can prosper until there's significant competition. Germany's social contract worked until the boundaryless economy made Germany's huge cost structure a killer—of jobs, of profits, of security.

Germany has the oldest students, the youngest retirees, the longest holidays, and the shortest workday in the developed world.[51] In 1997, the jobless rate reached 11.4 percent or 4.3 million people. Even if the economy grows by 2.8 percent in 1998, economists say the unemployment rate will still rise to 11.5 percent because of the high cost of labor.[52] Some believe the 1997 unadjusted unemployment rate is already at 12 percent and that omits an additional 4 to 5 percent who are unemployed but don't appear in the statistics because they're in government-funded training programs or they've been forced into early retirement.[53]

German capital is leaving the country and foreign direct investment is falling in the face of sustained high unemployment and dismally low corporate investment at home. Helmut Kohl's government made a start on some social and economic reforms, but they've been halfhearted.[54] A plan for major tax reform has been killed by the political opposition. Two recent studies by Swiss-based organizations found Germany is becoming increasingly uncompetitive.[55] While there has been some movement by local union members to agree to cuts in overtime and increases in productivity, national labor leaders have generally continued to resist efforts to lower labor costs. At labor rallies, speakers condemn "elbows-out" societies like the United States and continue to support social values. Norbert Walker, Deutsche Bank's Chief Economist, says the government hasn't really touched the welfare state and its social benefits. Because Germany's government spends 51 percent of the country's GDP, Germany remains, Walker says, much closer to socialism than to a market economy.

Spain

Spain was freed from the restrictions of the Franco government in 1975, and in the 1980s the economy grew enormously as multinational corporations moved to Spain to benefit from the opening of the market and its 39 million citizens.[56] In 1986, Spain became a member of the European Union, development funds flowed into the country, and wages shot up.

Spain moved easily from Franco's fascist welfare state to a socialist welfare state. During the boom years, the Spanish government increased the size of the bureaucracy and funded immensely generous social programs, including free health care and a heavily subsidized university education that was available to everyone. The government gave people more generous unemployment benefits than much richer European countries offered. A worker who earned about $1400 a month after taxes receives unemployment benefits of $1060 a month for two years.[57] Spending on social policies nearly doubled. As long as the economy was growing at nearly 6 percent in the 1980s, no one paid attention to those costs. But when Spain fell into a recession in 1991, the economy slumped and the fundamental weaknesses of the economy became visible. The consequences of the socialist government policies were an unemployment rate approaching 25 percent and a loss, since 1990, of 510,000 industrial jobs—17.2 percent of the nation's total employment. In 1997, the jobless rate is 22 percent—40 percent for people younger than 25.[58]

Very few Spaniards seem to grasp the idea that their labor laws, which were designed to protect jobs, had quite the opposite effect. Large layoffs or reorganizations in Spain require government and union approval, which can take anywhere from six months to three years. In order to stop worker protests over the company's plans to reorganize an obsolete plant, for example, Suzuki had to agree to wage increases of from 4 to 6 percent a year from 1993 to 1995 despite the fact that the Japanese automaker had lost roughly $140 million in that plant between 1990 and 1994. Because of Spain's labor laws, it takes five times as many workers and costs Suzuki 46 percent more to build a Samurai in Spain than in Japan. Suzuki left Spain.

Spain's labor law also requires that laid-off workers who are "fairly" dismissed receive 20 days' salary for every year they worked, but that those who are "unfairly" dismissed receive a minimum of 45 days' wages for every year they were employed by the organization. Thus far, the courts have declared almost every dismissal unfair. For an employee with 20 years experience, that's a severance payment of about $90,000. Since the cost of laying off long-term workers is so high, long-serving employees basically have guaranteed jobs and employers are stuck with these people forever. The virtually guaranteed job security means experienced workers have little incentive to be productive or restrain their wage demands. Naturally, the result is that even prosperous companies are reluctant to hire new, permanent employees.

The Spanish solution to employers' reluctance to hire was to create a two-tier labor market—one long-term and permanent, the other short-term. The Spanish call the short-term market *contratos basura,* which means garbage contracts, because it offers no job security at all. In 1996, 97 percent of the new jobs that were created were temporary and many younger Spaniards are now employed on short-term contracts. They work for six months or a year and are then replaced by a new employee who is also on a short-term contract. While that is arguably inefficient, many employers consider it a better choice than being stuck with a permanent employee they don't need. It remains to be seen whether or not Spain's prime minister, José Maria Aznar, succeeds in his 1997 goal of persuading labor to make it easier for private employers to hire and fire.

As Spain tightened its belt in order to qualify for the Economic and Monetary Union, in 1997 its economy is booming and inflation is running about 2 percent as the deficit is reduced, interest rates have fallen, and there's monetary stability.[59] In 1996, the economy generated 167,000 net new jobs. But one major problem remains: the unemployment rate is 22 percent, the highest in the 15-nation EU. Spain's rigid labor market laws have created high unemployment, high youth unemployment, and high levels of temporary jobs. A law moderating the cost of layoffs recently passed, but it applies only to new hires. In that agreement, which is perceived as a landmark, the normal 45 days of severance pay for each year of employment is reduced to "only" 33—in exchange for longer labor contracts for first-time job applicants and the long-term unemployed. Juan Perez Aparicio, chief executive of Radiotronica SA, wants to cut his Spanish work force from 1000 people to 500. He estimates that would cost him $21 million, 10 times the company's 1996 profit. His only choice, he feels, is to expand abroad and use those profits to gradually reduce his work force in Spain.

Sweden

Sweden was long admired as a model of how a nation could achieve both a lavish social welfare system and a healthy capitalist industrial sector.[60] But, ultimately, it didn't work. Acting as though the private sector had an infinite ability to fund every ambitious social agenda, Sweden's Social Democrats created subsidized housing, an ironclad full employment policy, extremely generous unemployment insurance, and a welfare state that encouraged people not to work. The government gave the unemployed, the sick, or people who simply wanted to quit working from 90 to 100 percent of their working income.

This expensive program requires very high taxes. Sweden had some of the highest capital and income taxes in the world. The top marginal income tax rate reached 85 percent and the state collected 70 percent of the nation's gross domestic product. As a result of the costs of the huge welfare state, the Swedish economy began falling sharply as the private sector began shrinking in the 1980s. Sweden's industrial production has plunged 15 percent since 1989 as Swedish businesses moved their operations outside of the country, the country's jobless rate reached 12 percent, and the budget deficit reached 13 percent of Sweden's GDP.

In the early 1990s Sweden's economy contracted three years in a row and the nation suffered its worst economic crisis since the 1930s.[61] As unemployment soared and the currency was devalued by 20 percent, a conservative government put its fiscal house in order. In 1991 Sweden elected Carl Bildt of the Conservative Coalition; Bildt cut the top marginal tax rate to 50 percent from 85 percent, cut capital gains taxes to 30 percent, tamed inflation, cut welfare payments, lowered government expenditures by $11 billion, privatized government enterprises, and lowered jobless benefits. In 1995 exports boomed and Sweden experienced high economic growth.

Alas, economic success brought the Social Democratic Labor Party back to power. The Social Democratic Party continues to push for programs that would recreate the comfort that was achieved when socialism piggybacked on Sweden's then-vigorous private sector.[62] The socialists want to raise jobless benefits for the many who remain unemployed and they want to increase spending on state welfare programs. But, just as in Canada, Britain, and the U.S., the left wing is being forced by fiscal crisis to behave like fiscal conservatives.[63] As Sweden has a huge budget deficit and high interest rates—the outcome of long-term social programs—the Social Democratic Labor Party has created a budget plan that will bring the deficit-to-GDP ratio down to 3 percent in 1997.

Lessons from Overseas

Europeans have defended their economic policies on moral grounds: their highly regulated and taxed labor market practices result in less wage inequality than is found in the freer markets of the United States and Britain.[64] Earnings for more highly skilled and educated people relative to the wages of less skilled people have climbed far more sharply in America and Britain compared with Europe. But the European practices have had an outcome that Americans find morally untenable. While insiders, those already employed, whose jobs are protected by law, seniority, and unions rules, prosper, European unemployment, especially long-term unemployment, has soared and that has especially impacted the young, the less educated, and women. Americans see work as a core part of being an adult and being responsible for oneself. Thus, a system that forces large numbers of the population out of the economy is far more immoral and unfair than one that rewards people proportionately to the value of what they contribute. In fact, recent data clearly demonstrate that the American economy remains extremely vibrant, so that even people in the lowest fifth of income earners are very unlikely to remain there.[65] Of the poorest fifth in 1975, only 5.1 percent remained there in 1991. By 1991, 14.6 percent of the lowest fifth moved to the second lowest fifth; 21 percent were in the middle fifth; 30.3 percent were in the second highest fifth; and 29 percent had moved up to the top fifth. The healthiest and fairest mechanism for creating economic redistribution is a robust market economy that generates jobs and opportunities for all.

Around the world, but most dramatically in Europe, the experiences and policies of the government public sector and the business private sector are the reverse of each other. In the twentieth century, public-sector social engineering created the good life—"free" schools, "free" health care, good salaries, long vacations, and guaranteed employment—while ignoring the fact that in multiple ways, social engineering is fantastically expensive. In contrast, around the world, most successfully competitive companies have cut costs, cut jobs, and cut benefits. The private sector is disciplined by the competitive open market, whereas the public-sector monopoly has chosen to buy votes and indulge voters until financial crises become glaringly evident.

Europe's expensive and extensive social welfare systems were designed, in part, to soften the blow of unemployment.[66] In the past 20 years, most of the job growth in the United States and Japan has been in the private sector. In Europe, during the same period, most job increases have primarily been in the public sector. The paradox of Europe's labor practices is that even when the economy grows, job growth does not follow. From 1970 to 1990 the number of people employed in the United States increased by 52 percent while real labor costs (wage and nonwage charges adjusted for inflation) rose only about 10 percent. In the 12-nation European Community, these ratios are exactly the reverse of those in America: In the EC, real labor costs increased by 60 percent while employment increased by only 10 percent. Most European governments have elected to not make the tax and spending cuts that would, in the longer term, increase the number of jobs and decrease unemployment levels.

While many European governments and unions are extremely reluctant to lessen or dismantle the systems of social protection that evolved in this century, the employers of Europe are clear about the need to increase their competitiveness by developing a lower cost structure and a more flexible labor force. That has to involve a reduction of the role of government and the power of the unions in European economies. While government officials and union leaders battle industries' efforts to cut costs and jobs, only the companies that have aggressively followed the American model of cutting costs and laying off people are currently profitable in competitive industries.[67]

It's no surprise that the majority of people, especially Europeans, want to keep if not expand their programs. But they can't afford them. In the early 1990s, Europe's universal health care coverage, pensions, and unemployment benefits took, on average, about 30 percent of the gross domestic product.[68] Increasingly, European employers are refusing to contribute any more money to social welfare programs because they are already responsible for more than half of those costs. In 1994, the governments of the European community absorbed between 45 and 62 percent of their national incomes, leaving very little available for investment.[69] The corresponding rate in the United States at the same time was about 35 percent.

The lack of job growth in Europe is the result of the costs of very generous government programs and mandates, as well as restrictions and regulations that take too much money out of the economy, reduce or eliminate profits, and make companies in those countries noncompetitive against companies in countries that are economically freer and offer far less social protection. The outcome, of course, is the higher costs of Western European labor are forcing the work to flee from Western Europe to Eastern Europe, Asia, and the United States, where costs are lower, productivity is higher, and quality is on a par with that in the home country.

Western European labor and social policies have had the paradoxical outcome that while they were created to ward off poverty, they have in fact become major disincentives to the creation of jobs. In 1993 in Spain, for example, because of government regulations and union power, average wages rose by more than 6 percent even though the economy contracted and unemployment was 22 percent. That's a powerful incentive to move anywhere else. As high wages and social security costs still pervade the EC, even recovery from recession will not increase employment because the majority of jobs will still migrate to lower-cost nations.

While European nations have done some tinkering to lower their costs—Spain's government made some changes in the law that made it prohibitively expensive to fire workers and Italy has ended the practice of giving people automatic wage increases tied to the rate of inflation—the really costly parts of the state are the enormously comprehensive welfare programs, government employment, and subsidized industries. Whenever EC nations have tried to cut them, the response has been protests and politically perilous strikes. With the exception of Great Britain and, to some extent, Holland, European political leaders have not made sweeping cuts in taxes, welfare, and other aspects of the safety net.[70]

There is a widespread perception in Canada and Europe that the government gives people "free goods." Does Paul not notice Peter? How can people not realize that the ostensibly "free" education, health care, unemployment benefits, long vacations, and the like are paid for by very high taxes and high unemployment rates? The answer is, people don't "see" when they're grabbing their own portions.

Assar Lindbeck, a Swedish economist, finds that the fundamental problem of the Western European welfare state is that "When it gives too much to those who are idle and takes away too much from those who are not, it destroys the incentives of both to work and produce."[71] Michael Novak, a theologian, calls this the moral hazard of the welfare state. Novak says the welfare state tends to generate idleness and ultimately dishonesty as people who want benefits begin to cheat on the rules and then the taxpayers who are most heavily burdened begin to cheat the tax collector. I would also add that whenever there's a welfare organization, those who distribute the welfare are exceedingly motivated to remain employed and they do so by increasing the number of recipients. Thus, these overgenerous social programs are reinforced by the self-serving behaviors of the bureaucrats who dole out the money as well as by the self-serving attitudes of its recipients at all class levels.

Practices designed to provide high levels of safety and security don't work over the longer term because they increase costs enormously. No nation can afford to be a high-cost player because its own businesses, as well as those of other countries, will move elsewhere. The economic outcomes of generous social programs are:

- Migration of work to lower-cost nations
- Little money available for investment in the entrepreneurial private sector
- Little or no job growth
- High rates of long-term unemployment
- Disproportionately high wages and benefits for those employed
- Low productivity rates
- High taxes to support high levels of government spending
- Low personal savings rate
- Many bureaucratic regulations impeding economic growth
- Restrictions on competition perpetuating costly practices
- High tax rates stimulating an underground economy

Net net: no matter how well-intended, programs designed to create artificial security result in high costs, a loss of jobs, and increased financial insecurity.

Worldwide, in less than a decade, there's been an enormous increase in the number of political leaders who have come to accept what Adam Smith saw 200 years ago: Economic progress requires market freedom. For three years, the Heritage Foundation (and now *The Wall Street Journal*) has published the annual Index of Economic Freedom, which tracks international progress toward freer economies.[72] The comparisons reveal a perfect parallel: The freest economies have the highest standards of living and the most restricted economies have the lowest standards of living.

Unfortunately, economic success carries the seed of destruction. Germany is a recent worst example. Rich countries introduce restrictions on economic freedom as they attempt to redistribute their wealth. When countries become wealthy, they create extensive social programs and legal restrictions in order to provide protections for people left behind economically. While that is an important objective, when it is carried too far—as we see in most of Europe, Canada, and, to a lesser extent, Japan—economic growth slows and living standards decline.

Although it's initially painful, most of the EC and Japan must free up their economies. They need to deregulate their labor markets, cut their bureaucracy, speed new product approvals, stop subsidizing noncompetitive businesses, deregulate state-owned businesses, permit restructuring, reengineering, and downsizing, eliminate many government controls, and allow competition to force higher efficiencies and lower costs.[73]

In reality, it is always hard to get rid of Entitlement programs as people understandably try to hang on to their "gains" and politicians try to veto the laws of economics. But basic change will occur. First, the perpetuation of costly Entitlement practices results in economic bankruptcy. Second, those social practices encourage moral bankruptcy as people lose the courage of self-reliance in exchange for being taken care of, and fight among themselves to gain whatever is "free." The experience of all nations with overgenerous social benefits and practices is that they ultimately:

- Strangle the economy and increase long-term unemployment

- Reinforce selfishness and greed

- Require political and business leaders with conviction who will act with courage in order to reduce them

CHAPTER

19

Creating a Future

WHAT SHOULD THE GOALS OF THIS COUNTRY BE?

- Greater prosperity achieved through an expanded economy
- A population of resilient, confident people who flourish in turbulence and risk
- People who are self-governed by moral criteria of right and wrong
- Respect for the civil aspects of society, its rules and responsibilities
- A strong sense of community
- Hope for the future

How these goals will be accomplished takes us to issues of economics, governance, and politics.

Capitalism is amoral, but civil societies need morality. Because unbridled capitalism easily leads to things that are repugnant—sweatshops, child labor, forced labor, dangerous working conditions, compensation under the legal minimum, physical and verbal abuse of workers, harassment, collusion between management/owners and police/military to control workers—civil societies impose restrictions on corporate freedom. Capitalism must be restrained through competition, law, and enforcement of the law. As Rudi Dornbusch says, "Society cannot function by rat race alone."[1] The necessary element is balance. Vibrant capitalism requires a balance of power. Balance is a difficult goal because the optimal balance will shift under varying conditions. Since balance is a moving target rather than a fixed outcome, continuous judgment is necessary to achieve the best balance between truly free markets and control by the state.

Beginning with the founders of this country, America has long mistrusted a concentration of power in very few hands. Our government is based on a system of checks and balances within any one government and between governments. For most of our history, small government was the ideal.

In this century, government grew large. Government can be large in different ways: when it employs many people in its bureaucracy; when it imposes many regulations, mandates, and requirements; when it runs many programs or operations; and/or when it collects a large percentage of the Gross National Product in taxes.

For the last 50 years (in this nation and in many others) large, powerful, centralized governments were seen as the best way to manage the economy and ensure a greater equality of people's standard of living. While well intended and conceptually plausible, large government involves a major drawback—since government is a monopoly, it always creates a culture and a psychology of Entitlement. Cultures where people feel owed are dangerous because not only is the economy harmed, democracy is threatened because personal integrity, character, and strength are eroded. Large, powerful, centralized government fails its people both economically and morally: people lose their ability to govern themselves and deal with hard issues.

Government is a heavy anchor dragging down economic growth because the majority of what it does is not an investment in the economy. In addition, the government is normally far less efficient than the profit-seeking private sector. That is, when government does something, it usually costs far more than it would if it were done outside of government. The basic reason for that is simple: Whenever there is a monopoly, the restrictions on cost, and the discipline of being the best that is required where there *is* competition, are missing. Without competition, organizations and those who work within them inevitably become self-indulgent, lax, inefficient, and therefore expensive. The ratio is obvious: The greater the protection from competition, the worse the performance. Government's monopolistic programs are intrinsically inefficient and ineffective in comparison with circumstances where customers have the power of choice.

Worse, many—if not the majority—of government's mandates, regulations, requirements, and programs involve collecting and redistributing money from a source to a recipient. That's not an economic investment. When government imposes high taxes with the primary goal of redistribution, it drains resources from the economy. The cost of collecting and redistributing the money and of enforcing the collection and monitoring its allocation is enormous, especially because it's done by the government's monopolistic bureaucracy. That money would be far more effective in terms of growing the economy if it were allowed to remain in the economy and be invested.

The most logical economic policy is to focus on growing the economy by reducing the size of government, by reducing the size of government activities, and by reducing the rate of taxation. Those actions would directly increase the money available for investment and expansion, which in turn would increase the number of jobs, profits, and tax revenues. That, of course, creates a sense of success and optimism that energizes an entire society. *America's can-do spirit arises from generations of upward mobility. Nothing should be allowed to jeopardize that.*

As with government, Americans have also long feared the effect of a concentration of power in corporations. At the beginning of the twentieth century, during the Progressive Era, there was real concern about the effects of big business because of the growing power of giant corporations. People were mostly concerned with how they could preserve a democratic government in the face of this enormous financial power. They feared the effect of large corporate power on the autonomy of local communities, which, for the most part, were the site of American self-government.[2] The Progressives' and the Roosevelt New Dealers' greatest concern, an issue that was voiced by Jefferson when the republic was founded, was that concentrated economic power would pose a threat to democracy because consolidated economic power results in the consolidation of political power.

After World War II most sectors of the American economy either dominated the world's economy or were protected, pampered, and regulated.[3] In the 1950s and 1960s, America enjoyed an unchallenged industrial supremacy; corporations regularly announced price increases as they granted significant wage and benefit packages to powerful unions because they knew they could extract those cost increases from consumers. Unskilled, poorly educated, unionized employees were paid high wages, which created the single-worker household standard of living we remember so nostalgically. Today, America cannot ignore the level of wages around the world. From 1988 to 1993, 2.5 billion people were brought into the world economy. Workers in western Europe, eastern Asia, eastern Europe, Latin America, China, and India are forcing American labor to become much more productive so as to be cost-efficient in order to be competitive. Otherwise, the work moves elsewhere.

There are continuous downward pressures on costs in an open economy as everyone is competing against people anywhere in the world who are able and willing to do the same job for less money. Today's economy is one in which Detroit autoworkers compete against counterparts in Mexico, and Silicon Valley software writers go head-to-head with programmers in India and Russia.[4] Jobs will be created and facilities built, depending on costs, skills, and overall competitiveness. In this world, capital knows no national boundaries. It will go anywhere on earth.

Andrew Grove, CEO of Intel, says, "The consequence of all this is painfully simple: If the world operates as one big market, every employee will compete with every person in the world who is capable of doing the same job. There are a lot of them and many of them are very hungry."[5] Nations, organizations, and individuals are faced with the reality that they either will learn to operate in a borderless world of ever increasing competition or they will fail. The need to run faster and smarter will never stop.

The new reality of ever increasing competition and inexorable change is viewed pessimistically by the many who don't perceive an increase in opportunities because they're preoccupied with the losses that boundarylessness creates. A widespread and profound loss of security naturally gives rise to anxiety and cynicism, which leads to serious disappointment in our "leaders." It is a very short journey from wishing that things would get better to insisting that some authority make it happen. Threats to people's sense of security always give rise to surges in desires for protection. But the essential reality is that we are participants in the borderless economy because it is in our own interest to buy and sell worldwide. No artificial boundaries of protective legislation or assertive actions on the parts of unions or politicians can change that.

As boundarylessness is a fundamentally new set of conditions, no one can know what the future holds. The past is not a prelude to this present. This present may not predict the future. The only thing we know is that we cannot extrapolate from yesterday to today and we probably won't be able to extrapolate from today to tomorrow. This is not incremental change. The world is experiencing a quantum change and there is no going back. Welcome to the new world of uncertainty and opportunity.

Creating!

Our culture has always valued the successful innovator. Small, young firms are key to an entrepreneurial economy because they're typically much more innovative than large, older ones. As they're swifter and more flexible, they're more creative and cutting-edge especially in terms of developing and using technology, generating new products and strategies, and using more effective management styles. Innovativeness challenges older and larger organizations; when the older and larger firms don't change, innovative young firms contribute directly to creative destruction. It is the genius of relatively unfettered capitalism that it sets competing forces against each other and lets the market decides which is best.

Governments that pursue identical *outcomes* instead of identical *opportunities* reinforce no-consequence cultures that, in the long run, strangle growth. Today's greater competition between an increasing number of reasonably free, capitalist economies guarantees that while some people and some sectors of any economy will experience significant hardship, others will experience major new opportunities for growth and success.

A vital capitalist economy will experience dynamic job growth and dramatic job cuts simultaneously—but in different companies and different industries. In the first half of 1996, unemployment fell to 5.3 percent. In the first half of 1996, companies announced the elimination of 270,513 jobs. How can we reconcile those two facts? In the first half of 1996, during a period of major cuts, companies were also adding jobs at the rate of 210,000 a month.[6] Companies are eliminating nonproductive jobs while they increase jobs where the business is growing. In 1995, the Fortune 500 companies increased their revenues by 9.9 percent but increased their employees by only 0.2 percent.[7] But, as the economy expanded in services and high tech areas, within those industries the growth in jobs in the Fortune 500 was very significant. Computer hardware positions increased by 11 percent; entertainment added 13 percent more jobs; computer services and software grew by 14 percent; and health care was up by 25 percent.

While there is downsizing, there is also growth. Mostly what there is, is change. Donald Hicks, a political economist at the University of Texas, measured the amount of job growth and destruction in two studies, one looking at what happened in Dallas and the other assessing outcomes in Texas.[8] Hicks found there was an extraordinary amount of job creation and destruction that is hidden in aggregate numbers. From 1986 to early 1989, during which Dallas had a recession and a recovery, the number of jobs in non-farm private industry went from 1,081,013 to 1,056,149. While the number of jobs looks pretty stable, during those years 26.7 percent of the existing jobs were lost and 24.4 percent were newly created. When Hicks looked at what happened to companies in all of Texas that produced goods from 1970 to 1991, he found the number of companies had grown from 12,437 to 28,413. But during that period, 94,000 manufacturing companies had opened—and closed.

Upheaval creates pain and fear. Reducing people's psychological and economic insecurity with contractual job security and wages tied to seniority appears at first to be a compassionate response. But we now have the data that reveal that the paradoxical outcome of imposed job security is that the cost of labor rises so much that jobs go elsewhere and the result is widespread long-term unemployment. Since buggy whips gave way to Model-Ts, capitalism has created losers as well as winners. What we've learned is that, as humane as they appear, government efforts to protect the manufacturers of buggy whips always end up incurring the law of unintended consequences and making things worse. The "compassionate" European system supports people for long periods of time, because the system makes it too expensive to create jobs. As Robert Samuelson says, "What Europe teaches is that societies can't outlaw job insecurity but they can inadvertently outlaw job creation."[9]

Though the transition is not complete, after being forced to give up no-consequence practices and become results-driven, American companies have every reason to expect to succeed in the competition of a worldwide market. America's entrepreneurs are well positioned to create new technologies, new products, new methods of distribution, and new, more efficient ways of doing real work. They are creating jobs and wealth.

Just as individuals often experience major personal growth when they have to cope with tough conditions, organizations and nations do too. While the dynamics of market capitalism are harsh, the outcome can be very positive. America's corporations started cutting costs and reorganizing in 1982, more than a decade before similar efforts began in Japan and Europe. While there are losers—the unemployed, the underemployed, and those forced into early retirement—the overall result has been significant gains in competitiveness and profitability.[10,11]

Between 1988 and 1994 American companies garnered 37 percent of sales in globally competitive industries and achieved 48 percent of the profits in global markets.[12] With some exceptions (for example, steel production), American industry is either the leader relative to Europe and Japan, or it is highly competitive. U.S. industries gave up market share in low-profit industries and captured market share where profits are high. The latter includes technically intensive industries like computers and pharmaceuticals, and also food, beverage, and personal care products. The increase in profits financed growth, including jobs. America created over 18,000,000 new jobs in the past decade, while Europe created 6.9 million, although Europe's population is larger than that of the United States. American business has created enough new jobs to provide work for both the people entering the labor force and the people who were laid off. In 1995 alone, more than a million new managerial and professional jobs were created and unemployment fell below 5.6 percent. And the entrepreneurial spirit is flourishing: From 1990 to the first half of 1996, more than 2300 private companies went public with an initial public offering (IPO).[13]

The pain of restructuring and downsizing, of moving out of mature industries with little potential and into those with high growth and profit potential, has made the United States the most competitive economy in the world. Our growth in productivity, manufacturing, job creation, investment, and standard of living is the highest it's been in decades.[14]

But within the dramatically improved competitive position of America's corporations, the losers hurt and many people's real compensation has not increased substantially in the last two decades.[15] This is fertile ground for the growth of populists and protectionists. Ross Perot and Pat Buchanan attracted millions by tapping into widespread resentment about stagnant wages and job insecurity by giving it a name—free trade—and making it an enemy. The cause of the pain, they said, is the great sucking sound of jobs going elsewhere where labor is cheap. The solutions they proposed—pulling out of NAFTA and GATT, raising tariffs, pulling out of international trade, and raising protectionist walls—have a strong emotional appeal to people who feel victimized and powerless.[16,17]

Free trade policies have actually resulted in many more higher-paying jobs in export industries than eliminated jobs in industries threatened by imports.[18] But, within that gain, free trade is likely to negatively impact particular industries and unskilled workers as it also impacts other industries and skilled employees very positively. While Boeing's profits soar and it employs more people in well-paying jobs, people that work in factories that process vegetables are likely to see their jobs move to Mexico.

In the last 50 years, jobs connected to exports have increased three times faster than those that aren't.[19] In the past decade, exports accounted for one-third of our economic growth, and the growth in exports is believed to be responsible for a third of the jobs created in 1995.[20] Eleven million jobs now depend on exports; that's more people than work in the automobile and housing industries combined. A study by the National Association of Manufacturers concluded that since the late 1980s, firms that export have created 20 percent more jobs than firms that don't, export-linked jobs pay an average of 10 percent higher wages and benefits than jobs unlinked to exports, and companies that export are more likely to survive. The overall outcome of free trade policies is they have created more and better jobs than those that were lost to imports.

The American Dream of upward mobility depends on an expanding economy, and exports have become a major engine of that growth. While free trade does put pressure on compensation, especially in lower-end jobs, it also creates growth by affording access to increasingly large markets. The reality is that the largest potential for growing markets exists in developing countries in which a large middle class is being created. Millions, if not billions, of people are new consumers, and if development continues on a worldwide scale, there will be billions more. Selling to worldwide markets is the key to enlarging the economic pie.

Educate People

The economy's largest growth is in both low-wage service jobs and high-wage managerial and professional positions. The income gap can be thought of as a skills gap. The largest part of the work force, about two-thirds, has lower-level skills and few opportunities, while highly skilled and educated people have many. Despite a reasonably strong economy and the growth of millions of jobs, the number of people whose incomes are flat or are declining, and the number of people who are working poor, is increasing.

To an enormous extent, the disparity in income growth reflects the market value of what people can do; it is the result of differences in education and the relevance of people's knowledge and skills. The difference in compensation between people who have little education and those who have a lot is widening.[21] But (and I'm ignoring the dumbing down of the curriculum) the average level of educational achievement is rising. In 1973, among people aged 16 to 65 in the civilian work force, about 30 percent had not completed high school. In 1993, that figure had fallen to about 10 percent.

Over the last 30 years, access to college education has increased enormously.[22] The proportion of people aged 25 to 29 who have a college degree has soared from one-ninth to one-fourth. And the reality that America has become even more of an open society is demonstrated by the fact that it was much harder to go to college if you were from a low-income family in the 1960s than it is in the 1990s. From 1972 to 1993, the percent of high school graduates who went directly to college from families in the bottom fifth of the income distribution increased from 26 to 50 percent.

Not many years ago, metaphorically speaking, most people took their last diploma, folded it neatly, put it in a pocket, and figured they were done with school. That's over. Everyone need to upgrade their skills continuously at work and, at least intermittently, in school. In the near future, it's a reasonable assumption that the great majority of people will be technologically literate because that will be a precondition for almost every kind of work. There will be a large demand for technicians—people who specialize in using technology or repairing it. As information keeps exploding, the shelf life of any knowledge will get briefer and briefer. Many jobs will come from industries that grow faster than anyone imagines, and many will come from industries that no one has yet imagined. The only way to ride this wave, much less get ahead of it, is for organizations to keep challenging their basic assumptions and for people to insist that work itself be a continuous education.

The nation's 1200 community colleges have become the most innovative and effective sector of education, because technicians are becoming the new middle class. Students often alternate or combine school and work, usually for two to four years; when they graduate, they are prepared to handle skilled jobs that are available locally. As the programs are targeted to local businesses, the curriculum is often jointly developed by the school and potential employers. Classes are given both in the community college and/or in the companies. Many community college instructors are full-time practitioners and part-time instructors. Teachers, students, and employers are in continuous dialogue, creating entire new programs as well as modifying existing course content, in step with changes in the workplace.

How will we pay for an enormous increase in lifelong education? My first impulse was to suggest a new version of the post–World War II American GI Bill of Rights, which supplied every veteran with enough money for college tuition and living costs. Any veteran who wanted to could go to college. That was the jump start of the vast increase in the nation's level of education. Today, 62 percent of Americans have some college education.

Fifty years ago, the GI Bill was an enormous and successful investment in the intellectual capital of the country. But, 50 years later, I don't think the same kind of huge investment would be a wise course. The difference is that the GIs were children of the Depression and most couldn't conceive of *not* keeping their nose to the grindstone. Often poor, they gratefully accepted the opportunity created by the GI Bill and they went to school in order to go to work. Today's basic culture is that of Entitlement. If education were free, for many it would simply be another fulfillment of what they believe they are owed. In the worst case, a new GI Bill could become perverted, with many people staying in school in order to avoid going to work. Responsibility and account-ability are not big values in no-consequence cultures.

We need a significant investment in appropriate and effec-tive education, and the sources of funds should include both the private and public sectors. But individual responsibility and accountability must be built into the financial relation-ship. In simpler terms, those who study have to be involved in earning the money for it. It's too easy not to value what you get for free.[23]

Cost makes it unlikely that single organizations will pro-vide education and customized experiences to develop skills. But the nation needs continuous learning as much as individuals do. Therefore, this country needs to initiate a widespread, shared responsibility among many institutions for the continuous reeducation of everyone. While it is a cor-porate responsibility, it is simultaneously a government responsibility. While it is an individual's responsibility, it's also a community responsibility. We must manage the con-tinuous transformation of what people know and what they are able to do because that's what reality demands.

Give or Invest?

We know that no nation can afford unrestrained benefits. No country can afford to supply unlimited economic secu-rity, health care, retirement benefits, and education, nor can countries afford the costs of the expanding government pro-grams that supply such benefits. These programs will come under harsher political and economic scrutiny. The political battle has already begun. Costs will force choices, and choices have to be made. The debate must be joined.

There's a core human conflict between *giving* and *invest-ing* in people. Usually, we *give* out of pity, out of guilt, or for humanitarian reasons. We don't require something in return because we don't expect to get it. When we *invest,* we believe we're contributing to growth and strength and we expect a rate of return.

When you give and ask nothing in return, you create and reinforce the belief that individuals are owed, and in the long run you ask them to accept the psychology of victimization. Giving, without requiring something in return, demonstrates a conviction that the recipient is incapable of being held responsible. Therefore, whenever we give some form of assistance and don't require any form of responsible behavior in return, we demean the recipient. In contrast, when we invest, when we demand a rate of return, regardless of its form, producing the return increases people's motivation, focus, discipline, and pride.

One of the choices that will never be resolved is whether to invest in the most promising or give charity to the least able. At the moment, the pendulum of a no-consequence culture has swung too far to charity at the expense of the best and brightest.

A special education teacher of severely retarded kids was asked, "How many students are in your class?" "Six," she replied, "but because some of the kids don't understand English, there's also another teacher who can speak Spanish." Stunned by the cost of two full-time accredited teachers allocated to only six children, someone blurted out, "How many of them do you think will ever be able to tie their shoes?" After a pause, the teacher said, "I think perhaps one might be able to do that."

Without abandoning charity, the pressures to remain competitive among the world's nations requires that the pendulum shift toward investment in the most promising because they are the nation's most important resource.

Still, there is a particularly difficult case in the investment-charity choice that involves people who are not and may never have been participants in the economy. We must change the economic, living, and educational conditions in the inner cities not only for humanitarian reasons, but because the economic, social, and moral impoverishment in the inner cities is dangerous to the entire nation.

How do we start? What do we know? Interventions designed as giving fail. Welfare, of course, is the epitome of giving. While welfare became the hallmark of the country's sense of social responsibility and generosity, when we contrast the economic success of the immigrant poor with the economic and life failure of those who spend a long time on the welfare rolls, we have a clear view of the destructiveness of "giving" generosity. The prolonged "kindness" of welfare programs informs participants that they are incapable of helping themselves. When recipients are glad to receive handouts and be relieved of responsibility for themselves, they are denied experiences that would lead them to challenge the idea of their incompetence. As it is, welfare participants never develop the confidence, determination, discipline, and patience required to achieve independence and accomplish anything significant. Without what George Will calls "the accumulated social capital of good habits," the underclass cannot rise from poverty.[24]

Roger Waldinger found that from 1970 to 1990 New York City lost more unskilled white workers than it lost unskilled jobs.[25] That should have created an opportunity for unskilled people in the inner city. But inner-city residents didn't go after those jobs even though unemployment was rising in the ghetto. Instead, the jobs were taken by immigrants. The reason inner-city residents didn't move into those jobs was explained this way by a 25-year-old father of two who works two jobs: "They try to find easier routes and has been conditioned over a period of time to just be lazy, so to speak. Motivation [is] nonexistent, you know, and the society that they're affiliated with really don't advocate hard work and struggle to meet your goals such as education and stuff like that. . . . They don't see nobody getting up early in the morning, going to work or going to school all the time. The guys they be with don't do that . . . because that's the crowd you choose—well, that's been presented to you by your neighborhood."[26] The availability of jobs counts, but looking at the experiences of recent immigrants, attitudes and values count more.

The outcome of generous giving is an impoverishment of the self, inadequate discipline and motivation, inadequate skills, and, therefore, highly reduced opportunities for entry-level jobs. This, the opposite of the American Dream, is surely the nation's nightmare.

Saving the inner-city underclass requires what every poor immigrant group has needed: a powerful sense of community and responsibility for one another; a strong sense of family; a commitment to the next generation; a determination to challenge discrimination through achievement; and the desire to move into the American mainstream and the goal of climbing up the ladder. Undergirding ambition are the core middle-class American values: pride in achievement; deferred gratification; hard work; responsibility, dependability, and accountability. The development of these values will require major initiatives based on investment.

Salvaging members of the inner city requires a mission of transformation with a goal of enabling people to manage their responsibilities. Experience, especially in the charitable private sector, reveals that the effort must be coordinated rather than piecemeal; at best, it's difficult and expensive. More than job training, people need preparation for adulthood and becoming members of the labor force. They have to learn the simple disciplines of being on time, of caring enough to do a good job, of thinking through beforehand what they'd do if a child got sick or the car broke down. In order to handle responsibilities, one has to learn to be responsible. The only way that can happen is for people to be held responsible for their actions.

How can we achieve effective compassion and help people become effective, confident, and independent? Dependency-creating programs of giving defeat these objectives. In all of the effective programs, people are accountable for performance; a wide range of long-term help is brought to each individual or family; and the medium-term costs are higher in the new system than in the old. These are all aspects of investment, and they are necessary.

Peter and Regina Bidstrup of Phoenix, Arizona helped create a nonprofit organization called Homeward Bound.[27] The program's participants are homeless families with children who are not so impaired that they cannot work to achieve goals. The families must also be willing to do the hard work that's involved in getting back on their feet.

Homeward Bound starts by getting the family stabilized, physically comfortable, and able to begin thinking about how they can solve their problems. Many of the program's participants have had so much recent tragedy—the loss of a job, being evicted—that they have not been able to think coherently. With help from case managers, family members create a set of goals that, if achieved, would solve their problems. Goals might be to get a job within 30 days or get some training. Everyone has goals: Kids in school have goals about what their grades will be and how much homework they'll do. Case managers have two roles: They help members of the family as they also monitor progress.

Homeward Bound wants people who, though debilitated, can earn a more normal lifestyle. Those are the people the program can help. Therefore, the people selected have the motivation, capacity, and ability to make progress. Homeward Bound is looking for people who don't want to be on welfare.

During the period the families are sheltered, they live in housing provided by the program and they're charged 30 percent of their income. Every time the program accepts a family, it gets a sponsor (a church or a professional firm) who provides volunteers and $300 a month. The program's homes are spread out in a large geographic area. As a result, no one knows the family is homeless—and appropriate role models live next door.

After a family's goals are set, the program provides a 12- to 18-month boot camp. Homeward Bound's staff and volunteers teach, help with achieving goals, and evaluate progress. Homeward Bound is not a welfare program. It's transitional. It gives families a limited time to meet their agreed-upon goals. If a family doesn't meet its goals, it is asked to leave and evicted if necessary.

Homeward Bound *invests* in its families. While participants receive a wide range of assistance, they have the responsibility of achieving their goals. If they don't meet those goals, they have to leave the program. With an annual expenditure of $3600 a family plus the capital cost of the house, Homeward Bound has a 90 percent success rate.[28] After completing the program, the families can afford regular housing and the program helps participants to buy a house. Some of the superstar families buy the house that was originally used to shelter them (or another Homeward Bound house). Investing in people who have the desire and at least some ability to succeed results in a much higher probability that they will.

The state of Wisconsin has created a model of effective, compassionate welfare.[29] The first step was changing the attitudes of social workers who had been trained to believe that caring for people meant putting them on welfare and giving them food stamps and clothing vouchers. Social workers had defined "good" performance as getting more and more people on welfare. That changed: Social workers became financial counselors who ask clients, "What can you do? What do you need in order to go to work?"[30]

Investment was instituted: Wisconsin's Governor Tommy G. Thompson's first change was to require that young people stay in school. If they had three unexcused absences, their share of the welfare check was eliminated. The second change, called Children First, required that parents pay child support or go to jail. When people claimed they couldn't find a job, they were assigned to 16 weeks of unpaid work,

32 hours a week, sweeping streets, clearing brush, or being crossing guards. Within 10 days most parents found a job and started paying child support. The third change was to allow AFDC-qualified people to get married. The fourth innovation was to insist that any parent younger than 18 had to take courses in parenting.

Wisconsin's biggest change is W2, or Wisconsin Works. The Social Service Department has been transformed into the Work Force Department, and everyone is required to work. Beginning in September 1997, recipients will not receive money from the state. Instead, the money will come from where they work.[31]

While the total cost to the state is higher now because the investment is greater, the state's AFDC checks declined from $46 million a month in 1987 to $21 million in 1996. Since 1987, Wisconsin has reduced the welfare caseload by 44 percent and has emancipated 40,000 women and 76,000 children from the welfare system. The state's most recent survey found the women starting out at $6.10 an hour, making more money than they ever received from AFDC. The investment is paying off.

Sometimes giving is replaced by investing and something wonderful happens. Some years ago I lived next door to a man who had a significantly retarded son. The young man was nice looking and very pleasant, but with an IQ probably near 75. He spent his days with other retarded people, essentially warehoused. One day he called out, "Mrs. Bardwick, Mrs. Bardwick!" I turned and saw him standing next to a moped, dressed in a white shirt, dark tie, and navy slacks with a sharp crease. "I got a job!," he called out. "You did?! Wow!" I replied. "Where?" "Sea World," he answered proudly. "My job is to show people where to go to the next show. My job is to help them have a good time." Begun out of kindness, for humanitarian reasons, Sea World ended up investing in people like that young man, and what they got in return were committed, loyal employees. Every morning, proud as could be, my neighbor's son rode his moped to Sea World, where he took his job seriously . . . and earned a salary.

Look to the Future with Hope

America's optimism has always rested on the Horatio Alger story. Many of us have achieved levels of prosperity far greater than the ones we knew as kids. Americans haven't resented wealthier people because of the belief and hope that any American, or his or her children, could work hard and prosper. Being able to climb up the ladder from whatever rung you started on has been key to Americans' hope for the future, belief in the nation, and trust in the government. Restricting that opportunity to a small sector of the population would be wrong and extremely dangerous.

In January 1996, after five years of economic growth, about 250 people of a sample of 1001 reported they were worse off than they had been four years before.[32] In contrast, about 500 people said they were better off, and about 250 reported no significant change in their economic status. While that's not as good as we could hope for, it's hardly terrible. However, only 410 people said they expected their children to be better off than they were. Among the baby boomers, many of whom are squeezed by college costs and the care of aging parents, pessimism ran deep. Two-thirds of the boomers were not optimistic about their children's future.[33]

There's a split among economists: Some believe there's been no basic change in how the economy operates, while others, including Alan Greenspan and many corporate leaders, believe there has. The latter believe the increased efficiencies of business in an open economy, plus the competition created by deregulation, have effectively capped costs. Because of the significant number of competitors and the availability of lower-cost providers, corporations are now hampered in terms of raising prices just as labor has been unsuccessful in gaining major wage increases above those of productivity improvements. If true, this means the danger of inflation is lower than it's been. The United States has had high employment rates, a high number of layoffs, and low inflation for almost 15 years. In a borderless economy, it may be possible to cut the deficit and simultaneously grow the economy without increasing inflation.[34]

"Growing the economy" is a phrase that doesn't pack much emotional punch. But it should. It's much more important than many people realize. When the economy grows robustly, so do the number of businesses, the number of jobs, and incomes. More people earn a living, achieve self-respect, and become homeowners and taxpayers. A high-growth economy is optimistic; people have a sense of hope about their own future and the future of their community.

After years of corporate upheaval, American manufacturers may be about to experience powerful gains in productivity. If we look only at the impact of deregulation on telecommunications, we find that in the years from 1994 to 1996, despite the visible and massive downsizing of the phone companies, employment in the phone industry rose by 54,000.[35] If we scan wider and look at the full range of the overlapping complex of communications, computers, and entertainment, in 1995 those industries generated 400,000 new jobs.

The great investor Peter Lynch observes that while the media keep reporting news of downsizings and other difficult dislocations in the new economy, when you look at the total employment figures the United States has experienced tremendous "upsizing."[36] American entrepreneurs started enough new businesses, or grew enough small and medium companies to giant size, that job growth far eclipses job loss. In the 1980s America lost 3 million jobs, but ended the decade with a net gain of 18 million. Between February 1992, the low point of the last recession, and the fall of 1996, the economy added 12 million new jobs. While the pain of those who were "rightsized" is undeniable, the number of people who gained from growth and "upsizing" is much larger.

A borderless economy involves the turbulence of change. Thus far, most of the focus has been on the negative consequences or the losses because of change. But change always generates opportunity as well as dangers. Chaos has not replaced absolute stability, though relative instability has replaced relative stability.

The country's anxiety is higher than the economic and employment numbers would justify. In addition to the sense that something fundamental is changing, the fact that there are people who had achieved significant career success, but have now become losers in the transition to a different kind of economy, increases the nation's sense of vulnerability. Among those victims are white male managers who had achieved the comfortable life of reasonably affluent Americans. Most of those men are middle aged and many had reached the vice presidential level. These are people who went to the right schools, joined the right companies, married the right women, became members of the right clubs. People who succeeded in achieving status can never be psychologically prepared for the loss of it. Being let go, being discarded, must be akin to a kind of death of these people's sense of themselves. Everyone has experience with death and divorce, but unemployment is the new catastrophe.[37]

The focus on the half-empty bottle jeopardizes our historic optimism and belief in the possibility of upward mobility. We and our leaders have not yet been successful in creating a powerful vision for the future. The people who will become our real leaders will be those who are able to convince us that though the future will surely be different, it can also be better.

The future is just beginning, and we have only started to find the path. The problems generated by a borderless economy are essentially new, so many of their solutions must also be new. Some answers, like some questions, are not yet imaginable. But the future promises opportunities created by the very turbulence that feels scary.

The only preparation for dealing with unpredictability and risk is to deal with them continuously. That means stepping up to what is now really real. As paradoxical as it sounds, we have to give thanks for hard times because adversity is the driver for extraordinary achievements. Extraordinary achievements are now the only way to succeed. Out of fear and pain, we are getting better and better. We are getting stronger as well as more flexible, tempered like a sword blade thrust between heat and cold, hammered over and over again.

I am becoming optimistic. We're the people for whom it has to get worse before it gets better. It got worse and we got better. While we must be wary of complacency, let us look to the future with hope!

To achieve a better future:

- Within constraints that balance power, the discipline of a competitive market is allowed to create a healthy economy.

- Investments are made in people.

- The economy grows fast enough to create jobs, opportunity, and hope for the future.

The Three-Dimensional Model

IN *DANGER IN THE COMFORT ZONE,* I DESCRIBED A PSYCHOLOG-
ical model that takes the form of a three-dimensional bell-
shaped curve. This description of the model is for people
who are unacquainted with the earlier book.

There are two important facts in psychology. The first,
the Yerkes-Dodson Law, says that performance increases as
anxiety levels rise. Performance reaches its highest level
when anxiety is at an ideal level. If anxiety levels increase
higher than is ideal, however, performance declines. If the
word *anxiety* feels strange, substituting terms like *risk,
uncertainty, accountability,* or *pressure to perform* is fine.
The second fact is that the motive to achieve reaches its
highest level when the probability of success is 50 percent.
In other words, people are most motivated to achieve something when it is in their middle range of risk or difficulty. In
plain English, that means people are not very motivated to
pursue a goal or master a task if it's either too hard or too

easy. We are most motivated to do something when it's a challenge or a stretch. This simply means we most enjoy a task when the goal is hard but there's a very good chance we can succeed. That's what we mean when we say people are pushing the edge of their envelope. That's when people feel most vibrantly alive.

Yerkes-Dodson and the motive to achieve can be described in a very simple graphic. There are two variables, one horizontal and one vertical.

The horizontal variable, which Yerkes-Dodson calls *anxiety,* but which we might also call risk, uncertainty, or pressure, refers to the extent people can take what they get for granted. Where there's little or no risk, people take everything for granted, and where there's total risk they can take nothing for granted.

In the left section of the horizontal variable, the level of risk is too low. That means people will pretty well take whatever they get for granted. In the right section of the horizontal variable, the level of risk or anxiety is too high.

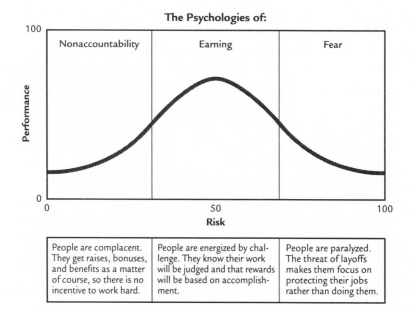

Nonaccountability	Earning	Fear
People are complacent. They get raises, bonuses, and benefits as a matter of course, so there is no incentive to work hard.	People are energized by challenge. They know their work will be judged and that rewards will be based on accomplishment.	People are paralyzed. The threat of layoffs makes them focus on protecting their jobs rather than doing them.

Under those conditions, people can take very little or nothing for granted. The ideal level of risk or anxiety is midway, or at 50 percent.

Yerkes-Dodson calls the vertical variable *performance.* Since the relationship is very powerful, we can also call it *productivity.* The vertical variable is also self-confidence.

This simple graphic makes it easy to see that having too little risk or anxiety is as detrimental to performance and confidence as having too much. While that is counterintuitive, that is the basic fact of Yerkes-Dodson.

This simple curve enables us to see that performance is highest where the level of risk or anxiety is medium (or 50 percent) for that person. When we say "for that person," we're recognizing that different people have very different relationships to risk. While some people are risk avoiders and are scared to death of it, and others are positively turned on by it, all have a level that is medium for them.

The bell-shaped curve is the graphic expression of the three psychological states generated by different levels of risk, pressure, or anxiety.[1] Where the level is too low, we have the psychology or attitude *You owe me.* This is by far the most common set of assumptions and practices in this country.

Fear is the flip side of nonaccountability, and it is equally destructive to confidence and performance. When anxiety or risk levels are too high, and especially when people feel they have no control over what is happening to them, turf defense replaces teamwork, cynicism and mistrust flourish, and people focus more on protecting themselves and their jobs rather than doing them.

Basically, productivity is low when people are in the nonaccountability sector of the curve because too many people either don't work or they work very hard at garbage activities. Productivity is low when people are in the Fear sector of the curve because people are exhausted by how they feel. They don't work well because they're drained of psychological energy.

Between Nonaccountability and Fear, between having too much security and too little, lies the psychology of Earning, which in this book I've usually referred to as *being Results-Driven.* While people face enough risk in Earning so they cannot take what they get for granted, the odds are good they can earn those outcomes. Earning is the attitude everyone must have if the organization is to prosper and if the individuals within it are to flourish. People and organizations need that medium level of risk that motivates them to achieve at levels they haven't reached before, and provides those successful risk taking experiences that result in ever increasing levels of confidence. The medium level of risk is exciting. It's the source of vitality, of *go for it!*

The psychology of Earning is the feeling that while there is downside risk, the upside potential is far greater. It's the sense we *can* do it if we strive and stretch and sweat. Ultimately, that's the real fun! at work. In the competitive boundaryless economy, everyone has to be in Earning—results-oriented, proactive, productive. That is the only sector from which one can compete. But nonaccountability and a presumption of rights is very seductive.

The facts are as follows. (1) When there is very little fear, there is a very high probability of nonaccountability. (2) Once a culture of nonaccountability and a presumption of rights begins, it tends to grow larger. (3) People like the security of nonaccountability, which makes it very hard to eliminate.

When we use the curve, we acknowledge the fact that there are degrees of the three psychological states and we impose positions from 1 to 9 on the curve. The strongest position in Nonaccountability is 1; 9 is the extreme of Fear.

When I published *Danger In The Comfort Zone,* I thought position 5 was the best place to be. But I've since learned that when an organization is at 5 for any significant length of time, the chances are very good that the organization and the people in it will become arrogant. Once you become arrogant, the inevitable journey is to the complacency of

The Earning Curve

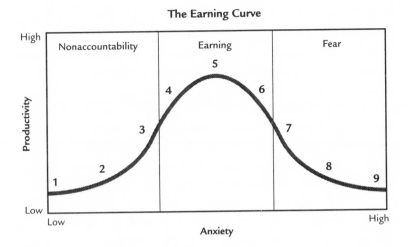

Nonaccountability. Therefore, I find the single best place is 6—in Earning, but a little tenser than is comfortable.

In 1992, the American Management Association conducted two surveys that tested the validity and usefulness of this model. The first survey reported responses from 408 human resource managers and the second analyzed feedback from over 1000 secretaries. Remarkably, the surveys found a powerful correlation between how profitable an organization was and where it fell on the Earning curve. Unprofitable firms and nonprofit organizations were in Nonaccountability. Highly profitable organizations were in Earning.

Unprofitable and not-for-profit organizations had many of the qualities of a no-consequence culture. Employees avoided risks, didn't innovate, and weren't flexible. With little confidence in the organization's ability to solve problems and little confidence in subordinates, performance requirements and performance levels were low, as were morale and the motivation to perform. People were neither held accountable nor given responsibility. Those organizations tended toward low levels of energy and, despite their objective lack of success, people in them felt complacent.

In profitable companies, people were not bound by strict rules and regulations. They responded to that by being proactive and productive. People in highly profitable companies tended to be confident, innovative risk takers, and they exuded energy. The organizations encouraged people to work together, count on each other, and bend the rules or create new ones. In Earning, these companies required performance and were focused and energetic enough to keep advancing. That's why they were very profitable.

Being in Earning means being in a meritocracy. It is an entrepreneurial mentality within an organization whose culture never loses sight of the fact that the only thing that matters is results. Being in Earning means being very, very clear about what the business of the business is, and assessing success only in those terms. Being in Earning means being focused, aggressive, creative, and proactive in figuring out the best ways to achieve what really matters within ethical boundaries.

- Nonaccountability is a set of conditions in which performance is *not* a precondition for security.

- Fear is a set of conditions in which there is no way to earn security.

- Earning is a set of conditions in which performance is the criterion for (some) security.

NOTES

INTRODUCTION

1. Dana Milbank, "Birth of the Welfare State," *The Wall Street Journal,* April 24, 1995, R10 and R12.

2. A technical explanation for this assertion can be found in the Postscript.

CHAPTER 1

1. David Hage, Linda Grant, and Jim Impoco, "White Collar Wasteland," *U.S. News & World Report,* June 28, 1993, 42-51.

2. Matt Murray, "Amid Record Profits, Companies Continue to Lay Off Employees," *The Wall Street Journal,* May 4, 1995, A1 and A5.

3. Louis S. Richman, "Getting Past Economic Insecurity," *Fortune,* April 17, 1995, 160-168.

4. Hage, Grant, and Impoco, op. cit.

5. Ibid.

6. Michael J. Mandel and Christopher Farrell, "Jobs, Jobs, Jobs— Eventually," *Business Week,* June 14, 1993, 72-73.

7. Hage, Grant, and Impoco, op. cit.

8. Murray, op. cit.

9. Roger M. Haughen, "Changing the Employment 'Game,'" *Benefits & Compensation Solutions,* September 1995, 22–27.

10. Hage, Grant, and Impoco, op. cit.

11. Murray, op. cit.

12. Challenger, Gray & Christmas, Inc., "Happy Labor Day," *Time,* September 4, 1995.

13. Gene Koretz, "Downsizing Isn't Down Enough," *Business Week,* December 4, 1995, 24.

14. Aaron Bernstein, "Who Says Job Anxiety Is Easing?" *Business Week,* April 7, 1997, 38.

15. Michael J. Mandel, A. T. Palmer, and Alice Cuneo, "Whatever Happened to Economic Anxiety," *Business Week,* September 23, 1996, 34–36.

16. Bernstein, op. cit.

17. Ibid.

18. Ibid.

19. George Melloan, "Why All This Downsizing? Ask Washington," *The Wall Street Journal,* March 25, 1996, A15.

20. Richard Wintermantel, JD, vice president and director, Motorola, personal communication, May 1, 1996.

21. Greg Stricharchuk, "Affecting Change Is a Lot Like Moving a Rock," *Dayton Ohio News,* October 17, 1993, B1.

CHAPTER 2

1. On December 3, 1997, Steve updated this information. He expects 1998 sales to be in the $80 million range. The number of employees has risen to about 300. ICS just constructed and moved into a 132,000-square-foot corporate headquarters and manufacturing facility.

CHAPTER 3

1. Steve Mason, CEO, Mead Corporation, personal communication, May 10, 1996.

2. Ned Barnholt, executive vice president and general manager, Test and Measurement Organization, Hewlett-Packard, personal communication, May 10, 1996.

3. Barnholt, op. cit.

4. Al Derden, director of quality, Texaco, personal communication, September 22, 1995.

5. Ronald G. Shafer, "Cut Entitlements," *The Wall Street Journal,* July 29, 1994, A1.

6. Allen Bell, executive vice president, human resources, Toronto Dominion Bank, personal communication, April 22, 1996.

7. Craig Cantoni, personal communication, August 20, 1996. Cantoni, a consultant, says people who are dependent on the protection of Entitlement exaggerate the negative aspects of change and deny the positive. When the Entitlement culture is pushed to change to a strong commitment to people and hitting business targets, fear and resentment lead people to claim that the real goal is to create a culture where people don't matter very much.

8. Anne B. Fisher, "Making Change Stick," *Fortune,* April 17, 1995, 121–128.

9. G. Dowell Schwartz Jr., executive vice president of general services, Baltimore Gas and Electric, personal communication, May 7, 1996.

10. Richard Champion, director, corporate relations, Florida Power Corporation, personal communication, May 27, 1996.

11. Mason, op. cit.

12. Dennis Coleman, group personnel manager, Hewlett-Packard, personal communication, May 1, 1996.

13. Steve Gardiner, director, management education and development, Champion International Corporation, personal communication, June 5, 1996.

14. David Morrison, vice president, human resources development, Toronto Dominion Bank, personal communication, May 7, 1996.

15. Robert Newton, Ph.D., director of macrophage pathology, DuPont Merck, personal communication, February 11, 1994.

16. John Thompson, "The One Hundredth Monkey: An Anthropological Model for Change," *Index SMI Review,* 4th quarter 1993, 15.

17. Ibid.

CHAPTER 4

1. Norman Lorentz, vice president for quality, U.S. Postal Service, personal communication, May 13, 1996.

2. Walter Boomer, CEO, Rogers Corporation, former CEO, Babcock-Wilcox and General, USMC, Retired, personal communication, July 11, 1996.

3. The president went on to tell me that opening the books turned out to be an awfully good idea. Over the next month, on Saturdays, he held a voluntary course in basic finance and over 90 percent of the tool and die makers attended.

CHAPTER 5

1. Kerry Pechter, "Rebooting Big Blue," *Human Resource Executive,* September 1993, 1 and 23.

2. Gilbert Fuchsberg, "Why Shake-Ups Work for Some, Not for Others," *The Wall Street Journal,* October 1, 1993, B1.

3. Michael J. McCarthy, "New Shuttle Incites a War between Old Rivals," *The Wall Street Journal,* December 1, 1994, B1 and B6.

4. "A Bureaucrat's Guide to Smaller Government," *The Wall Street Journal,* April 7, 1995, A10.

5. Personal communication, March 1994.

6. Richard Champion, director, corporate relations, Florida Power Corporation, personal communication, May 27, 1996.

7. Norman Lorentz, vice president for quality, U.S. Postal Service, personal communication, May 3, 1996.

8. G. Dowell Schwartz Jr., executive vice president of general services, Baltimore Gas and Electric, personal communication, May 7, 1996.

9. Margot Kyd, vice president of human resources, marketing, and customer service, San Diego Gas and Electric, personal communication, May 2, 1996.

10. Susan Chandler, "Sears' Turnaround Is for Real—For Now," *Business Week,* August 15, 1994, 103.

11. Charles M. Farkas and Phillipe DeBacker, "There Are Only Five Ways to Lead," *Fortune,* January 15, 1996, 108-112.

12. Robert Frey, "Empowerment or Else," *Harvard Business Review,* September–October 1993, 80-94.

13. Ibid.

14. Noel M. Tichy and Ram Charan, "The CEO as Coach: An Interview with AlliedSignal's Lawrence A. Bossidy," *Harvard Business Review,* March-April 1995, 69-78.

15. David Kirkpatrick, "Intel Goes for Broke," *Fortune,* May 16, 1994, 62-68.

16. Ibid.

CHAPTER 6

1. This explains the common conflict between those who want to lead others through turbulent times and those who refuse to become followers as they insist it's still peacetime.

2. Raju Narisetti, "Mead Corp. Decides to Go Back to Its Roots, Literally," *The Wall Street Journal,* May 27, 1994, A10. Some leaders do come from inside the no-consequence culture organization. Steven Mason, CEO of Mead Corporation and a third-generation Mead employee,

surprised analysts by the toughness of the demands he's made since he became the top officer in 1992. In his first two years he eliminated about 1000 jobs, or 5 percent of the workforce, and his target is to cut costs a further $60 million a year. When Mason installed a 680-pound rock in the lobby of corporate headquarters, he told Mead's employees that changing Mead into a nimble, risk-taking company would be as hard as literally moving that rock.

3. Abraham Zaleznik, "Managers and Leaders: Are They Different?" *Harvard Business Review,* May–June 1997, reprinted March–April 1992, 126-135.

4. Elizabeth Lesly, Zachary Schiller, Stephen Baker, and Geoffrey Smith, "CEO's with the Outside Edge," *Business Week,* October 11, 1993, 60-62. Of the 51 new CEOs hired in the first half of 1993, for example, 35 percent were outsiders. That's the highest percentage since Eugene Jennings started tracking this practice in 1949.

5. Richard Stengel, "The Making of a Leader," *Time,* May 9, 1994, 36-38. Leaders need a repertoire of techniques to gain followers: sometimes telling, sometimes listening, sometimes patient, sometimes driving for speed. Nelson Mandela, for example, sometimes moves out front, ahead of everyone else, with an aggressive policy. At other times, he drives change from behind by suggesting, pressuring, and waiting. He has described that leadership style as the one he learned herding cattle as a boy: "When you want to get a herd to move in a certain direction, you stand at the back with a stick. Then a few of the more energetic cattle move to the front and the rest of the cattle follow. You are really guiding them from behind. That is how a leader should do his work."

6. Winston Churchill, speech on Dunkirk, House of Commons, June 4, 1940.

7. Communicating persuasively and behaving with integrity are dealt with more briefly here than the other topics because they are described fully in Chapter 11.

8. Laurie Hays, "IBM's Finance Chief, Ax in Hand, Scours Empire for Costs to Cut," *The Wall Street Journal,* January 26, 1994, A1-A6.

9. Lee Smith, "New Ideas from the Army (Really)," *Fortune,* September 19, 1994, 203-212. General Gordon Sullivan, the army chief of state, for example, believes that in 1994 about 5 percent of the army's active duty officers were still mentally locked into the Cold War. Sullivan estimates that some 65 percent have moved up to the Gulf War. But only 30 percent, he thinks, can stand with him 15 years into the future, imagining what that will be like and figuring out how to get there.

10. Marshall Loeb, "Leadership Lost—And Regained," *Fortune,* April 17, 1995, 217-218.

11. Just as we can't confuse what we deliver with how we get there, we can't confuse criteria of involvement with a strategy for winning. When, for example, Jack Welch, CEO of General Electric, decided that if GE couldn't achieve the number one or number two position in an industry, it would get out of that business, he was defining a criterion of whether or not to remain involved, but that is not strategy. There's often a basic confusion between the strategic choice and the process of how the strategy is achieved.

12. Processes include improving how the work is done; improving the market and delivery system; improving financial effectiveness; and improving the synergy of the parts. Here are specific examples:

- Improving how the work is done, i.e., TQM, empowering employees, creating teams, reengineering, centralizing or decentralizing, partnering.

- Improving the marketing and delivery system, i.e., JIT, information technology, new retail channels, advertising, changing the structure and/or mission of the sales force.

- Improving financial effectiveness, i.e., downsizing, capital investments, vertical integration, outsourcing, creating alliances, getting suppliers to cut prices, making R&D focus on commercial products.

- Improving the synergy of the parts, i.e., realigning people and their mission, reorganizing structures, changing compensation from individuals to teams or units, improving communication, changing management's style.

13. Dennis Coleman, group personnel manager, Hewlett-Packard, personal communication, May 1, 1996.

14. Margot Kyd, vice president of human resources, marketing, and customer service, San Diego Gas and Electric, personal communication, May 2, 1996.

15. Henry Mintzberg, "The Fall and Rise of Strategic Planning," *Harvard Business Review,* January–February 1994, 107–114.

16. Richard Champion, director, corporate relations, Florida Power Corporation, personal communication, May 27, 1996.

17. Brian Dumaine, "Why Do We Work?" *Fortune,* December 26, 1994, 196–204.

18. "Making Daimler-Benz Dance," *Sky,* May 1995, 58–74.

19. Christopher A. Bartlett and Sumantra Ghoshal, "Changing the Role of Top Management: Beyond Strategy to Purpose," *Harvard Business Review,* November–December 1994, 79–88.

20. Coleman, op. cit.

21. Stratford Sherman, "A Master Class in Radical Change," *Fortune,* December 13, 1995, 82-90.

22. Warren McFarlan, "Reaching for the Technology Dividend," *Index SMI Review,* 4th quarter 1993, 24-26.

23. Brian O'Reilly, "J&J Is on a Roll," *Fortune,* December 26, 1994, 178-192.

24. Malcolm S. Forbes Jr., "Fact and Comment," *Forbes,* May 9, 1994, 25.

25. John Rutledge, "Just Do It," *Forbes,* February 14, 1994, 142.

26. Thomas A. Stewart, "How to Lead a Revolution," *Fortune,* November 28, 1994, 48-61.

27. G. Dowell Schwartz Jr., executive vice president of general services, Baltimore Gas and Electric, personal communication, May 7, 1996.

CHAPTER 7

1. Robert H. Nelson, "Old Bureaus Never Die," *Forbes,* October 11, 1993, 50.

2. That "critical" effort cost the treasury $1.4 billion, and that debt is still on the books. Despite the spectacular insignificance of what the Bureau does, I find it interesting that while the President's Office of Management and Budget has repeatedly asked for reductions of between $20 and $30 million a year in the Bureau of Mines' budget every year since 1983, Congress has consistently turned down that request. In fact, Congress has increased the Bureau's budget by 20 percent since 1983.

3. Daniel Pearl, "Rolling Along," *The Wall Street Journal,* April 27, 1994, A1 and A4.

4. Even though it has nothing to do, the ICC has become the "agency that won't die," because efforts to cut its $45 million budget have failed in Congress.

5. John A. Byrne, "The Pain of Downsizing," *Business Week,* May 9, 1994, 60-69.

6. David Kirkpatrick, "Could AT&T Rule the World," *Fortune,* May 17, 1993, 55-62.

7. Al Derden, director of quality, Texaco, personal communication, May 13, 1996.

8. I saw the award given at the National Accounts Sales Meeting in Tampa, Florida, January 1996.

9. Richard Wintermantel, JD, vice president and director, Motorola, personal communication, May 1, 1996.

10. Thomas A. Stewart, "Another Fad Worth Killing," *Fortune,* February 3, 1997, 119-120.

11. Nancy A. Nichols, "Medicine, Management and Murders: An Interview with Merck's P. Roy Vagelos," *Harvard Business Review,* November–December 1994, 108.

12. Dennis Coleman, group personnel manager, Hewlett-Packard, personal communication, May 1, 1996.

13. Noel M. Tichy and Ram Charan, "The CEO as Coach: An Interview with AlliedSignal's Lawrence A. Bossidy," *Harvard Business Review,* March–April 1995, 69–78.

14. Karin D. Mayhew, vice president of human resources, SNET, personal communication, December 19, 1996.

15. Christian Poindexter, chairman and CEO, Baltimore Gas and Electric, personal communication, July 10, 1996.

16. G. Dowell Schwartz Jr., executive vice president of general services, Baltimore Gas and Electric, personal communication, May 7, 1996.

17. Margot Kyd, vice president of human resources, marketing, and customer service, San Diego Gas and Electric, personal communication, May 2, 1996.

18. There is an important exception to this rule: When the highest priority is to increase teamwork or collaboration across the organization, the largest percentage of compensation will reflect how the organization as a whole has done.

CHAPTER 8

1. "Now Hear This," *Fortune,* February 7, 1994, 20.

2. Patricia McCracken, "In the Cause of Change, Think Twice," *December* 1993, 1–6.

3. Stratford Sherman, "Is He Too Cautious to Save IBM?" *Fortune,* October 3, 1994, 78–90.

4. Raymond W. Smith, "Managing Change and HR: A CEO's Perspective," Executive Human Resource Conference, Sanibel Island, Florida, October 4, 1993.

5. Benjamin Franklin, at the signing of the Declaration of Independence.

6. Walter Boomer, CEO, Rogers Corporation, former CEO, Babcock-Wilcox and General, USMC, Retired, personal communication, October 12, 1996.

7. Stratford Sherman, "A Master Class in Radical Change," *Fortune,* December 13, 1995, 82–90.

8. Alex Taylor III, "GM Some Gain Much Pain," *Fortune,* May 29, 1995, 78–84.

9. *Mon Valley/Fairless Today* 8, no. 1 (Summer 1993).

10. Anne B. Fisher, "Making Change Stick," *Fortune,* April 17, 1995, 121–128.

11. Alex Taylor III, "Will Success Spoil Chrysler," *Fortune,* January 10, 1994, 88–92.

12. Richard Wintermantel, JD, vice president and director, Motorola, personal communication, May 1, 1996; Ned Barnholt, executive vice president and general manager, Test and Measurement Organization, Hewlett-Packard, personal communication, May 10, 1996.

13. Rob Norton, "New Thinking on the Causes—And Costs—of Yes Men (and Women)," *Fortune,* November 28, 1994, 31.

14. Captain John V. Reschar, U.S. Marine Corps, "Cohesion and the Corps," *Proceedings,* November 1993, 37.

15. John H. John, *Cohesion in the U.S. Military* (Washington, DC: National Defense University Press, 1984).

CHAPTER 9

1. Kirk Lawrie, president and CEO, Richmond Savings, Richmond, British Columbia, Canada, personal communication, April 21, 1994.

2. James Ferrell, CEO, Ferrellgas, personal communication, November 1995.

3. Thomas A. Stewart, "New Ways to Exercise Power," *Fortune,* November 6, 1989, 53–64.

4. Note that while the reasons for the changes in leadership are logical, clear, and persuasive, successful leaders won't always use a participatory, collegial style of decision making. Just as sometimes CEOs are praised for decentralizing or centralizing, they are praised for sharing power if profits go up; but if the business slides south, they are accused of losing control. While it's sometimes necessary to use a more traditional kind of leadership style in which the boss makes decisions for reasons of efficacy and efficiency, decision making styles never need be authoritarian. There is no substitute for judgment. We may further note that collaboration does not relieve senior management of the duty of setting overall goals and priorities. Direction and inspiration must still come from the top.

5. Noel M. Tichy and Stratford Sherman, "Control Your Destiny or Someone Else Will," *HarperBusiness,* 1993.

6. Lucy McCauley, "Employee Performance," *Harvard Business Review,* March–April 1994, 14–15.

7. Ibid.

8. Ned Barnholt, executive vice president and general manager, Test and Measurement Organization, Hewlett-Packard, personal communication, May 10, 1996.

9. Robert Newton, Ph.D., director of macrophage pathology, DuPont Merck, personal communication, May 29, 1996.

10. John Teet, former CEO of Dial Corporation, personal communication, March 28, 1994.

11. Steve Mason, CEO, Mead Corporation, personal communication, May 10, 1996.

12. Brigid McMenamin, "What Kind of Duck Are You," *Forbes,* March 14, 1994, 126–128.

13. Barnholt, op. cit.

14. Henry Dubroff, "Trujillo's First Task: Fix the Phones," *The Denver Post,* June 20, 1995, 1C.

CHAPTER 10

1. Rich Teerlink, CEO of Harley-Davidson, quoted in *Fortune,* August 22, 1994, 20.

2. Mark Ivey, "The Ecstasy and the Agony," *Business Week,* October 21, 1991, 40.

3. Nitin Nohria and James D. Berkeley, "Whatever Happened to the Take-Charge Manager?" *Harvard Business Review,* January–February 1994, 128–137.

4. This list is by no means inclusive. Ronald Ashkenas and Robert Shaffer list some more: computerization, quantitative management, diversification, management by objectives, T-groups, centralization, decentralization, matrix management, conglomeration, zero-based budgeting, portfolio management, entrepreneuring, management-by-walking-around, skunk works, quality circles, wellness programs, broadbanding, and supply-side management. Ronald N. Ashkenas, Robert H. Shaffer, et al., "Beyond the Fads: How Leaders Drive Change with Results," *Human Resource Planning* 17, no. 2, 1994, 25–44.

5. David Robinson, "Overcoming the Odds," *Index SMI Review,* 4th quarter 1993, 11–13.

6. Gene Hall, Jim Rosenthal, and Judy Wade, "How to Make Reengineering Really Work," *Harvard Business Review,* November–December 1993, 119–143.

7. Thomas A. Stewart, "Reengineering the Hot New Managing Tool," *Fortune,* August 23, 1993, 41–48.

8. *CSC Index,* State of Reengineering Report, North America and Europe.

9. Lewis J. Perelman, "Kanban to Kanbrain," *Forbes ASAP,* June 6, 1994, 84–95.

10. James Champy, "Reengineering Management," *Insights Quarterly* 7, no. 1 (Spring 1995), 4–15.

11. Ashkenas, Shaffer, et al., op. cit.

12. Stratford Sherman, "Quality Time," *Fortune,* May 16, 1994, 151.

13. Steve Gardiner, director, management education and development, Champion International Corporation, personal communication, June 5, 1996.

14. Nohria and Berkeley, op. cit.

15. Ibid.

16. Norman Lorentz, vice president for quality, U.S. Postal Service, personal communication, May 3, 1996.

17. William G. Lee, "Deming's Not for Us," *The Wall Street Journal,* January 31, 1994, A14.

18. Robinson, op. cit.

19. Nohria and Berkeley, op. cit.

CHAPTER 11

1. Al Derden, director of quality, Texaco, personal communication, May 13, 1996.

2. Steve Mason, CEO, Mead Corporation, personal communication, May 10, 1996.

3. Ned Barnholt, executive vice president and general manager, Test and Measurement Organization, Hewlett-Packard, personal communication, May 10, 1996.

4. James Wetherbe, "How to Be a Master Communicator," *Index SMI Review,* 4th quarter 1993, 17-19.

5. Ibid.

6. Dennis Coleman, group personnel manager, Hewlett-Packard, personal communication, May 1, 1996.

7. Walter Boomer, CEO, Rogers Corporation, former CEO, Babcock-Wilcox and General, USMC, Retired, personal communication, October 12, 1996.

8. Editorial, "Companies Suffer When Pay Splits Execs, Workers," *USA Today,* May 17, 1996, 12A.

9. "People," *U.S. News & World Report,* March 25, 1996, 20.

10. Letters, *Business Week,* May 30, 1994, 14.

11. "Companies Suffer When Pay Splits Execs, Workers," op. cit.

12. John A. Byrne and Joseph Weber, "The Shredder," *Business Week,* January 15, 1996, 56-61.

13. Ibid.

14. William L. Berry, "Nucor Corporation, A Case Study," *Preparation Guide,* n.d., 8 pages.

15. Thomas A. Stewart, "Watch What We Did, Not What We Said," *Fortune,* April 15, 1996, 140-141.

16. "Companies Suffer When Pay Splits Execs, Workers."

17. Allen Bell, executive vice president, human resources, Toronto Dominion Bank, personal communication, April 29, 1996.

18. Michael Rothschild, "When You're Gagging on E-mail," *Forbes ASAP,* June 6, 1994, 25 and 26.

19. Ibid.

20. T. J. Larkin and Sandar Larkin, *Communicating Change* (New York: McGraw-Hill, 1994).

CHAPTER 12

1. Those kinds of assumptions on the part of the employees who had worked for a long time in any of our "best" companies led to my personal rule: employees from those organizations could not work with us until they had been out on their own for at least two years.

2. Janet Novack, "Is Lean Mean?," *Forbes,* August 15, 1994, 88 and 89. The size of the contingency labor force depends on how "contingent workers" is defined. Some statistics report that there are already over 35 million people who are contingent workers, which is almost 30 percent of the U.S. labor force. Nearly 11 million contingent workers are self-employed professionals. The percentage of such professionals hasn't really changed very much over the last 25 years. Another 22 million people who are called contingent workers work part-time. The June 1994 Bureau of Labor Statistics Survey found that of the 22 million contingent workers, 17 million prefer that arrangement. While there's a lot of media visibility given to the nearly 5 million people who work part-time who would prefer full-time work, the number of people who are involuntary part-time employees actually reached its highest level in 1983.

3. James Aley, "The Temp Biz Boom: Why It's Good," *Fortune,* October 16, 1995, 53–56.

4. "The Post-Capitalist Executive: An Interview with Peter F. Drucker," *Harvard Business Review,* May–June 1993, 115–122.

5. Brian O'Reilly, "The New Deal—What Companies and Employees Owe One Another," *Fortune,* June 13, 1994, 44–52.

6. Robert H. Waterman Jr., Judith A. Waterman, and Betsy A. Collard, "Toward A Career-Resilient Workforce," *Harvard Business Review,* July–August 1994, 87–95.

7. Keith H. Hammonds, Kevin Kelly, and Karen Thust, "The New World of Work," *Business Week,* October 17, 1994, 76–87. In 1994, U.S. employers spent only 1.4 percent of payroll on training. While U.S. companies that employed more than 100 people spent $50.6 billion a year on training in 1996, that sum was actually only an 11 percent increase from 1990, a percentage that was lower than inflation.

8. Kerry Pechter, "Rebooting Big Blue," *Human Resources Executive,* September 1993, 1. Training, while unarguably a good investment for individuals and organizations, is also extremely expensive. IBM, for example, wants its employees to be fully aware and appreciative of the fact that they have been receiving $2 billion worth of education a year.

9. I recently met a 20-year employee of a Fortune 500 company who is pursuing a Ph.D. while working full-time. The company is footing the bill for this education. The employee said he was too busy to integrate what he's learning in school into his responsibilities at work—no benefit to the corporation there!—and besides, the degree is his route out of the organization.

10. Robert J. Samuelson, "R.I.P.: The Good Corporation," *Newsweek,* July 5, 1993, 41. To date, the mobility of employees has been grossly exaggerated. Compared with 15 years ago, fewer people today and in the future will spend their whole careers with a single employer; still, most people are likely to remain with an employer for 10 or more years. Samuelson reports that stable jobs have definitely not vanished. Among men, the typical employee between the ages of 45 and 54 has been with his present employer 12 years. About one-third of these male employees have been with their employers 20 years or more. And, as more women are pursuing careers, their job tenure has actually increased.

11. James Olson, senior vice president, 3Com Corporation, personal communication, May 2, 1996.

12. Ned Barnholt, executive vice president and general manager, Test and Measurement Organization, Hewlett-Packard, personal communication, May 10, 1996.

13. Steve Peltier, CEO, Industrial Computer Source, personal communication, April 29, 1996.

14. Keith H. Hammonds, "The Issue Is Employment, Not Employability," *Business Week,* June 10, 1996, 4.

15. "For Now," *The Economist,* July 17, 1993, 13-14.

CHAPTER 13

1. Bob Newton of DuPont Merck says research, which is what his group does, is long-term and "Ninety-nine percent of what we do involves failure. We screen 100,000 compounds to find 1 good one. Last year in one program we went through 48,000 compounds. We haven't found a good one for that target in two years. It's easy to be defeated and it's hard to feed people enough success to keep them motivated. Once they have a taste of success, it snowballs. But it has to be real. You find that you often have to find success in learning. Even a lack of success can be buried with honor. We acquired a lot of knowledge even

though we didn't get the product. You have to find small victories along the way."

2. Al Derden, director of quality, Texaco, personal communication, May 13, 1996.

3. William Stover, department manager, plate scheduling, U.S. Steel, personal communication, October 11, 1995. Stover sent me a letter contributing a critical idea about implementing stretch goals. He wrote, "The top manager must tell each of his subordinates what the subordinate's portion of the central organizational goal is and give an appropriate deadline. This action must be replicated at each level of management so everyone knows what they are expected to do and when it is due. Breaking the goal up into defined pieces that contribute to the central goal all the way down to the lowest organizational level and communicating the pieces correctly is very difficult. An analogy may be drawn to the questionable accuracy of the message at the end of a Chinese telephone. If this step is missed, lower levels of the organization experience general anxiety in response to the top executive's pressure and don't know what to do. For example, the goal at Gary Works was 94 heats a day, which has now increased. Many people don't know their part of the goal because they do not work in steel producing. Contributory goals for other portions of the organization should have been identified. In fact, maybe employees should have been asked for their thoughts on specific goals, which was not done. For example, contributory goals could be downtime targets for maintenance or information requirements from systems. There is great anxiety but no defined goal for much of the organization. As a result, prioritization of tasks is not happening and the latest request is the hottest, even if previous jobs aren't complete. Since we did achieve the goal, I'm not belittling the success. However, the whole organization might be better if everyone felt they contributed rather than just people in steel producing."

4. Ronald N. Ashkenas, Robert H. Shaffer, et al., "Beyond the Fads: How Leaders Drive Change with Results," *Human Resource Planning* 17, no. 2, 1994, 25-44.

5. James Olson, senior vice president, 3Com Corporation, personal communication, May 2, 1996.

6. Norman Schoenfeld, consultant, one-page summary, April 23, 1994.

7. Personal communication, AT&T Meeting, Atlanta, GA, May 23, 1993.

8. Judith M. Bardwick, *The Plateauing Trap* (New York: AMACOM, 1986). Paperback version published by Bantam, 1988.

9. Julie Connelly, "Have You Gone as Far as You Can Go," *Fortune,* December 26, 1994, 231-232.

10. The grief involved in coming to terms with this disappointment can be seen in reinterpretations of reality that are sometimes amazing. I have seen employees insist that every one of their job changes was a promotion, even though their salaries and grades remained the same. One manager said to me, "In my career thus far I have had eleven laterals and all of them were developmental. I consider them promotions."

CHAPTER 15

1. "Fortune 1000 Ranked within Industries," Fortune, April 28, 1997, F-49.

2. Brian O'Reilly, "The New Deal—What Companies and Employees Owe One Another," *Fortune,* June 13, 1994, 44-52.

3. Anne Murphy, "Too Good to Be True," *Inc.,* July 1994, 34-43.

4. Ibid.

5. Thomas P. Murphy, venture capitalist, personal communication, August 14, 1994.

6. Ronald B. Lieber, "How Safe Is Your Job," *Fortune,* April 1, 1996, 72-80.

7. Walter Kiechel III, "A Manager's Career in the New Economy," *Fortune,* April 4, 1994, 68-72.

8. Ben Stein, "Whining And Dining," *New York,* April, 11, 1994, 14 and 15. People who have taken steps to improve their situation are dramatically better off overall than people who haven't. In 1991, for example, the median income of households in which the householder had a professional degree was significantly higher than twice the income of families where the householder did not have a degree. In families where the householder had a professional degree, 67 percent were in the top fifth of all families in terms of earnings and more than one-third of that group were in the highest 5 percent. In families where householders had masters degrees, more than half were in the top fifth in earnings. Education usually pays off an awful lot in the long run.

9. Jane Gross, "A New Spin on Car Pools in the Suburbs," *The New York Times,* November 30, 1997, 45.

10. "The Post-Capitalist Executive: An Interview with Peter F. Drucker," *Harvard Business Review,* May-June 1993, 115-122.

11. Kiechel, op. cit.

12. "The Post-Capitalist Executive," op. cit.

13. Ronald Henkoff, "So, You Want to Change Your Job," *Fortune,* January 15, 1996, 52-56.

CHAPTER 16

1. June Kronholz, "Clinton's Plan for Tough Student Tests Is Expected to Bring High Failure Rate," *The Wall Street Journal,* February 6, 1997, A16.
2. Richard A. Melcher and Paul Magnussen, "Education: More Reform, Please," *Business Week,* December 9, 1996, 178-184.
3. Thomas Toch, Robin M. Bennefield, Dana Hawkins, and Penny Loeb, "Why Teachers Don't Teach," *U.S. News & World Report,* February 26, 1996, 62-71.
4. Tom Kelley, personal communication, Young Presidents Organization Regional Meeting, November 7, 1991, St. Thomas, United States Virgin Islands.
5. Tom Loveless, "The Academic Fad that Gave Us Ebonics," *The Wall Street Journal,* January 22, 1997, A18.
6. Pat Ordovensky, "Two Top Teachers Have a Few Ideas," *USA Today,* May 17, 1996, D1 and D2.
7. Gary Putka, "Forceful Educator Gets Teachers and Children to Be More Productive," *The Wall Street Journal,* June 5, 1991, A1 and A4.
8. Toch et al., op. cit.
9. Sarah Lubman, "Breaking Away," *The Wall Street Journal,* May 19, 1994, A1 and A6.
10. Diane Ravitch, "Challenging Monopoly," *Forbes,* October 21, 1996, 56.
11. "Charter Schools Gain," *The Wall Street Journal,* December 20, 1996, A1.
12. Richard Melcher, "School Solution?" *Business Week,* February 3, 1997, 14EB.
13. Jeffrey Taylor, "Dole Calls Clinton Teacher Unions' 'Pet,' Offers Plan to Let Parents Choose Schools," *The Wall Street Journal,* May 30, 1996, 14.
14. Sol Stern, "Why the Catholic School Model is Taboo," *The Wall Street Journal,* July 17, 1996, A14.
15. Diane Ravitch, "Testing Catholic Schools," *The Wall Street Journal,* October 1, 1996, A22.
16. Tim Goeglein, "School of Devotion," *The Wall Street Journal,* March 31, 1997, A14.
17. Jonathan Kaufman, "Grade Inflation," *The Wall Street Journal,* March 1, 1996, A1 and A8.

CHAPTER 17

1. Michael Barone, "What Worries Americans Most Is Their Country's Social and Moral Decay," *The San Diego Union-Tribune,* July 28, 1996, G1 and G6.

2. Clifford Orwin, "All Quiet on the (Post)Western Front?" *The Public Interest,* no. 123 (Spring 1996), 3-21. The anthropologist Franz Boas introduced cultural relativism, the view that all cultures had to be considered equal because there aren't any neutral principles that allow an evaluation of differences between cultures. This position was enthusiastically embraced by people with progressive values because it supported diversity and egalitariansm, and by 1950 it had become the dominant view in universities.

3. Howard Fineman, "The Virtuecrats," *Newsweek,* June 13, 1994, 30-39. A group of educators and philosophers met in 1992 and produced the Aspen Declaration. That report listed "six core elements of character" that included trustworthiness (including honesty and loyalty), respect, responsibility (including hard work and self-discipline), caring ("compassion"), fairness, and citizenship (which involves obeying laws, staying informed, and voting). William Bennett has a similar list, but he adds courage and faith, describing the latter as reverence.

4. Daniel Yankelovich, "Question and Answer," *The San Diego Union-Tribune,* March 31, 1996, G5.

5. The name of the company can be disclosed because this story was reported in the newspapers.

6. Not his real name.

7. He didn't succeed.

8. Dana Milbank, "Instant Justice," *The Wall Street Journal,* August 15, 1996, A1 and A4.

9. This phenomenon is not restricted to the United States. Wherever there are perceived advantages, people will naturally try to gain them. Perhaps the most absurd but most telling illustration can be found in India, where there have been reports of Brahmins (members of the highest caste) claiming to be Untouchables because of the "set-asides" for the latter group.

10. But, increasingly, we are pulling the pendulum back to center. We have begun to blame people for illnesses that arise as a direct result of lifestyle choices. AIDS and lung cancer are obvious examples.

11. Heather S. Richardson, "Bobbitt: A Verdict that Kills Justice," *The Wall Street Journal,* January 24, 1994, A14.

12. Myron Magnet, "Is Culture the Culprit?" *The Public Interest,* no. 113 (Fall 1993), 110-118.

13. William Bennett, *The Index of Leading Cultural Indicators* (New York: Simon and Schuster, 1994).

14. Gertrude Himmelfarb, "Moral Renewal," *The San Diego Union-Tribune,* December 24, 1995, G1 and G4.

15. Milbank, op. cit.

16. People are angry because the common good is being violated by the overwhelming preponderance of individual rights or freedoms. As the multiplication of rights and victims has jeopardized people's ability to be safe in their own communities, regaining that safety has become paramount. New laws are being written and old ones enforced that prohibit aggressive panhandling and open containers of alcohol. Old rules are being reinstated against trespassing and sleeping in public places. More than 200 cities are enforcing new or revived curfews. Communities are reasserting their rights against panhandlers, public drunks, the drug market, and irresponsible parents whose kids break the law.

17. George F. Will, "The Cultural Contradictions of Conservatism," *The Public Interest,* no. 123 (Spring 1996), 40-57.

CHAPTER 18

1. Brian Bremmer, William Glasgall, and Peter Galuzka, "Two Japans," *Business Week,* January 27, 1997, 24-28.

2. Mark Memmott and John Hillkirk, "Japan Inc. Has Lost Aura of Invincibility," *USA Today,* March 3, 1994, B1 and B2.

3. Brenton R. Schlender, "Japan's White-Collar Blues," *Fortune,* March 21, 1994, 97-104.

4. Gale Eisenstodt, "Job Shokku," *Forbes,* July 31, 1995, 42-43.

5. Shintaro Hori, "Fixing Japan's White-Collar Economy: A Personal View," *Harvard Business Review,* November-December 1993, 157-172.

6. Brenton R. Schlender, "Japan: Is It Changing for Good?" *Fortune,* June 13, 1994, 124-134.

7. Edwin W. Desmond, "The Failed Miracle," *Time,* April 22, 1996, 60-64.

8. Robert L. Simison and Valerie Reitman, "Toyota Says It May Have to Shut Down Plants in Japan; Layoffs Are Possibility," *The Wall Street Journal,* May 12, 1995, A6.

9. Caspar W. Weinberger, "Japan: Mid-1995," *Forbes,* June 5, 1995, 37.

10. Jathon Sapsford, "Unemployment in Japan Hits a Seven-Year High," *The Wall Street Journal,* August 31, 1994, A7.

11. "Alberta on the Right Track," *The Economist,* February 15, 1997, 28.

12. David Frum, "Ontario Quake: Tax Rates Suffer Most," *The Wall Street Journal,* June 12, 1995, A14.

13. W. Bilal Syed, "Ontario's Elite Still Can't Smell the Coffee," *The Wall Street Journal,* June 16, 1995, A11.

14. Mark Heinzl, "Ontario Tax-Cut Plan Gets Cool Response," *The Wall Street Journal,*" March 12, 1996, A2 and A13.

15. David R. Henderson, "Canada's High Unemployment Is No Mystery," *The Wall Street Journal,* February 7, 1997, A17.

16. Todd G. Buchholz, "Northern Lights," *Worth,* October 1996, 88–89.

17. "Canada—Fiscal Virtuosos," *The Economist,* October 25, 1997, 36.

18. Richard C. Morais, "I'm Entitled," *Forbes,* April 26, 1993, 82–94.

19. Paula Dwyer, "Should We Praise Maggie or Bury Her?" *Business Week,* August 28, 1995, 17.

20. Irwin M. Stelzer, "What Thatcher Wrought," *The Public Interest,* no. 107 (Spring 1992), 18–51.

21. Dana Milbank, "Unlike the Rest of Europe, Britain Is Creating Jobs, but They Pay Poorly," *The Wall Street Journal,* March 28, 1994, A1 and A5.

22. Howard Banks, "Has Labour Changed Its Spots," *Forbes,* May 20, 1996, 86–92.

23. "Blair Takes His Partner," *The Economist,* February 1, 1997, 62.

24. "The Vision Thing," *The Economist,* September 27, 1997, 18.

25. "All Mod Cons," *The Economist,* September 27, 1997, 59–92.

26. Toby Helm and George Jones, "Blair in First Clash with Brussels," *The Daily Telegraph,* June 5, 1997, 1.

27. "Tony Keeps It Tight," *The Economist,* September 20, 1997, 61.

28. Peter Gumbel, "French Official in Uphill Battle Seeks to Win Favor for Proposed Labor Rules," *The Wall Street Journal,* March 14, 1994, A10.

29. Thomas Kamm and Douglas Lavin, "The Strikes in France May Pose a Challenge for European Union," *The Wall Street Journal,* December 22, 1995, A1 and A7.

30. Ibid.

31. Youssef M. Ibrahim, "France's Addiction to Benefits Makes More Strife Likely," *The San Diego Union-Tribune,* December 25, 1995, A48.

32. "Daylight Jobbery," *The Economist,* September 20, 1997, 56–59.

33. "Heading for a Coma," *The Wall Street Journal,* July 23, 1997, A18.

34. "Funny Figures," *The Economist,* October 18, 1997, 52–53.

35. Greg Steinmetz and Matt Marshall, "How a Chemicals Giant Goes about Becoming a Lot Less German," *The Wall Street Journal,* February 18, 1997, A1 and A6.

36. Karen Lowry Miller, "Are the Easy Times Gone for Good?" *Business Week,* January 29, 1996, 48-49.

37. Greg Steinmetz, "Americans, Too, Run Afoul of Rigorous German Rules," *The Wall Street Journal,* February 2, 1996, A6.

38. Daniel Benjamin, "Germany Is Troubled by How Little Work Its Workers Are Doing," *The Wall Street Journal,* May 6, 1993, A1 and A4.

39. John Templeman, "When Will Germany Stop Sleep Walking?" *Business Week,* May 29, 1995, 48.

40. Paul Hofheinz, "When Will Germany Come Back?" *Fortune,* April 4, 1994, 112-116.

41. Malcolm S. Forbes Jr., "Fact and Comment," *Forbes,* July 17, 1995, 23-24.

42. Amity Shlaes, " 'Re-employment' that Kills Jobs," *The Wall Street Journal,* April 26, 1994, A20.

43. Steinmetz, "Americans, Too, Run Afoul of Rigorous German Rules," op. cit.

44. Amity Shlaes, "Germany Buys Itself a Miracle," *The Wall Street Journal,* July 6, 1995, A8.

45. William Echikson, "In the Fast Lane in a Slow Market," *Fortune,* June 13, 1994, 118.

46. Cacilie Rohwedder, Matt Marshall, and Thomas Kamm, "Germany, France Unveil Economic Plans," *The Wall Street Journal,* January 31, 1996, A12.

47. George Melloan, "Germany's 'Flagship' Casts off as Kohl Fiddles," *The Wall Street Journal,* January 13, 1997, A17.

48. Cacilie Rohwedder, "Germany's Continental AG Sets Up Shop Farther East to Escape Costs at Home," *The Wall Street Journal,* July 15, 1994, A6.

49. Peter Gumbel and Audrey Choi, "Germany Making Comeback, with Daimler in the Lead," *The Wall Street Journal,* April 7, 1995, A6.

50. John Templeman, "The Economy that Fell to Earth," *Business Week,* January 15, 1996, 46.

51. "German Lessons," *The Economist,* October 18, 1997, 70.

52. "No Thanks," *The Economist,* November 1, 1997, 52-53.

53. Howard Banks, "Deutsche Hegira," *Forbes,* May 5, 1997, 130-133.

54. "Germany Makes Haste Slowly," *The Economist,* July 12, 1997, 43.

55. Greg Steinmetz, "Germans Falter in Struggle to Regain Competitive Edge," *The Wall Street Journal,* June 12, 1997, A14.

56. Judith Valente and Carlta Vitzthum, "With Boom Gone Bust, Spain's Social Agenda Still Haunts Economy," *The Wall Street Journal,* June 13, 1994, A1 and A6.

57. Lawrence Ingrassia, "Out of Work, but Not Out of Luck, in Spain's Cadiz," *The Wall Street Journal,* November 30, 1995, 10.

58. "Spain: Consensus versus Jobs," *The Economist,* February 1, 1997, 54.

59. Thomas Kamm and Carlta Vitzhum, "Bullish Arena," *The Wall Street Journal,* May 20, 1997, A1 and A10.

60. Paul Klebnikov, "The Swedish Disease," *Forbes,* May 24, 1993, 78-80.

61. Gene Koretz, "Economic Trends," *Business Week,* February 26, 1996, 26.

62. Editorial, "Sweden's Reactionaries," *The Wall Street Journal,* August 25, 1994, A12.

63. Buchholz, op. cit.

64. Gary Becker, "Job Markets: Europe Doesn't Have Anything to Boast About," *Business Week,* March 17, 1997, 23.

65. Gregory Fossedal, "The American Dream Lives," *The Wall Street Journal,* February 14, 1997, A14.

66. Peter Gumbel and Charles Goldsmith, "ED's Growing Unemployment Provokes Questions about Economic Practices," *The Wall Street Journal,* June 18, 1993, A6.

67. Audrey Choi and Neal Templin, "Europe's Auto Industry Faces Dilemma on Cutbacks," *The Wall Street Journal,* March 10, 1994, B4.

68. John Templeman and Paula Dwyer, "Europe's Social Cushion Is Looking Rather Frayed," *Business Week,* July 5, 1993, 50.

69. Richard C. Morais, "Les Miserables," *Forbes,* February 28, 1994, 50-51.

70. Peter Gumbel, "Europe Faces Pressure to Cut Social Spending," *The Wall Street Journal,* May 8, 1995, A1.

71. George Melloan, "Europe's Gloomier View of the Welfare State," *The Wall Street Journal,* February 14, 1994, A15.

72. Kim R. Holmes and Melanie Kirkpatrick, "Freedom and Growth," *The Wall Street Journal,* December 16, 1996, A16. Ten key areas of 150 economies are evaluated using 50 independent economic criteria: trade policy, taxation, government intervention, monetary policy, capital flows and foreign investment, banking policy, wage and price controls, property rights, regulation, and black market activity.

73. Terence Roth, "Gordian Knot," *The Wall Street Journal,* September 30, 1994, R4. Of course, this also applies to eastern Europe, Latin America, and many other nations.

CHAPTER 19

1. Rudi Dornbusch, "Sure, Fight Inequality, but Set the Markets Free," *Business Week,* June 27, 1994, 14.

2. Sandel, Michael J., "America's Search for a New Public Philosophy," *The Atlantic Monthly,* March 1996, 57–74.

3. Ron Chernow, "Ferocious Competition," *The Wall Street Journal,* April 1, 1994, A8.

4. Editorial, "Welcome to the Age of Disinflation," *Business Week,* November 15, 1993, 186.

5. Andrew S. Grove, "A High-Tech CEO Updates His Views on Managing and Careers," *Fortune,* September 18, 1995, 229–230.

6. Reuters, "Job Cuts Soar in 1st Half of Year," *The San Diego Union-Tribune,* July 9, 1996, C1 and C3.

7. Joe Spiers, "The Fortune 500: The Profits Flowed," *Fortune,* April 29, 1996, 260–261.

8. Louis S. Richman, "How Jobs Die—And Are Born," *Fortune,* July 26, 1993, 26.

9. Robert J. Samuelson, "Down-sizing for Growth," *Newsweek,* March 25, 1996, 45.

10. Robert J. Samuelson, "Reinventing Corporate America," *Newsweek,* July 4, 1994, 53. Alan Greenspan, chairman of the Federal Reserve, says that total productivity grew about 1 percent a year in the 1970s and 1980s. From mid-1990 on, he reports that it has averaged about 2 percent a year. Because increases in wages and profits are tied directly to improvements in productivity, it's very important that total productivity growth in manufacturing doubled after 1981, from 1.4 percent a year from 1950 to 1981 to 3.3 percent a year from 1981 to 1990.

11. Michael C. Jensen, "A Revolution Only Markets Could Love," *The Wall Street Journal,* January 3, 1994, 6. Real labor compensation rose by 0.3 percent a year, but real labor costs declined 25 percent because of the increased productivity. Labor productivity increased from 2.3 percent in 1950–1981 to 3.8 percent from 1981 to 1990. While real median income had been declining 1 percent a year from 1973 to 1982, from 1982 to 1989 it grew by 1.8 percent a year. These are significant gains in both productivity and compensation.

12. Daniel Strickberger, "The Other American Dream Team," *The Wall Street Journal,* February 15, 1994, A14.

13. Mortimer B. Zuckerman, "Creators of the 21st Century," *U.S. News & World Report,* July 1, 1996, 64.

14. Ibid., ref. 9, cites The World Economic Forum and The Council on Competitiveness. Additional sources include Steve Kichen, "Keeping Score," *Forbes,* July 17, 1995, 228, which refers to *The World Com-*

petitiveness Report. Terence Roth, "U.S. Is Ranked Most Competitive Economy in World," *The Wall Street Journal,* September 6, 1995, A2, refers to a survey conducted by the World Economic Forum in Geneva and the International Institute for Management and Development in Lausanne, Switzerland.

15. Wage Stagnation? It depends on who's answering the question . . . I give economists an A in confusion and an F in clarity. Here's a sample of some "answers" (different measures italicized):

- "Stagnant *wages* are a 20-year problem . . ." Robert Rubin, Ronald Brown, Robert Reich, Joseph Stiglitz, and Laura D'Andrea Tyson, "What's a Minimum Wage Job Worth?" *The Wall Street Journal,* April 1, 1996, A14.

- "But *overall compensation—wages and salaries plus benefits—* have grown at a steady rate in recent decades. Non-wage perks such as health insurance and vacation pay account for more than 40 percent of all remuneration, up from less than 20 percent in the 1950s." Tony Snow, "Clinton Zapping Business Unfairly," *USA Today,* September 11, 1995, A10.

- "Stagnant wages could be justified in the 1970s and 1980s when productivity gains were low, but not so easily today. Now, productivity is moving up smartly, but incredibly, *average wages and salaries* are still dropping." David Gergen, "Squeezing American Workers," *U.S. News & World Report,* January 22, 1996, 68.

- "Using the Commerce Dept.'s new *chain-weighted price index for consumer spending,* real wages have been increasing steadily since 1993." James Cooper and Kathleen Madigan, "Why Rising Pay Isn't Courting Inflation," *Business Week,* February 26, 1996, 27–28.

- "*The share of corporate revenue going to employees* has in fact remained remarkably constant ever since World War II, while the share going to profits is actually low by postwar standards . . . True, profits have improved in recent years, but they were coming off a very weak base . . . According to Commerce Department figures, corporations in the 1990s have paid out some 65 percent of revenues to employees in wages and fringe benefits, slightly more than in the halcyon 1950s and 1960s . . . Meanwhile, after-tax profits in the 1990s have tumbled to 6 percent of revenue, down from 8 percent in the Seventies, 9 percent in the Sixties and more than 10 percent in the Fifties . . . A key reason that corporate employees think they're getting shortchanged . . . is that compensation has increasingly been paid out as benefits rather than as take-home pay. Benefits have jumped from 4.4 percent of corporate revenues

in the 1950s to 11.5 percent in the 1990s . . . [and] federal programs . . . siphon off funds that would otherwise be available for
wages. Corporate contributions for Social Security and Medicare
climbed from $12 billion in 1966, when Medicare began, to more
than $200 billion last year (1995), doubling the share of revenue
absorbed to 5 percent. . . . business is lifting compensation nearly
as much as productivity gains permit. The trouble is that the costs
of services produced outside the corporate sector, like rent and
school tuition . . . property taxes, water and sewer fees and public
transportation charges . . . are rising relatively quickly, squeezing
workers' incomes." Joe Spiers, "The Myth of Corporate Greed,"
Fortune, April 15, 1996, 67–68.

- "In deftly convoluted language, [chief economist Joseph] Stiglitz
  writes that 'Two-thirds (68 percent) of the *net job growth in full-
  time employment* between February 1994 and February 1996
  occurred in industry/occupation groups paying above-median
  wages.' The implication is that the actual jobs paid good wages. . . .
  But that's not quite what Stiglitz said, or what his statistics show.
  Since wage inequality has been increasing within occupations and
  industries, you can't assume that a job pays a high wage just
  because it is located in a high-wage sector. For example, a new
  pilot on a fast-growing commuter airline will be paid far less than
  the pilot of a big trunk airline . . . The real bottom line is *the economy's actual median wage.* In the past year (1995), that number
  declined again, as it has in six of the last seven years. Whatever is
  really happening with new jobs, more than 50 *percent of all workers* are earning less than a year ago." Robert Kuttner, "New
  Statistics, but Same Old Problem," *The San Diego Union-Tribune,*
  April 26, 1996, B9.

What is going on? How can economists come up with such violent
disagreements about what's happening? Figures don't lie, but liars figure.
Economic policies and decisions are driven by political motives.
Opposing political factions justify their views with economic numbers.
Economists are unusually skilled in creating numbers that justify their
positions. Another way to say that is that economists appear to feel free
to make assumptions and use measures that justify a political position.

16. Stephen Golub, an economist at Swarthmore College, reports
that American labor does compete with apparently low-wage workers
overseas because of the low productivity of the latter. When the productivity of workers in a developing nation improves, wages and the value of
that nation's currency rise. Golub compared factory wages and other

compensation in the United States and Korea, Thailand, Malaysia, and the Philippines in 1990. While compensation ranged from only 14 to 32 percent of American levels, actual unit labor costs in Korea were 71 percent of American levels, and in Thailand the percentage was 86. The unit labor costs in Malaysia and the Philippines were higher than those in the United States. In addition, there were differences in productivity between different industries. In Thailand, for example, wages and productivity were 15 percent in overall manufacturing. But Thai productivity is probably higher than 15 percent in the manufacture of simple items like fabrics and lower than 15 percent when the product is complex, like machinery. Thus, it is to Thailand's advantage to export fabrics while importing machinery. Golub feels that fears about unfair competition from developing nations have been very exaggerated. This information can be found in: Gene Koretz, "The Equalizer: Productivity," *Business Week*, September 11, 1995, 26.

17. "Buchanan Fires, and Exporters Fire Back," *U.S. News & World Report*, March 11, 1996, 8. While we have a substantial trade deficit, as a percentage of our Gross Domestic Product it had shrunk to 1.5 percent in 1995 from a high of 3.3 percent in 1987. Between 1994 and 1995 our trade deficit with Japan declined by almost 10 percent and our exports increased by 12 percent (those to Japan rose by 20 percent).

18. George J. Church, "Where He Rings True: Free Trade Isn't Always Fair," *Time*, March 4, 1996, 29.

19. Mortimer B. Zuckerman, "Protectionism? Just Say No," *U.S. News & World Report*, April 8, 1996, 64.

20. Gene Koretz, "How Exports Create Jobs," *Business Week*, August 12, 1996, 22. Koretz reports that the 20,000 jobs supported by $1 billion worth of exports in 1981 had fallen to 14,200 in 1995 because of American gains in productivity and America's ability to charge high prices in the world's markets.

21. Herbert Stein, "The Income Inequality Debate," *The Wall Street Journal*, May 1, 1996, A16.

22. Stephan Thernstrom, "Alien Nation," *The Public Interest* no. 122 (Winter 1996), 103-107.

23. Just to kick off a national discussion, here are some possibilities:

- An expanded Job Corps or Peace Corps that pays tuition and some living costs after the successful completion of a tour of duty.
- An increase in the number of work-study programs.
- Deducting education costs from taxes.
- Developing pretax portable tuition savings accounts.

- Giving people the right to borrow from their pension funds for more education with the responsibility to repay the fund with interest by a given date.

- Money for education as one choice from a range of employee benefits.

24. George F. Will, "Clinton's Legislative Laundry List," *The San Diego Union-Tribune,* August 31, 1996, B8.

25. Roger Waldiner, *Still the Promised City: African-Americans and New Immigrants in Post-Industrial New York* (Cambridge, MA: Harvard University Press, 1996).

26. William Julius Wilson, "Work," *The New York Times Magazine,* August 18, 1996, 27–54.

27. Peter Bidstrup, former chairman and CEO, Double Tree Hotels, personal communication, February 4, 1997.

28. Ibid.

29. Tommy G. Thompson, "Question and Answer," *The San Diego Union-Tribune,* September 1, 1996, G5.

30. Wisconsin learned there are four things that are critical in terms of getting people off welfare. The first is medical coverage for the mother and her children. Second is some kind of training to increase the recipient's sense of self-esteem. Child care is third, and that part of the budget increased from $12 million to $60 million a year in the first few years and will rise to $160 million in 1997. The fourth requirement is transportation. Wisconsin loans people several hundred dollars to fix their cars so they can go to work.

31. There are several levels of work:

- People who have never worked, who may be young, who are likely not to have graduated from high school, or who have always been on welfare are required to go to a sheltered workshop or a nursing home where they have to put in an eight-hour day. They may remain in that transitional workplace for several years.

- Subsidized public work involves working for a school district, a city, or a county, in a job subsidized by the state.

- Subsidized private work where the state pays employers $300 a month for as long as two years to defray the cost of training or the employee's wages.

32. David Wessel and Gerald F. Seib, "Americans, Especially Baby Boomers, Voice Pessimism for Their Kids' Economic Future," *The Wall Street Journal,* January 19, 1996, A10.

33. Much of our economic news is pretty good. Why, then, the decrease in optimism for the future? In addition to the downward pres-

sure on compensation created by the boundaryless economy, we have other factors contributing to a sense of gloom:

- Catastrophe is always more newsworthy than anything ordinary. Draconian downsizing by one corporation is far more likely to get lots of media attention than the gradual increase in jobs in many companies. The threat of aggressive international competition is far more visible than American corporate growth overseas. And the media themselves have become more vivid and thus more memorable as television supplants print.

- Women's labor force participation, which contributes greatly to household upward mobility, peaked in recent years and appears to be in slight decline.

- Jobs are increasing at the bottom of the wage scale and at the top in the $50,000-$80,000 range. But there aren't a lot of jobs in the middle, at the $35,000-$40,000 level. There's been a net reduction in the number of jobs in manufacturing; in addition, flat organizations don't have many jobs in the middle.

- The intractability of inner city poverty after 30 years of effort and 3 trillion dollars assaults our sense of *can-do!* Many people start out poor and it's okay because that's just their starting place. In the ghetto it has become an ending place—along with high levels of crime, drugs, broken families, and physical and mental abuse.

34. Christopher Farrell, "The Great Growth Debate," *Business Week,* October 30, 1995, 160-162.

35. Catherine Arnst and Michael Mandel, "The Coming Telescramble," *Business Week,* April 8, 1996, 64-66.

36. Peter Lynch, "The Upsizing of America," *The Wall Street Journal,* September 20, 1996, A14.

37. Tony Horwitz, "Jobless Male Managers Proliferate in Suburbs, Causing Subtle Malaise," *The Wall Street Journal,* September 20, 1993, A1 and A6.

POSTSCRIPT

1. Readers who want more detail about the model are directed to the earlier book, *Danger In the Comfort Zone.*

INDEX

Values (*Continued*):
  of leaders, 74, 83, 89, 129-130, 151
  and power, 86, 125
  role of, in mergers, 110
  societal, 234-235, 243, 246, 248
Variable compensation, 55, 105, 106,
  157-158
Victimization:
  and entitlement, 237, 238, 240-244,
  248
  and free trade policies, 286
  psychology of, 291

Virtual organization, 169, 170, 174
Voluntary severance, 33, 45

Work:
  creating meaningful, 28, 94-96, 99,
  187
  definition of, 17, 18, 35
  vs. "garbage," 16, 147
Workers, *see* Labor force
Work ethic, traditional, 234

Yerkes-Dodson Law, 169, 301-303